Cohesion
and
Conflict

Cohesion
and
Conflict

Lessons from the Study of
Three-Party Interaction

DAVID WILKINSON

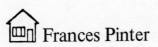 Frances Pinter

Published in Great Britain in 1976 by
Frances Pinter (Publishers) Limited
161 West End Lane, London NW6 2LG

ISBN 0 903804 14 X

Printed in Great Britain by offset lithography by
Billing & Sons Ltd, Guildford, London and Worcester

Published in association with
the Richardson Institute for Conflict and Peace Research, London

CONTENTS

LIST OF TABLES

AUTHOR'S PREFACE

The study of the triad, or three person group, does not fit nicely within the scope of any one single traditional discipline. In recent years however a new discipline, Conflict Studies, has emerged which embraces the relevant fields of enquiry.

There is a large amount of relevant work from the fields of International Relations, Behavioural Science, and Sociology dealing with specific conflicts, but Conflict Studies is concerned chiefly with conflict in the abstract i.e. we are dealing with the basic structures of conflict. While conflicts in the real world exist at all levels e.g. between people, groups or nations, their basic structures may be similar. Thus Conflict Studies strips the conflict of most of its real world trimmings and looks at the skeleton features underlying it. Mathematics is a very useful tool for this sort of approach and a large part of the field is concerned with the building of mathematical models to analyse the situations and make predictions. A certain amount of experimentation is also possible and some has already taken place using students as decision makers. Lack of finance has however prevented any experimentation in connection with the subject matter of this study though some which has been carried out by others is given consideration.

The original title of this study was 'The Influence of Third Parties in Conflict Situations'. It was intended to look at the influence of a third party on the interaction process taking place between two others. Some situations such as the mediation of a dispute between two parties are obvious examples. But there are certain other triadic situations which, though providing information which is relevant, would not fit into a field so narrow as that implied by this title. The title was therefore altered in order to include all such situations, and this work is a general study of the triad.

My work has been carried out at Lancaster University under the guidance of Dr. M. B. Nicholson to whom I am indebted for his comments and ideas. My thanks are also due to the many colleagues and acquaintances I have consulted in connection with this work, and to Althea Culpin for correcting my rather bad grammar in the earlier draft.

DAVID WILKINSON

As my husband died before being able to prepare this manuscript for publication, the task was very kindly undertaken by his colleagues, Dr. Michael Nicholson and Dr. David Chapman.

ALTHEA WILKINSON

FOREWORD

Cohesion and Conflict is an original work of scholarship which significantly adds to our theoretical knowledge of the formation of alliances and coalitions. Because of its scope, and the fact that it is not a traditional area of study with established convention, this book is not easy to classify. It is clearly to the political scientist that the central core of the argument is directed, but it has explicit interest for people outside this area. It would be a pity if the readership were confined to political scientists, and I want in this introduction to try to provide a background for the scholar who is not actually working in this field.

If one is interested in conflict — whether international conflict, industrial conflict, internal political conflict or conflict of any kind — one must become interested in alliances. A few conflicts take place between two parties, obviating the need for an analysis of alliances, but by and large conflict situations do not have this convenient characteristic. Thus a theory of conflict needs a theory of alliances. Why for instance does one alliance form rather than another? Why are some alliances in some contexts stable, whereas others are unstable and prone to break up? When, and this is a rarity, do alliances not form at all? A theory of alliances aims to answer these general questions about alliance formation and stability, and not merely particular questions about particular alliances. It is towards this end that this book is directed.

While the problem of alliance and coalition formation has been readily admitted it has not, until recently, lead to a great deal of theory, scientific or testable theory in Political Science is relatively new. What has been called political theory is more properly described as political philosophy, coupled with some propositions about the world which may or may not have been testable, but which were certainly not tested. It has not been theory in the sense that the word is used in 'economic theory', which has been about in ostensibly testable forms for perhaps two centuries. Unfortunately though, despite their theoretical inclinations, economists have shied away from the problem of alliance formation in their own discipline, even though it is one which invades very forcibly into many economic situations, such as the formation of labour unions or the problem of oligopoly. Thus we are found with a problem which, in view of its importance, has occupied theorists surprisingly little.

As in so many other fields, theoretical complacency was shattered by the advent of the Theory of Games. While it is arguable that nothing in the original Theory of Games and Economic Behaviour is a theory of anything which one would be interested in for its own sake, as the problems are too simplified or unreal, it cannot be doubted that there are few branches of social theory which do not show the effect of the work. The theoretical development of alliance formation is no exception to this. The theory of n-person games (n being greater than two) is as much a theory of alliances as anything else. Riker's *Theory of Coalitions* was an explicit development of n-person game theory. This book can be said to have given coalition theory its own identity and defined a set of problems which, even if they are later dismissed, must be commented on. He defines his problems as zero-sum problems and works for this basis. In such cases as elections, with which Riker is particularly concerned, the identification of the problem as zero-sum may not be unreasonable. However, for many purposes this is clearly inadequate.

While clearly in the same tradition as Riker, David Wilkinson approaches the problem using a different set of assumptions in order to get at an expanded class of issues. He abandons Riker's zero-sum assumption which though perhaps justifiable in some contexts is not justifiable as a general assumption. However, Riker made it to keep the problem within a bearable degree of complexity. Wilkinson's simplifying assumption is to restrict the problems he is dealing with to the triad, that is to the conflict between just three actors. This is less artifical than it sounds. While it is true that the world does not conveniently split into three-person conflicts so that triadic conflict is commonplace, the analytical problems involved in more than two-person conflicts are found as soon as one moves up from two to three actors; there is little reason to assume that the move from three to a greater number of actors brings any new analytical problem. This is not to say that, for example, seven-person conflict may not be more complex than three-party conflict, but that the problems are more complex varients of those found in the three-party situation. This is not true in the move from two to three, where the nature of the whole activity is altered so that it is a different type of problem — one in which alliances can occur.

Wilkinson's concentration on the triad is most illuminating and it is hard to see how a satisfactory theory of alliances could be achieved without a thorough analysis of the problems posed in this book. Just as the device of the two-person situation was psychologically, though not logically, necessary to clarify some of the essential problems of conflict, so the problems of alliance formation can be most profitably analysed in the very simplest social system in which alliances are possible — namely the three-party social system. By sweeping away the complexities one can get at the essentials, and once one has got the three-party situation straight, can then draw in the complexities of greater numbers. This seems to me a major contribution of Wilkinson's work — to have posed the problem bluntly and then gone on to work at it in this light. The removal of the zero-sum restriction draws attention to the significance of the relative pay-offs, and it is by thorough analysis of these that the frequent instability of triadic conflict becomes apparent. Wilkinson poses the question, when is a triadic conflict stable? That is, when do the parties continue their conflict each against the other and refrain from forming alliances? He finds under most configurations of pay-offs and with various innocuous behavioural assumptions, that alliances are likely to form, and he is able in most cases to predict which one will do so.

This theory of the triad is not restricted to just one form of conflict situation. It is a theory of a particular process relevant to conflict which has general application, given that the relatively moderate assumptions about the ordering of pay-offs can be met. Thus business alliances, intergovernmental alliances, political party alliances, and personal alliances can all be interpreted within this framework. Experimental approaches, which are given a considerable amount of attention, also, of course, fall within this framework. Wilkinson himself has not done experimental work but his analysis of what has already been done is illuminating to the general argument.

This study is interdisciplinary in the sense that the theory covers a wide variety of situations, a form which is becoming widespread; various forms of behaviour are identified, analysed, and then applied to many different contexts. Thus there is a widely discussed theory of bargaining behaviour which is frequently developed in the form of bargaining models which are intended to have general application to all forms of bargaining behaviour — from industrial bargaining, to international bargaining to inter-personal bargaining. Each class of behaviour has its own peculiarities just as each individual event within its class does, but nevertheless these activities have sufficient in common for us to regard them provisionally as different versions of the same thing. It is true of the theory of games in general, and of the various offshoots from the theory, that they are intended to have general application to all sorts of different social contexts. This leads to a redifinition of categories within the social sciences. Traditionally groups of activities are classified together because of their common subject matter. When we classify the world according to forms of behaviour (whether bargaining behaviour, alliance behaviour, conflict behaviour or whatever) we cut across the traditional boundaries and set up new ones. This should not discomfit us unduly.

The methodological spirit in which this book is written is sadly yet to receive its due amongst political scientists particularly in Britain. Even in the United States, where methodological innovation is regarded with a less jaundiced eye, it would be hard to pretend that formal and mathematical political analysis was sweeping the campuses. To my prejudiced and committed eye however the approach seems the main hope for developing a Political Science which is not just an *ad hoc* collection of plausible hypotheses stuck together by a few case histories. Theories must be developed which make generalisations about behaviour which are part of an integrated deductive system. These generalisations must be built up painstakingly from simple models of situations, which are then made more and more complex until they form a set of statements which can be tested against reality and rejected if found incorrect. This does not mean that the simple model exists purely as the handmaiden of the complex theory which it is hoped it will result in. It also has explanatory value in its own right, if it is a good model which reveals some of the underlying characteristics of various processes, enabling a greater understanding of particular events. Alliance formation is not the only area of Political Science which has been penetrated by the model builders. Voting theory is another conspicuous example; so is the theory of interactive processes such as arms races; and of course there is the theory of collective goods — which is another good example of a problem which does not lie neatly within any disciplinary boundary being a mixture of Economics and Political Science.

There are of course two problems in adopting such approaches. First can theory be developed at all and secondly, assuming it can, is the building of formal models which can then be complicated the most appropriate way of going about it? The second is almost a straw man. It is hard to dispute that it is a possible way of developing theory. Given one's uncertainty about the nature of the creative process if it is a possible path, then some of us should follow it. If there is another path to which others are inclined then it would seem churlish to curb their inclinations.

The first question is the substantive one. Let us consider it in the case of alliances. There are some students of politics who would argue that it is impossible for there to be a general theory of alliances, but only *ad hoc* explanations of particular alliance formations. However, to explain things on an *ad hoc* basis is to have at the back of our minds the view that actors under particular circumstances do certain sorts of things. If we are to explain things then we do so in terms of generalisations and if this is so then it is our obligation to work for the best set of generalisations we can get to — that is a theory of testable and tested propositions which covers as wide a domain as possible.

The path to a theory of alliance which meets the criteria expressed in the last sentence is still a long one. No-one, and certainly not the scholar who wrote this book, would want to claim otherwise. However, that this is a significant step along the way cannot be doubted. We can only regret that it must be David Wilkinson's last work.

Michael Nicholson
London 1976

CHAPTER 1

INTRODUCTION

1.1. CONFLICT RESEARCH

For centuries conflict has been recognised as something very basic in life. Research workers in such fields as Economics, Sociology, Psychology and International Relations have all made contributions to the study of this phenomenon. But it is only in the past couple of decades that Conflict Research has emerged as a separate discipline worthy of its own department in a University. In view of this fact it is fitting that a study in this field should include at least a short section dealing with the methodology and philosophy of the subject.

Taking any academic discipline we must look at the questions it poses and seeks to answer and the techniques it uses to arrive at such answers. Dealing as it does with human beings as decision makers, Conflict Research is undoubtedly a social science. A science exists to make generalisations about the behaviour of observable events. The social scientist is concerned with the behaviour of human beings in given environments, and looks for consistencies in order to formulate theories of general classes of behaviour.

The generalisations which the conflict researcher looks for are those concerned with conflict. The assumption is that conflict between units at all levels of interaction from the personal to the international level exhibit certain consistencies that can be observed or measured. Thus he is looking for a general theory of Conflict as opposed to the special theories developed by the sociologist or psychologist for instance. This general theory seeks to demonstrate the abstracted similarities between

15

conflict situations at all levels of society and thereby to provide a greater understanding of each particular kind of conflict than can be provided by the relevant special theory. Consequently the general theory will provide a better account of all conflict phenomena than could be provided by the amalgamation of all special theories.

The conflict researcher's approach is different from that of the historian or traditional international-relations theorist. Whilst the historian would choose a particular event and study it fully, the conflict researcher takes the event and strips it of many of its real-world trimmings, looking at its basic underlying structure. He may then do this with other events too, and end up making generalisations about these basic structures. His research is extensive rather than intensive, concentrating on many units or events but on few variables. The historian's research on the contrary is intensive, concentrating on a single event but many variables. Only by abstracting in the way he does can any orderliness be observed and the conflict researcher make his generalisations. The generalisations usually refer to certain aspects of situations rather than the situations in total. Generalising may contribute relatively little to the solution of some specific problem, but considerably more light may be thrown on some specific aspect of the problem.

As with any science, the idea of generalising and looking at basic underlying structures suggests mathematics as a convenient tool of analysis. Mathematical models have in fact been used widely in conflict Conflict Research, but as many authors have stressed, the type of mathematics required is not necessarily that which serves the natural sciences so well. True, certain techniques have successfully been applied, a notable example being Richardson's use of calculus in building models of arms races.[1] But the social sciences must develop the kind of mathematics which best fits situations in which human decision making is involved. One very promising branch of mathematics is Game Theory, and this is discussed at length later in this study.

Three types of mathematical model can be distinguished — descriptive, prescriptive and predictive. Having abstracted some aspect of the situation being considered we may build a model to describe the underlying features which we see. Such a model enables us to clearly analyse the situation, and if we are lucky may provide us with insights which were not apparent from a mere verbal description. A prescriptive model enables us to make recommendations to a decision maker about what to do when confronted with a given situation. In order to do this we must first decide on what his objectives are, and the usual assumption is that he is trying to maximise something. We can then tell him that in order to maximise this something he must behave in a certain way. Traditional Game Theory is a prescriptive theory. Given that the decision makers behave in the prescribed way we can then make predictions about what the outcome will be. In this thesis several models concerning coalition formation are built. We assume that decision makers are attempting to maximise something and we prescribe ways in which rational decision makers should act. If they do behave thus we can predict which coalition should form.

A model which predicts something can be tested either by observing historical data, or by experimentation and comparing observations or results with predictions. Gaming experiments are very popular in Conflict Research and related fields. Here human subjects are confronted with a simple choice situation. The choices actually made can be compared with any predictions. One must be careful here in drawing any conclusions since even if the predicted outcome results it does not necessarily follow that the criteria used by the decision makers were those postulated by the model. Conceivably experiments could be arranged to prevent this sort of thing happening, but when human beings are the units being studied, so many psychological variables may be at work that it is difficult to arrange an experiment which eliminates all but a few. One can attempt to solve this problem by performing the experiment on different classes of subjects between whom one believes these variables differ. Thus similar experiments may be carried out using male and female subjects, differences in decision making noted and attempts made to relate these differences to the variables which could not be eliminated. More will be said on these topics when we deal with gaming in chapter 3.

Perhaps expectedly in a field which has developed out of many isolated fields of study the problems facing conflict researchers have been made more difficult by the lack of conformity on basic definitions. Fink has illustrated this problem with respect to the definition of conflict itself, and other terms such as competition and power are open to many definitions and interpretations.[2] It is a pity that more work has not been done to iron out these basic problems. But as things stand we have opted here for certain definitions which are stated in the appropriate places and adhered to thereafter. Whilst these may not be the best definitions and may be totally unacceptable to some people, it was felt that in order to get anywhere with this research a stand had to be made somewhere.

1.2   WHY STUDY THE TRIAD?

Some writers have argued that the ultimate end of Conflict Research is the prevention of war and that Conflict Research is therefore a branch of International Relations. It is admitted however that since conflict exists in other spheres there may be work emanating from other disciplines, such as Sociology and Social Psychology, which should also be considered because it may provide insights on the problems at the international level.

Insofar as it is one aim of this study to integrate research which, though connected, has been carried out in isolated fields, this work hopes to fulfil to some extent this second need. But the end of this study is not solely to investigate three-nation wars. Rather it is to look at triads in general and provide some ideas about their formation and viability.

Much of the sociological theory on the triad insists that such a group is unstable and fraught with conflict, two of its members always tending to identify with each other far more than with the third. The two may form a coalition or act as one with respect to the third and so the group effectively degenerates into a dyad. Witness the popular sayings "Three never agree" and "Two is company, three is a crowd". But is this split always likely to occur? If not, under what conditions does it occur? Which particular two members will join forces? What role will the third party play? These are some of the questions which must be answered.

There are also triadic situations where these are not the relevant questions. With such phenomena as 'mediation' and 'divide and rule' where a third party intervenes on some existing dyadic process (or interaction between two others) such questions as "Will the mediator succeed in resolving the dispute?", "Will the divider succeed in fomenting conflict between others?" and "What sort of qualities are desirable in such third parties?" arise. Analysis of triadic situations of these types may throw some light on the process taking place after the split in the previous kind of triad.

A further useful aspect of this study is that it takes the dyad out of isolation. Much work in Conflict Research has been concerned with the two-person group and this is logical since it is the lowest group in which there is an interaction. But to take two people of two nations out of their environment and analyse this interaction may mean that one arrives at false conclusions because certain features have been neglected. The influence of third parties on the decisions of the pair may be missed. A study of the triad may help one to understand the dyadic process more fully.

Finally, the triad is the lowest-order group in which coalitions or

18

sub-groupings are possible. In mathematics, the transition from the two-variable to the three-variable case (corresponding to the dyad and triad respectively) involves many complications but these are fewer than those encountered in higher cases. At least a geometric representation is still comprehensible and the number of possible re-groupings is small. It is therefore fitting that a study of coalition formation should begin with the triad.

1.3   THE MONAD AND THE DYAD

Below the level of the triad we encounter the single person and the two-person group. As these are the entities into which the triad may disintegrate, it is important to consider them in some detail. We use the term 'person' here to describe any entity such as a human being, a group of people or a nation, which may be considered as one unit or decision maker. Equally we can and do use from time to time, the terms 'party' and 'actor'.

During its lifetime any party has to make decisions on the issues with which it is confronted. The Oxford Dictionary defines an issue as "The point in question, especially between contending parties in action". The decisions a party has to make are determined by its aims or goals with respect to the issue. These in turn are influenced by its present position which in turn is influenced by its past decisions and extraneous factors. We can represent the system diagramatically as shown in fig. i.

Having set out its aims the party considers what actions are available and what the possible outcomes from a given action may be. Each outcome is associated with a payoff which may be positive if it is a reward and negative if it involves a cost. This payoff may be in real terms such as money or it may be purely psychological. Even if it is in real terms we still have to enter the realm of the psychological to determine the true value of the outcome to the party concerned. It is not within the scope of this study to discuss the notion of utility and its many associated problems but we note in passing that such problems do exist, especially in the comparison of the payoff of two different parties.

In evaluating the payoffs the party considers the various extraneous factors and the way he believes they will operate. A decision is made and the actual outcome is determined by the way in which these factors really do operate. The party then arrives back at the starting position, modifies his aims if necessary and proceeds in the same manner. This goes on until no further decisions on the issue are required.

It is perhaps a contradiction in terms to say that the monad or single

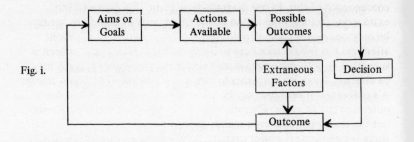

Fig. i.

party is the lowest group but since its analysis as far as we are concerned is pretty trivial, this point need not bother us. In our context an analysis of the monad must be an analysis of those decisions which are not affected by the decisions of other parties. Thus the extraneous factors in the above scheme are only natural forces such as the weather. Psychology is the field in which the individual human being is studied in this way, while the purely internal decisions of a single nation are studied by the government specialist. In studying the triad we shall only be interested in the decisions made by any member with respect to the other members, so the monad as conceived here need concern us no longer.

The dyad on the other hand is very important. The triad can split up into three possible dyads and isolates and we have to consider the relationships both between the members of the dyad and between the dyad and the isolate. In the latter case the dyad may act as one party and the isolate as another so that in effect we are considering a dyad.

Strictly speaking any two entities can form a dyad and these entities need not be of the same type. A dyad may consist of two people, two nations, an individual and a group of people and so on. In passing it is worth making a note of what is referred to as the 'identification problem'. This poses the question "Who is the real decision maker?". In dealing with nations for instance the decisions made, though in the name of a nation, are actually made by one or a few individuals. While important in some contexts this problem need not worry us, for we shall be primarily concerned with triads in their more abstract form and all that we require is that there be three decision makers.

Any two entities, then, constitute a dyad but that dyad is only of real interest if there exists an interaction between its members. Interaction is defined by saying "Two parties interact over some issue if the actions of one or both, taken with respect to that issue, influence the outcomes of the other". Note that it is the outcomes i.e. payoffs which are affected. Behaviour may also be affected but only as a

20

consequence of this. In our diagramatic scheme (fig. i) one of the extraneous factors is the action of the other party. The influence may be only one-way e.g. the decisions of the Prime Minister might well affect me but my decisions are unlikely to affect him. If the influence is exerted in both directions it may still be very unequal. Party A may be able to change B's outcomes to a far greater extent than B can change A's outcomes. A decision may be taken specifically to alter another's outcomes but often the alteration may take place quite passively without the decision maker even realising what is happening. Sometimes a party is said to exert power over another because by controlling the others' outcomes he can make him behave in a certain way. Power will be dealt with extensively in later sections.

The sequence of decisions and actions taken through time and their consequences on the parties involved are called the 'Interaction Process' or in this case the 'Dyadic Interaction Process'. It should be noted that this process does not necessarily involve any communication between the two parties. Sometimes, in cases where purely psychological payoffs are concerned, it is sufficient for party A to keep note of what B does in order for B to exert an influence, and sometimes a party may not know who is affecting its payoffs when they are of a material nature.

When two parties interact they find themselves in a certain state which may be characterised by conflict, co-operation or a mixture of the two. This state refers to the particular issue in question. A state of conflict is said to exist if the parties pursue goal states which are incompatible.[3] This means that only one party can experience the outcome which he desires. If the only possible outcomes are those in which one party attains this position and the other does not, the situation is one of complete conflict. If certain compromise outcomes are also feasible, the situation is said to contain elements of conflict and co-operation. A state of pure co-operation exists if by co-ordinating their actions the parties can achieve outcomes which are mutually beneficial. In other words their best outcomes are not incompatible.

From now on the issue at stake, together with its possible outcomes and decisions available to the parties, will be referred to as a *game*. The parties themselves will be called *players* of the game. If the two parties interact over some issue they are said to play a game. If they interact over several issues they play several games but it may be possible to combine the choices open to the players and the payoffs involved in such a way that in effect we need consider only one game composed of all the smaller ones. For instance if two nations go to war many issues are usually at stake and not all of these are necessarily issues involving conflict. But the decision whether to go to war or not is taken when all these issues have been assessed together. The dyadic interaction process is the actual playing of the game. All games have rules and it is these which determine in part what decisions are available to the players. The player's resources may also limit the number of choices he has.

Time is another important factor when considering interactions. We may pose the questions "How does a game start?", "How long does it last?" and "When does it end?".

In answering the first question we distinguish two types of game — those played out of choice and those played not out of choice. The former are chiefly of the co-operative kind. Two parties with common aims may find that they can further these or improve their payoffs, by acting co-operatively. One party may go to great lengths to seek out another. The marital pair is a good example. Sometimes games involving conflict are played out of choice, sporting events being an obvious example. But most games of conflict are forced on one or both players. They will perhaps find they are making claims which are incompatible e.g. two car drivers travelling in opposite directions in a narrow street may find themselves at an impasse. There are also cases of co-operative games being played because circumstances force them, as when two people finding themselves seated together in a railway compartment chat together to pass the time.

The duration of a game depends on the decision-making process, and on the time it takes for actions to be carried out and the payoffs to accrue. The decision making may end long before the payoffs are complete. Some games require a once-for-all decision while others require many spread over time. Often a choice has to be made many times for the same repertoire of possible actions. It does not necessarily follow, in such circumstances, that the payoffs accompanying the same choice are invariant through time.

A game ends or ceases to exist when no further decisions are necessary and payoffs have been completed. Games of conflict end when one player surrenders or is defeated i.e. he no longer wishes to occupy or is incapable of occupying a goal state incompatible with that of the other player. Alternatively, some compromise solution may be found if this is possible. Games of co-operation end when one or both players' goal states change in such a way that they can no longer improve their payoffs by their continued association.

A convenient method of representing a game is by the use of a matrix. Some games, such as bargaining, are better represented in other ways but the matrix can be used to describe a large number of situations. This use of the matrix takes us into the realm of Game Theory and it is to this which we now turn.

1.4 TWO-PERSON GAME THEORY

In this section it is assumed that the reader is already familiar with
Game Theory and much of what is said is intended as a resumé. A
fuller account of the basic ideas is given by Rapoport.[4] Other authors
have dealt with the subject in greater detail from a mathematical view-
point, but such detail is not required by us.[5]

Game Theory is chiefly of use as a descriptive or analytic tool, a
device to help one to see the basic structure of, and to provide
insights into, a situation. Occasionally it does offer prescriptions to
the decision makers. Although there is a theory of games for any
number of players it is as yet poorly developed for cases of more than
three players, and even two- and three-person Game Theory leaves much
to be desired. In this section we deal only with the two-person case,
leaving the three-person case to Chapter 3.

$$B$$

		β_1	β_2
	α_1	a_{11}, b_{11}	a_{12}, b_{12}
A	α_2	a_{21}, b_{21}	a_{22}, b_{22}

Fig. ii.

Fig. ii represents a game played between two players A and B each
having two choices α_1, α_2 and β_1, β_2 respectively. These choices are
sometimes known as strategies. The payoffs to A and B are seen in the
cells of the matrix. The suffixes refer to the choices made. Thus a_{12} is
A's payoff when A chooses α_1 and B chooses β_2.

Before going any further some of the shortcomings of Game Theory
should be mentioned. It assumes that the players have complete
knowledge of the set of alternatives available to them and the possible
payoffs which might result from each choice. In the real world
neither of these statements may be true. Further, in the real world,
payoffs may change over time, as may the rules of play. This means
that different matrices may be needed to represent what is essentially
the same interaction.

Another point to note is that the rules may or may not allow
communications between the players. The term 'negotiable game' is
used to describe a game where it is allowed as opposed to a 'non-
negotiable game' where it is not allowed. Further the rules may or may

not prescribe an order of play. Sometimes players must make decisions simultaneously, sometimes one can make his choice, knowing the choice of the other.

Game Theory assumes that players are rational in the sense that they seek to win or maximise their payoffs. Thus any prescriptions it makes are for rational players.

Let us look first at the matrix representation of an interaction in which one player (A) can affect the payoff of the other (B) but B cannot affect A's payoff.

		B	
		β_1	β_2
A	α_1	1, 0	1, 0
	α_2	1, 2	1, 2

Fig. iii.

A's payoff is constant no matter what B does. B's payoff however can be 0 or 2 depending on whether A chooses α_1 or α_2.

		B	
		β_1	β_2
A	α_1	1, 1	1, 0
	α_2	2, 3	2, 2

Fig. iv.

In fig. iv. the differences are that B has some control over his own payoffs — he can improve them by playing β_1, and though A can still influence B's payoffs he can only lower them (by playing α_1) at some cost to himself.

Coming to these interactions in which the influence works in both directions we find that states of complete conflict are represented by what are called 'Zero-Sum Games'. This means that in any cell of the matrix whatever A gains, B loses and vice versa. Fig. v. represents such a game.

The entries in each cell always add up to zero. It is games such as these in which Game Theory does prescribe an optimal strategy or method of decision making for the players.

24

B

	β_1	β_2
α_1	5, −5	−1, 1
α_2	−2, 2	3, −3

Fig. v.   A

Suppose A and B have a large number of possible choices from which A chooses α_i and B chooses β_j. The payoffs are a_{ij} and b_{ij} respectively. A seeks to choose some α_i in order to maximize a_{ij} and B seeks some β_j in order to maximise b_{ij}. For any α_i A is guaranteed the minimum a_{ij} in that row of the matrix. He therefore chooses that α_i for which his guaranteed minimum is greatest.

In the above matrix A should choose α_1 because his guarantee of −1 exceeds that of −2 from choosing α_2. By similar reasoning B should choose β_2. The resulting outcome can however be improved for A if he switches to α_2 so there is no equilibrium or 'saddle point' as it is called, in this matrix.

Suppose the matrix had been that in fig. vi.

B

	β_1	β_2
α_1	5, −5	−1, 1
α_2	3, −3	−2, 2

Fig. vi.   A

α_1 and β_2 would again be played but there would be no incentive to move away from the outcome (−1, 1). Such a cell represents a saddle point and the payoffs therein represent the value of the game to the players, i.e. −1 for A and 1 for B in this case. If this game is played many times over we expect the outcome to be in this cell each time. If there is no saddle point we expect the outcome to vary. We can easily tell if a game has a saddle point. Consider A's payoffs. If one payoff is at the same time the minimum in its row and the maximum in its column, the cell in which it falls is a saddle point.

We have seen that not all zero-sum games have a saddle point; so what strategy should the players then follow in order to maximise their payoff? The answer is a mixed strategy i.e. select an α_i or a β_j at

25

random with known probability. These probabilities are obtained quite easily as follows.

Suppose A chooses his α_i with probabilities x_i (where $\sum\limits_{\text{all i.}} x_i = 1$),

and B chooses his β_j with probabilities y_j (where $\sum\limits_{\text{all j.}} y_j = 1$).

If A played just one α_i against B's mixed y, A's average expected payoff is $\sum\limits_{\text{all j}} a_{ij}\, y_j$. If A played a mixed strategy, x, against B's mixture, A's average payoff would be $\sum\limits_{\text{all i}} \sum\limits_{\text{all j}} a_{ij}\, x_i\, y_j$.

A is guaranteed the minimum of $\sum \sum a_{ij}\, x_i\, y_j$ over the various y's which B may adopt. He therefore choses his x's to maximise this minimum. Similarly B may be thought of as choosing his y's in order to minimise the possible maximum he would have to pay A. The Minimax Theorem then says

The $\dfrac{\text{(Maximum for)}}{\text{(possible x's\ \ )}}$ of the $\dfrac{\text{(Minimum for)}}{\text{(possible y's\ \ )}}$ of $\sum \sum a_{ij}\, x_i\, y_j$

= the $\dfrac{\text{(Minimum for)}}{\text{(possible y's\ \ )}}$ of the $\dfrac{\text{(Maximum for)}}{\text{(possible x's\ \ )}}$ of $\sum \sum a_{ij}\, x_i\, y_j$

= V, the value of the game.

Another theorem states: "If one player plays his optimal strategy then the payoff will remain equal to the value of the game no matter what mixture of good or worthwhile strategies the other player uses".

We make use of these theorems to solve the zero-sum game without a saddle point. As an illustration consider the game in fig. v. Let A play α_1 and α_2 in proportions x and $1 - x$. Let B play β_1 and β_2 in proportions y and $1 - y$. If B plays β_1, A can expect an average payoff of

(5) $(x) + (-2)(1-x) = V$, the value of the game to A.

i.e. $7x - 2 = V$

If B plays β_2, A can expect

$(-1)(x) + (3)(1-x) = V$

i.e. $3 - 4x = V$.

26

Solving the simultaneous equations we find

$$x = \frac{5}{11} \qquad\qquad V = \frac{13}{11}$$

This means that A should play α_1 and α_2 in the proportions 5 : 6 over different plays of the game. We can similarly show that B should play β_1 and β_2 in proportions 4 : 7. The value of the game to B is $-\frac{13}{11}$ so the game favours A.

In practice zero-sum situations rarely occur and even when they do the players would probably not know of this method of solution since there is nothing intuitively obvious about it. Also if we assume we can randomise the choices we are assuming a long series of plays of the game whereas in practice it may only be played once. In this case the best the player could do would be to use some random device, with probabilities as suggested above, to select one of the strategies and hope for the best.

Most conflict situations permit of some bargaining or accommodation between the two sides i.e. there is an element of co-operation. Game Theory can still help us for there is a large class of games known as non-zero-sum games which are applicable here. The drawback here is that the majority of non-zero-sum games do not have a solution in the above sense so no prescriptions can be offered. Those which have solutions are of a fairly trivial nature such as that of fig. vii.

B

	β_1	β_2
α_1	4, 4	2, 3
α_2	3, 2	1, 1

Fig. vii.   A

It is obvious that A will play α_1 and B will play β_1 since each then gets his best payoff. Nor will it be difficult to achieve this outcome because each player has what is called a 'dominant strategy'. This means for example that whatever B plays, α_1 is always the best choice for A, always earning him a better payoff than does α_2. Likewise β_1 dominates β_2 for B.

One of the best known and most extensively studied games in this

27

class is that known as the 'Prisoners' Dilemma'.[6] This game is structured in such a way that the second strategy is dominant for both players, and they end up in the bottom right hand cell. But the payoff here is considerably worse than that if both play their first strategy. A typical payoff structure is:

B

		C	D
A	C	5, 5	−10, 10
	D	10, −10	−5, −5

Fig. viii.

The strategies have been labelled C and D following the usual notation of Co-operative and Defective choices. From the individual's point of view it is best to defect but viewed collectively strategy C is the best choice. This is the dilemma. Once in the bottom right hand cell it is difficult to move out since anyone who does so alone will be punished.

Such a matrix describes a wide variety of real life situations. Price cutting in duopoly is one instance. If one party cuts his price he does well at the expense of the other, but this motivates the other to cut his price and then both are worse off. The problem of disarmament is another example. Both major powers may be considered to be in the bottom right hand cell of a matrix where they are making large spendings on armaments. If both disarmed together both would be better off, but if only one of them did so the other would gain at its expense.

As Game Theory cannot prescribe a satisfactory solution to these games, behavioural scientists have used experimentation to investigate them. Pairs of students have been confronted with the matrix and told to make their choices over a long series of plays of the game or trials. The frequencies of co-operative and defective choices have been tabulated, graphed and analysed. Models based on certain psychological propensities have been built in attempts to predict the patterns of play.

Such games have been played under a variety of conditions. Usually no communication is allowed between players but even if it is there is no guarantee that they will stick to their stated intentions, so the dilemma still exists even here. Other factors which have been investigated are the characteristics of the players — their sex, age, status, etc., the motivation e.g. the players may be told to maximise their own payoff, the combined payoff or the difference between payoffs.

Sometimes a stooge is used to try to induce some play in the subject or to investigate reactions to certain moves. Some interesting results have come out of these experiments and no doubt many more will do so.

One other aspect of Game Theory needs a brief mention and that is the idea of side payments. If communications are allowed before choices are made the players may be able to strike some bargain whereby one player agrees to transfer some of his payoff to the other. Of course this involves the notion of trust or some type of binding agreement. In some situations this sort of thing may be more realistic since the possible outcomes may not be confined to three or four alternatives but a large number. Sometimes however the payoffs are indivisible and there is no question of side payments.

Closely connected with side payments but not strictly within the realm of Game Theory is a body of work concerned with the process of bargaining. Again most work has considered the two-person case and perhaps the best known theories are those advanced by Zeuthen and Hicks[7] and Nash[8].

1.5 DEFINING THE TRIAD

The time has now come to attempt some definition of the triad. Just as any two entities (people, groups or nations) may be considered a dyad, any three may be considered a triad; but again the group is only of interest if there is some interaction between its members. For the dyad we have seen there are three possibilities — no interaction, interaction with one-way influence and interaction with two-way influence. A triad can be split up into three pairs and for each pair there are these three possibilities giving rise to sixteen essentially different triads.

Simple representations of these follow. Arrows represent interactions, the heads pointing in the direction of influence. The first is rather trivial since all three parties are in no way linked.

1. No interactions

B

A   C

2. One interaction, one-way influence

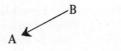

3. One interaction, two-way influence

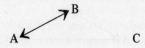

   In the next six types there is no interaction between B and C. Often in these types such an interaction may be later induced because of their relationship with A.

4. Two interactions, one party influencing the others

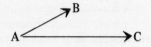

5. Two interactions, two parties influencing a third

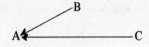

6. Two interactions, chain of influence

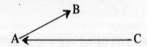

7. Two interactions, one with two-way influence

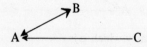

8. As 7, but one out of the pair with two-way influence influences the third party

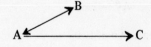

9. Two interactions, both two-way influence

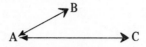

In the final seven, all members interact.

10. Three interactions, circle of influence

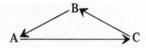

11. Three one-way interactions, one member free of influence

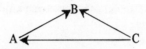

12. As 11 but one of two-way influence

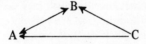

13. Three interactions, one being two-way influence

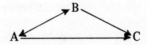

14. As 13, but the party which is influenced by one out of the pair in two-way influence, in turn influences the other one in the pair

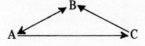

15. Three interactions, two of two-way influence

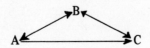

31

16. Three interactions, all of two-way influence

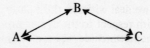

We can distinguish firstly the triad in which all interactions refer to the same issue. All three players might be involved in the same way, e.g. three people bargaining over the division of something. They may find themselves in a state of complete conflict, complete co-operation or a mixture. The new feature, aside from those of the dyadic inter-action, is that the aims of two members may be more compatible with each other than with the aims of the third. It is here that we encounter the possibility of coalition formation. Two members may find that by acting together they can benefit mutually at the expense of the third. So with respect to this particular issue they may form a coalition. Later we will spend some time defining a coalition more precisely.[9]

Sometimes the same issue may involve two players in a way which is different from that in which the third is involved, e.g. mediation. The interaction is essentially dyadic insofar as (a) it exists before the third party becomes a relevant force and (b) the payoff in real terms only goes to two members. But the third may derive some psychological payoff influenced by the actions of the others and in turn his opinions or actions may influence their decision making.

We can distinguish secondly a triadic situation in which each pair interacts over a different issue. Insofar as the choices of a player in one game are dependent on his choices in another, the three games can be combined into one overall game by re-defining the choices available and combining the payoffs from the different games. If the choices in the original games are independent each dyad can be treated separately without reference to the third party.

1.6 THE SCOPE AND OUTLINE OF THIS STUDY

This study is of a purely theoretical nature. It is concerned basically with the triadic interaction process, the way it begins, its course and its ending. In particular it is concerned with coalition formation in the triad. If a coalition forms we are effectively back to a dyadic inter-action process and so the triad, as three separate decision makers, has ceased to exist. Under what conditions does this take place and given these conditions which coalition is likely to form?

We shall be concerned almost entirely with situations where three parties interact over the same issue, though not always with those triads in which all members occupy a similar role with respect to the issue.

Thus in Chapter 2 we deal with the third party standing in a special relationship with respect to the dyadic process going on between the other two. This chapter includes sections on mediation, divide and rule, delegation, competition, intervention etc. and attempts a classification of these based on the role of the third party. The different third parties are compared using simple graphical representations.

Chapter 3 deals with the theory and experimentation on the triad which has been accomplished so far. It attempts to integrate this work and give a critical assessment of the present state of theory and usefulness of the experimental work. Included here are sections on Game Theory and several theories of coalition formation.

Chapter 4 examines more deeply the notion of stability and the factors which contribute to the stability or instability of the triad. It recognises the importance of power as an important determinant of coalition formation and points out some of the shortcomings of previous models. It goes on to suggest a different game and analyses this by building a mathematical model of the situation.

Chapter 5 again takes up the notion of power and the problem of predicting coalition formation in general, with power as the main variable, defined in a particular way. Returning to the dyad a measure of the amount of conflict in a given situation and a measure of the amount of power exerted by a player are developed. These are applied to several different two-person games.

In Chapter 6 we use these measures to build a model to predict coalition formation in three-person games, i.e. to decide whether it will occur, and between which players if it does occur. Several situations with different patterns of influence are considered. Some predictions are compared with experimental results.

Chapter 7 returns to some of the situations elaborated in chapter 2 and applies the model to these in an attempt to examine certain properties of the third party and the likely outcomes of the triadic interaction process in these cases.

An overall summary of this book and its conclusions is given in the final chapter.

Notes

1. Lewis F. Richardson, *Arms and Insecurity* (Pittsburg: Boxwood, 1960).
2. Clinton F. Fink "Some Conceptual Difficulties in the Theory of Social Conflict", *Journal of Conflict Resolution* Vol. XII, No. 4 (Dec. 1968), 412–460.

3. Throughout this study we use the term 'conflict' to refer to a state rather than a process.
4. Anatol Rapoport, *Two Person Game Theory* (Ann Arbor, Michigan: Michigan University Press, 1966).
5. See for example Duncan R. Luce and Howard Raiffa, *Games and Decisions* (New York: Wiley, 1957).
6. Anatol Rapoport and Albert M. Chammah, *Prisoners' Dilemma* (Ann Arbor, Michigan: University of Michigan Press, 1965).
7. See R. L. Bishop, "A Zeuthen Hicks Theory of Bargaining", *Quarterly Journal of Economics,* 77, (1963), 559–602.
8. J. F. Nash, "The Bargaining Problem", *Econometrica* 18, (1950), 155–162.
9. Section 3.2 below.

CHAPTER 2

THE INFLUENCE OF THIRD PARTIES

2.1 INTRODUCTION

Sometimes a third party becomes a relevant force in what was originally a dyadic process. In our scheme in fig. i. (page 6), the third party's actual or possible actions become one of the extraneous factors, i.e. the third party can affect the outcomes of the others. This can take place through an alteration in the possible payoffs, or a change in the number of choices available to the others. The effect may be a change in the behaviour of the pair. Certain outcomes may become more desirable and others less desirable, depending on the new payoff structure. In exerting an influence the third party alters the payoff matrix and this sometimes causes the members of the dyad to act differently from what they would have done if the third party had not been there.

Also relevant for consideration in this chapter is the situation where the third party is present from the outset of the dyadic interaction process but stands in a special relationship with respect to the other parties. The dyadic interaction may arise simply because the third party is there, or the third party may take steps to initiate the process. These situations will be clearer when we give examples later.

In refering to the third party we are using the term to refer to the third party as a decision maker. The decision maker is usually a person or group of people, acting on behalf of themselves or some larger body which they represent. Occasionally non-human entities have been suggested as third parties. The law and the market mechanism are often quoted, and Schelling considers traffic lights and the line down the middle of the road as mediators of possible traffic disputes.[1] This work is interesting but not strictly of concern to us though we do touch upon the subject in the section Potential Intervention.[2]

Before going further let us list some simple examples of triads of the types to be considered in this chapter.

a) A bystander intervenes to stop a fight between two other people.
b) In a traffic jam a bystander steps in and is given the authority to direct.
c) The U.N. intervened in Cyprus in the war between Greek and Turkish Cypriots.
d) Courts of arbitration in management-trade unions disputes.
e) Russia offered to act as mediator in the dispute between India and Pakistan over Kashmir.
f) The referee in a football match.
g) Faced with some external enemy, two mutually hostile neighbouring tribes may combine and fight together.
h) Stalin utilized the notion of 'capitalist encirclement', a potential enemy, when faced with internal opposition.
i) The action of the major powers in the world may be constrained somewhat by the presence of neutral countries.
j) The U.S.A. intervened on one side of the Vietnamese war.
k) Two small boys are fighting and one threatens to call in an older brother.
l) A criminal, confronted by the police, takes a hostage.
m) A large buyer of some goods hires a bidder to prevent the seller knowing who is really interested, thereby possibly getting his goods cheaper.
n) One person blackmails another by threatening to tell some secret to a third person.
o) Two men compete for the hand of one woman in marriage.
p) Two sellers compete for one market.

Examples (a) to (f) are all types of mediation. Sometimes this mediation is imposed, sometimes it is offered, sometimes it is invited. (g) and (h) are examples of intervention of a hostile nature. (i) represents a sort of mediation where the mediator takes not active part but exerts some influence merely by being there. (j) to (n) afford examples of a third party intervening on the side of one disputant. He may be invited, or his ally may merely threaten to invite him — for that may be sufficient to achieve the required result. The

36

final two examples are those in which the third party is responsible for the conflict between the members of the dyad.

2.2 A CLASSIFICATION OF THIRD PARTIES

Third parties are classified initially into two broad categories depending on the way in which they exert their influence. Firstly there are *active* third parties which actually take actions to influence the dyadic interaction process. Secondly there are parties, which, though they take no actions, because they are believed to be capable of such, do influence the dyadic process. Such third parties will be called *potential* third parties.

A potential third party may not be aware of the influence he is exerting. An active third party must have some interest in the dyadic interaction process i.e. the latter must affect his payoff otherwise there would be no motive for the action. This payoff, as stated earlier, will often be of a nature different from those made to the other parties. The outcomes for the potential third party however, might well be unaffected by the dyadic interaction process. All that is necessary is that one or both members of the dyad *believe* that the potential third party is an interested party.

Third parties can also be classified depending on when they enter the dyadic process. They may in fact initiate or instigate this process or they may exert an influence on an existing process. Both active and potential third parties may operate in either of these ways. We use the term *active instigation* where a dyadic process begins because of actions taken by the third party. The term *passive instigation* is used to refer to those cases where an interaction begins because the members of the dyad have considered a potential third party. Under active instigation we find all cases of competition — where two parties compete for something controlled by the third party, and instances of the principles known as 'divide and rule' and 'unite and fight'. The latter may also occur under passive instigation and cases of interactions involving blackmail may begin in this way.

We use the term *real intervention* to refer to that influence exerted by an active third party on an existing dyadic process. *Potential Intervention* refers to the influence exerted by a potential third party on an existing dyadic process. The nouns real intervener and potential intervener refer to these third parties respectively. *Intervention* is defined as "An action taken by an actor designed to change in some way the dyadic interaction process going on between two other actors'. Real intervention refers therefore to a situation in which actions are *actually* being taken by the third party, whilst potential intervention refers to a situation in which such actions *might* be

37

taken.

It should be noted that even under real intervention the members of the dyad consider actions which *might* be taken by the third party. The difference from potential intervention is that at least some actions are being taken or threatened by the third party whilst under potential intervention they are not.

Real intervention may occur in any of the following ways. The third party may

a) be invited by both sides e.g. mediation

b) be invited by one side e.g. the ally, hostage or delegate

c) intervene on its own initiative e.g. law courts.

We must consider the intentions of the third party and the dyad's perceptions of these. The ultimate aim of the third party is sometimes the existence of a certain state between the members of the dyad. Thus a dyadic interaction must be instigated or an existing one modified by intervention. Sometimes a state of conflict is desired because the third party derives his greatest satisfaction out of this. Sometimes a state of co-operation or resolution of conflict is desired, as in the case of mediation. Often it is desired to resolve this conflict in favour of one particular side. To achieve these ends the third party attempts to influence the behaviour of one or both members of the dyad by manipulating the payoff structure. Often however the third party has no intention of starting or altering the dyadic interaction but in fact does so.

The success of the third party in his bid depends to a large extent on the others' perceptions of his aims. Their perceptions influence the evaluations these players put on various possible outcomes. In situations involving potential third parties it is only these perceptions which matter. The intentions and the perceptions of them may not of course coincide but where there is an active third party they are more likely to do so, since the dyad has some evidence of the intentions from the actions of the third party.

For each possible decision available to the members of the dyad there are a number of possible outcomes, and by considering these the parties somehow arrive at an expected payoff for each decision. If the third party's action causes the expected payoff to a decision to fall, the action is said to *oppose* that decision. If the action causes the expected payoff to rise, it is said to *favour* that decision. If the expected payoff is unaltered, the action is *neutral* to that decision. The actions of the third party will generally affect different decisions in different ways though sometimes all decisions may be affected in the same way.

We now move on to analyse some particular three-person situations using the Game Theoretic approach. This should enable us to see better the similarities and differences between the various types of third parties. As we make our analysis we shall use illustrations from the real world and consider some of the research already carried out. Sections 2.3 and 2.4 deal with the main areas of instigation. 2.5 gives a general discussion on real intervention and 2.6, 2.7, 2.8 and 2.9 analyse particular examples of this. 2.10 is a general discussion on potential intervention and 2.11 deals with blackmail as a particular case. Finally 2.12 considers the relationships between the various types in more detail.

2.3 COMPETITION

In dealing with the third party as instigator we encounter the large field of competition. We are not concerned with competition between a multiplicity of parties but only with that between two parties to sell something to, buy or gain something from, or impress, a third party. Much of what we say is however relevant to competition with more than two competitors.

We encounter competition at all levels e.g. two men court one woman, two office clerks both seek promotion to one post and their boss must decide who gets it, two firms try to sell a similar product to one market, two art collectors both wish to buy a unique painting and the two Great Powers compete by means of aid or favours to win over some smaller country to their camp. Sometimes the prize is divisible so that both competitors can get something; sometimes only one can win.

But what exactly is meant by the term competition and how is it related to the term conflict.

We said in section 1.3 above that conflict exists between two parties if they pursue goal states which are incompatible. Conflict therefore characterises a situation or state which the parties find themselves in. There are two basic types of conflict:— conflict of interest, which arises from the scarcity of some resource, and conflict of values or beliefs. The former in a way presupposes a consensus, for both parties place some positive value on the good being sought after. Interest conflicts emphasise the similarity of the contestants, their common needs and aspirations.[3] Conflict of value on the other hand is based on a dissensus — the parties do not value the same things and tend therefore to keep apart. It is often difficult however to classify concrete cases of conflict as belonging to either type, since there may be elements of both kinds of conflict.

There has been much debating and much confusion over the terms

39

competition and conflict.[4] As conflict has been used to describe a *state*, we shall use competition to describe a *process*. It is one form of inter-action process which results because of the existence of conflict. Just as fighting is one form of interaction process between two parties in conflict, bargaining is another and competition yet another.

Simmel distinguishes two types of competition. In the first the prize is not in the hands of either adversary, and victory over the competitor, though of the first necessity, means nothing in itself. The goal of the action is attained only with the availability of a value which does not depend on the fight but the choice of the third party. This is the type of competition which is of interest to us. The other type has nothing really to do with third parties. Here each competitor aims at the goal without using his strength on the adversary. Typical of this type is competition in scientific research.[5]

It might be objected that popular usage of the term competition, even when of Simmel's first type, often does not involve a third party. A football match for instance may be considered a competition. Our answer to this is that whilst not apparent a third party is implicit in the rules of the game. The rule 'the side scoring most goals will win' is equivalent to a statement something like 'the side scoring most goals will impress the third party most so he will award the prize to that side'.

Competition may arise out of either of the two types of conflict mentioned above. It is obvious that it will result from conflicts of interest but it will also arise out of conflicts of value because these are often accompanied by some conflict of interest which derives from the scarcity of power and authority. Thus two religious organisations may compete for one man's allegiance.

It should be remembered in dealing with the question of competition for allegiance, that though it is classified under "instigation by the third party" the third party may take no active steps to initiate the process; instead, the competitors themselves may do so. Nevertheless the third party is still responsible, for if he did not exist the situation would not arise.

The position of the third party in competition is a strong one. Sometimes the third party is in a strong position anyway. In cases of competition for promotion, for example, the competitors are usually subordinates of the third party. But the third party's strength in the competitive situation itself derives from his control over the scarce resource which the others want. Control of this means that the third party can easily manipulate the behaviour of the competitors to his own advantage. Miron Rush, in dealing with the succession problem in a dictatorship stresses the problem facing the dictator when appointing his heir. If one person is selected and stands out too much, he may gather too much support and usurp the dictator's position. The solution is to appoint two heirs and 'play them off' against each other so that no one can be sure who will eventually be chosen.[6]

Though he stands in a strong position with respect to the issue over which there is competition, the third party is sometimes weaker than the competitors in other respects. For instance, in a three-party parliamentary system a party winning just a few seats may exert a disproportionate influence, because by allying with one of the other parties, with a large number of seats, it can give that party a parliamentary majority. The others might therefore compete for his allegiance by offering to adopt parts of the third party's programme.

Two situations regarding the choice of the third party can be distinguished. Firstly the choice can be a once and for all affair as in the case of the office clerks. Each member of the dyad attempts to persuade the third party that he is the best choice. He does this by various actions to which the third party may or may not react favourably. The reactions of the third party give the competitors some idea of what his final choice will be. Reactions in the case of the office clerks might be opinions expressed on their work. Once the choice is made the process ends.

Sometimes the choice may be delayed indefinitely and the third party benefit greatly because of the favours conferred on it by the other parties as they compete. Thus the Great Powers both give aid to India. Even if India does not decide in favour of joining either camp each side goes on giving aid to prevent her being too greatly influenced by the others. It is a sort of Prisoners' Dilemma situation. Once both sides have started competing it is difficult to stop because the first to do so may lose and the costs would be great. But in other situations a delay often means that one or both competitors drop out through exhaustion, boredom or inefficiency.

The second situation is that in which the competitive process goes on indefinitely, there being no one final choice in view. The resources at stake are divisible and the competitive process seeks to affect their distribution e.g. two firms compete to increase their share of the market, two political parties compete for votes and two religious organizations compete for followers. The absence of a central decision maker for the third party does not stop effective decisions being made. Each unit making up the third party makes its own choice and the result is the same as if some single person had decided on some allocation between the competitors.

In both situations, while a state of conflict exists between the competitors, such a state may also arise between either of the competitors and the third party. If the situation is one of rewards given over a long period of time, conflicts may arise over distributive injustice. The actions of the third party may be perceived by the competitors as favouring his opponent's decisions and opposing his own to too great an extent.[7] This fact and the possible consequences of a delay in choosing place limits on the third party's actions.

Economists have dealt extensively with competition, much of their work considering the cases of duopoly (two sellers) and duopsony (two buyers). But few of the models built consider the third party — the buyer and the seller respectively — except indirectly via the demand curve.

Shubik offers a simple model of the situation of two buyers B_1 and B_2, and the seller S of some unique indivisible good. This good is valued at u, v and w by B_1, B_2 and S respectively. We consider the case where $u < v < w$.

Suppose the outcome of the transaction is represented by a vector $(\alpha_1, \beta_1, \beta_2)$ where α is the share of S and β_1 and β_2 the shares of B_1 and B_2 respectively. By share we mean something like the derived utility and we assume this is expressible in terms of money. As we shall see later with other three-person games, it often happens that there are an infinite number of solutions. This is true here but the solutions fall into two parts.

(i) $v \leqslant \alpha \leqslant w, \beta_1 = 0, \beta_2 = w - \alpha$

There is no co-operation between the buyers here. The weaker one, B_1 is excluded and B_2 pays a price somewhere between v and w. His net gain in utility is therefore the value he placed on the good less what he paid for it.

(ii) $u \leqslant \alpha \leqslant v$. β_1 and β_2 are decreasing functions
of α and $\alpha + \beta_1 + \beta_2 = w$.

By co-operating the two buyers can force down the price to the interval $u \leftrightarrow v$. The stronger buyer B_2 will purchase the good and pay compensation to B_1. The compensation will be a decreasing function of α i.e. the more B_2 has to pay, the less the compensation. The example illustrates how the seller can benefit from the conflict or lack of co-operation between the buyers.[8]

It should be noted that competition cannot arise from passive instigation because the third party, controlling the objective of the competition, must make certain decisions. Competition is not a process which can take place while the third party remains unaware of it.

2.4 'DIVIDE AND RULE' AND 'UNITE AND FIGHT'

The other major contributions to the class of triads where the third party instigates the dyadic process are aptly described by these well known phrases. It is often said for instance that the British colonists used the technique of divide-and-rule in many of their possessions. If the opposition is divided it is easier to conquer. The success of the third party in his divide-and-rule bid depends on his skill in keeping the others apart, i.e. preventing their co-operation, and on their perceptions of what he is doing. Given that he wants them to behave in a certain way, which is usually some non-collusive way, he must try to make the outcomes from such behaviour appear more desirable than those from any alternative behaviour. If the third party's benefits accruing as a result of their non-co-operative behaviour are seen to be at their expense, the pair may place a greater value on co-operation.

While some cases of divide-and-rule fall strictly under the class of instigation, others fall in the class of intervention. With the latter the difference is that the conflict usually exists before the third party makes his bid. The third party utilises an existing conflict situation to his own advantage and may attempt to intensify that conflict in order to increase his advantage.

When the third party uses the situation to his own advantage the sociologists call him the *'tertius gaudens'* or exploiting third party. In using this term they are usually referring to the case just mentioned where an antithesis already exists between the members of the dyad. They use the motto *'Divide et impera'* to refer to the case where the third party creates that antithesis i.e. our class of instigation.

From the point of view of the members of the dyad it is in their interests to avoid actions which would encourage a would-be divider. They may however fail to see what the intruder is doing until it is too late. If there is insufficient consensus, cohesion or a united front may be impossible. It is worth noting here what Simmel says. Some groups may actually 'attract' enemies or invent enemies in order to maintain or increase group cohesion.[9] Thus we have the example of Stalin justifying some of his policies towards internal dissenters by pointing to capitalist encirclement.

The international sphere provides many examples of the divide-and-rule principle. There are other examples on this scale which deserve a somewhat less strong motto; perhaps tertius gaudens is sufficient. Thus the Soviet Union by means of propaganda about imperialism and neo-colonialism attempts to widen splits between the Western powers and their underdeveloped allies.

Sometimes an interaction of the co-operative kind is induced in the dyad by the third party i.e. by the third party acting as instigator. It may occur because a third party simultaneously attacks two others which previously had no interaction. They find it best to unite and fight against their common enemy. Again we may find a similar principle operating where a third party intervenes on an existing dyadic process. We will consider such examples in the next section.

Under divide-and-rule the third party actively promotes the state of conflict. To do this he might only need to influence the behaviour of one of the others, thus acting in a partial manner. For instance he could persuade A to make some claim on something owned by B. B's behaviour is then only indirectly influenced by the third party. The third party could of course act in an impartial manner if necessary.

Under unite and fight the state of co-operation is not actively promoted by the third party but rather comes about against his wishes. It exists because of his actions but his actions were not directed to that end.

So far the examples considered have arisen from active instigation. Obviously divide-and-rule could not arise from passive instigation because the third party has to take actions to induce the conflictful behaviour. Conflict can be induced however by passive instigation. Blackmail is one such example and is dealt with later. Co-operative behaviour can be induced by passive instigation as when two parties both perceive a third as a potential attacker and perhaps sign a pact of mutual assistance.

2.5 REAL INTERVENTION

In this section we deal broadly with the concept of intervention by a third party on his own initiative. We have already defined intervention in section 2.2. The third party's action may vary from an offer or threat to do something to the actual carrying out of such a deed. The existing dyadic interaction process will generally involve conflict but this is not always true.

The subject of intervention was touched upon in the previous section. Now we consider the divide-and-rule and unite-and-fight principles a little further, assuming the dyadic process already exists when the third party intervenes.

Suppose the third party wishes to intensify or perpetuate a state of conflict between the others. To further this aim he tries to make the others behave in ways which are more and more conflictful e.g. making greater demands, fewer concessions and placing less value on a compromise settlement. He may do this by means of propaganda, threats, promises, deception, separate deals with both sides, attacks etc. As we said previously his success depends on his skill and the perceptions of the other parties. Divide-and-rule will succeed if the third

44

party can maintain a state where the others place a greater value on remaining in conflict rather than on co-operating. If the dyad does reach a sufficient degree of consensus, seeing the third party as a common enemy, the pair may at least temporarily forget their original conflict. The effect of the intervention is then to resolve the conflict i.e. the opposite of what the third party intended.

This resolution may be short lived however. Simmel points out that defensive alignments contain only the minimum of unifying elements necessary to conduct the struggle because the participants frequently have only one interest in common — a concern for survival as independent units. Once this survival is assured the parties may lapse back to their previous state of conflict.[10]

These points are well illustrated by three examples cited by Coser. World War II forced some unification on east and west, partners who had little in common but the enemy, Nazi Germany. Differences were temporarily obliterated because co-operation was the only way to increase their chances of survival. But once the enemy was defeated these differences were too deep to remain in the background, and so the co-operative process terminated.

Also during World War II the Japanese aimed propaganda at the Negro population in the U.S.A., advocating "solidarity between dark and yellow races". The propaganda failed to produce the required conflict between the white and coloured Americans because the Negroes did not abandon their identification with American values.

On the other hand, the enemy attack in British and Dutch possessions in South East Asia resulted in disintegration because the natives saw the attack as aimed only against the colonising powers and not against themselves also.[11]

Sometimes the intentions of the third party are not basically hostile but the results are the same as if they were. Consider for instance the marital pair and the old friend who comes back into contact. Since each member of the dyad is likely to act differently in his presence the pair relationships may be changed. Changes may be observed in the partner and traits become evident which were not preceived before. Such changes may make for antagonism between the pair.

A third party may intervene with the intention of resolving or diminishing the state of conflict between the others. He tries to foster co-operative behaviour because he derives satisfaction from this. His motive may spring from a desire for general peace, respect for the law, or possible gain in prestige from success in this bid. The techniques he uses are set out partly under mediation in the next section but sometimes he enjoys a special position of power which enables threats to be used. Thus the mother of two small children who persist in squabbling may threaten a good hiding if they do not stop. The law is another example. The policeman who intervenes in a street fight is more likely to be heeded than the stranger who does so. As Aubert says the law is a case of an institutionalised readiness to intervene and one thing which makes this acceptable is the quality of distance from the disputants.[12]

The intervention, however good the intentions, may well backfire. Certain basic qualities are really necessary if the intervener is to be acceptable as a mediator. He must appear to be unbiased, i.e. his actions must not appear to favour the interests of one side more than the other, and he must be independent of both. Salience and respect as well as experience and reputation are also important.[13] It is of course the dyad's perception of the third party's intentions which determine their initial reactions, i.e. whether to accept it or not, assuming they have the choice. The bystander who intervenes in a fight may be seen as an interfering busy-body by both parties. They may resent such interference and both turn on the bystander, treating him as a common enemy. For a moment at least they turn to co-operative behaviour, but not in the way which the third party intended.

The success of the intervention bid also depends on the nature of the conflict. If it is one of complete deadlock, such as the traffic jam, intervention is likely to be welcomed. Even those cars which get away last will have got away faster than they would have if no intervention had taken place. The cost of continuing the conflict is the relevant factor here. The loss of face which may ensue if either party makes a concession may not seem to be so great if a third party suggests that such a concession should be made.

Finally the third party is more likely to be effective where the margin of power in the dyad is small. This is because a relation of submission and dominance is far less likely to develop here than one of deadlock.

If intervention is successful a process of conciliation, as covered in the next section, will follow. In terms of power and authority the third party will stand to gain by assuming some position between the rival claims. If he does suggest a middle-of-the-road settlement he emerges as the one who has taken the normatively correct position and his prestige may grow. So to the interests of the pair in reaching a compromise is added the interest of the third party in keeping his unique role and avoiding complete alliance. It may be the case however that one party is predominantly right in its claims, so the third party ought to be independent of both the need for alliance and the opportunity to enhance his position by a middle-of-the-road policy. Hence there is a need for social agencies strong enough to avoid alliances and with a secure status. The law courts are one such agency.[14]

In other cases of intervention the third party may not intend to affect the dyadic process but this does in fact happen. Thus a relationship involving conflict may turn into one of co-operation because the pair see the intervener as a common enemy even though he is not. On the other hand such intervention may promote conflict even though the third party does not intend this.

The intervention will usually be of an impartial nature in the above instances but there are also important examples of partial intervention. Here the third party seeks to change the behaviour of just one member of the dyad, usually in a direction which is favourable to the other member. His intention is to resolve the conflict in a particular direction. Such intervention is perhaps more likely to follow an invitation by a member of the dyad but there are cases where it occurs on the third party's initiative. The person who goes in to aid the under-dog in a fight is one such example. A nation making a declaration of support for or offering assistance to one side in an international conflict is another. Such intervention will be more effective the more credible the declarations and the stronger or more capable the third is. We shall consider this type in more detail under a later section on the ally.

2.6 MEDIATION

Mediation falls in the class of real intervention and may take place on the third party's initiative but is perhaps more likely at the dyad's invitation. In practice a third party might make an offer which is accepted by an invitation. The term mediation is popularly used to cover a large field of conciliation and adjudication. It is one area from which much theory and research has emanated probably because mediation is such an important method of conflict resolution. The third party is assumed to be added to the dyad because of the conflict and with the purpose of terminating the strife. He symbolises the desire that the dispute be disposed of peacefully and expeditiously.

The third party's role can vary greatly. As we move through different levels of conciliation — good offices, inquiry and mediation proper, to adjudication which embraces arbitration and judicial settlement, we see the third party playing an ever-increasing part and being vested with greater powers. While conciliation is based upon persuasion with no binding force, adjudication is of a binding character — the disputants are committed to accept the decision of the third party and the rule of law is paramount. Conciliation can take into account such things as 'honour' and 'face' but adjudication must keep to the letter of the law regardless of the cost or embarrassment to the contending parties. Settlement through conciliation, though it lacks

47

a legal base, is not necessarily inferior to that reached by legal means. Some disputes just cannot be dealt with in the latter way. Conciliation is generally preferred at the international level, since the States involved can retain a veto over the proposed settlement. One thing which makes conciliation acceptable is its flexibility.

Galtung defines mediation as "a debate where the mediator is to direct two antagonists towards mutual acceptance of some point in the compatibility region. His task is not necessarily to decide on that point, only perhaps to indicate it and serve as a debate regulator so as to make the contestants better aware of the structure of the goal space".[15]

Usually the conflict will have existed for some time before the mediator is invited or accepted. The presence of the mediator indicates a certain willingness to negotiate by the contestants and the whole character of the interaction process may be changed. Often the conflict has become charged with non-rational, aggressive overtones and subjective passions loom high. The mediator has the advantage of being outside this emotional field and he can bring an air of cool collectedness to the proceedings.

Often the contending parties have found it difficult to assess their relative strengths. As Coser says, one key function of the mediator is to make such indices available to both parties. In taking some of the responsibility for the outcome of the dispute the mediator thereby reduces the responsibility of the others.[16]

Usually it is not difficult to find a mediator as the presence of comparatively disinterested parties is characteristic of most disputes. There is usually some party which has a vested interest in seeing the peace kept. If however the conflict completely divides a local, national or international community i.e. there are no outsiders, solutions become very difficult because there are no available mediators.[17]

We have already mentioned the basic qualities necessary in the mediator for him to be acceptable to the disputants. For the various techniques which the mediator may adopt, which are outlined below, he will also need certain physical capabilities.

The field of conciliation is divided into three parts depending on the third party's role. Under 'good offices' the third party acts as a go-between but never takes an active part in the proceedings themselves. He may for instance provide facilities for negotiations, a neutral meeting ground. Under 'inquiry' we find the third party playing a more critical role, seeking out information, setting forth clear-cut statements, interpreting ambiguities and making these known to both sides. But it is only when we come to mediation proper that we find the third party actually participating in the process of negotiation, making suggestions, proposing solutions and persuading the parties to accept them. Control of the communications structure may enable the mediator to bring pressures to bear on the others which involve an element of deception. Techniques and tactics include suppression of information which might be disrupting, timing of messages, selecting material for emphasis and de-emphasis and distortions in the appropriate direction. This could of course be used in a self-interested fashion.

But the effectiveness of conciliation depends basically on the acceptance by the disputants, and the third party's role is always auxiliary. The main purpose of the third party is to facilitate the reaching of a solution by the disputants *themselves*. While inquiry and good offices could conceivably result from the suggestion of just one party, mediation must be acceptable to both. Mediation ends either when the dispute is successfully terminated or when it is declared by either side or by the mediator himself, that the means of reconciliation proposed by him are not acceptable.

Coming to adjudication we find processes relying on legal and quasi-legal methods of settlement. The Hague Convention defined arbitration as "settlement of disputes between states by judges of their own choice on the basis of respect for the law". Holsti lists three prior agreements required before arbitration:— that some form of settlement is definitely preferred to continued conflict, that the confict will be resolved by legal standards rather than military, political, economic or social standards and that a special court shall have jurisdiction over the proceedings.[18] These decisions being reached the parties must negotiate a compromise or preliminary agreement on the details of the composition, procedure etc. of the tribunal. Occasionally, as in the case of management-labour disputes, these have been institutionalised. At the international level a formula frequently used has been that of a three-member tribunal or commission, two of whom are appointed by the litigant states and the third being designated by agreement between the two. Both parties are bound to accept the decision of the arbiter who after hearing their evidence, decides on the future value distribution and hence terminates the conflict. The third party therefore enjoys a good deal of power in arbitration.

But the third party's power is greatest when we reach judicial settlement for here the rules of procedure are no longer laid down by the disputants themselves. Often the law will intervene itself and the disputants are bound to accept it. On the other hand two parties may decide to take their case to court but perhaps more likely just one of them will call in the law and this is sufficient. In judicial settlement everything is institutionalised. A solution is reached by an outsider who knows the rules of evidence and is able to perform logical manipulations within a normative structure.

Since litigation involves the risk of total loss for one side, why then, asks Aubert, does not one party try to buy himself out of the situation beforehand? There are a number of reasons. In criminal cases the law forbids bargaining between the parties involved. Sometimes the parties may simply overestimate their chances of winning since arguments favouring one's own side are more readily available and count for more than those favouring the opponent. Occasionally one party may have interests which transcend the individual case and, in order to 'test' the law, risk making a loss. Insurance companies often do this. Sometimes the object of the dispute is completely indivisible so the outcome is bound to be all or nothing. Finally some parties take their case to court because they perceive the law as a manifestation of divine justice.[19]

2.7   THE ALLY

Here the third party comes in to support one member of the dyad. This may be by the invitation of that member, on its own initiative or as the consequence of some prior agreement or pact to ensure intervention in certain contingencies. The existence of such a pact or the considered possibility of such intervention may itself be sufficient to moderate the actions of the other member of the dyad. For example a child with an older and stronger brother may be less susceptible to attack by the school bully. Recognition of the existence of the ally by the other member of the dyad will alter the dyadic interaction and the bargaining position of the side gaining the ally will generally be improved. His opponent may make lower demands and greater concessions.

The ally may enter the process for a number of reasons. It may be a sense of justice — a feeling of a need to support the weaker party. A crowd at a sporting occasion can often seem to be on the side of the losers, particularly if the score is greatly in favour of the winning side. Intervention sometimes comes because the ally fears for his own security. A nation may come to the aid of its neighbour when asked for help in a war between the neighbour and an external party because it feels that if its neighbour falls it will itself in turn suffer. Here we are dealing with our old unite-and-fight problem but from a slightly different angle.

Closely connected with the ally is the idea of Balance of Power and the balancer, found chiefly in studies on International Relations. This concept will turn up again later but at the moment we note that in such a situation so long as the two sides are balanced the balancer or third party does not intervene. But if one side gains in strength sufficiently to tip the scales, the balancer joins the weaker side in order to restore the balance. Whichever side becomes stronger, he will join the other. He must therefore be strong enough to tilt the scales decisively, so he must at least be as strong as the margin of power between the other two. The smaller the margin of power, between the two contenders, the more relevant is the total power of an intrinsically weak third party.[20] We are reminded here of competition for an ally dealt with in section 2.3.

2.8   THE HOSTAGE

Just as a disputant can attempt to improve his position in the dyadic interaction process by calling in an ally, he may also attempt to do this by taking a hostage. This is the one example of a party calling in a third party who happens to side with the opponent. But the hostage must be a party whose position or welfare definitely means something to the opponent.

By making threats of what he might do to the hostage, the disputant hopes to extract concessions or favours out of the other side. But hostages may also be used to deter aggressive action. Schelling notes that under the 'balance of terror' the population on one side is effectively the hostage of the other side. The presence of long-range missiles renders it possible to take a hostage without physical abduction.[21] Morton Deutsch has suggested the use of hostages in a crash programme of disarmament. During this period, for instance, the government of the U.S.A. would reside in Moscow and the government of the U.S.S.R. in Washington. Alternatively there could be an interchange programme for large numbers of citizens. This places a severe penalty on the side which initiates an attack. They now have a vested interest in protecting certain people located in the target country.[22] Such hostages are rather different from the type mentioned first since they are held by mutual agreement of both parties.

The third party as hostage takes an active part insofar as he is either physically abducted or placed in some vulnerable position. But he has very little or no control over the situation and his fate lies entirely in the hands of the disputants.

2.9   THE DELEGATE

The delegate offers another example of a member of the dyad bringing in a third party to influence his opponent's actions. But the delegate acts rather differently from the ally. The dyad member turns over his interest or initiative to a third party to whom his opponent reacts differently. The third party's intentions are directed by the dyad member. Sometimes the third party has some special skill for which purpose he is hired. A well known example, quoted by Schelling, is the use of thugs.[23] Another occurs when parties employ lawyers to settle disputes instead of taking them to court. Here both sides bring in similar third parties.

Often the third party is brought in to conceal the identity of the real party. Thus the well known buyer of antiques may employ some-one else to bid for him at an auction because the seller would be likely to charge a higher price if he knew with whom he was really dealing.

If the disputants are themselves groups of several members, some of them may be appointed as delegates to go to the bargaining table. This is not quite the same sort of delegation since it does not amount to the calling in of any external party.

An example of delegation in the international sphere is furnished by the Korean War. Firstly U.S. troops went in under the name of the United Nations. Then China intervened on the recommendation of the Soviet Union. Had the latter itself intervened it may have meant a third World War, but it could have China do this since a U.S. attack on China would be deterred by consideration of Soviet reaction. Many cold war disputes have been fought out not directly by the Great Powers them-selves but by minor countries backed up by aid from these powers.

2.10 POTENTIAL INTERVENTION

In stating that the mere existence of possible allies is often sufficient to deter an enemy we have already encountered a case of potential intervention. If one party threatens to call in a third the opponent may well change his behaviour, so that the third party has exerted an influence even though he has taken no actions. We also mentioned that the mere presence of the mediator, even before he does anything, may fundamentally alter the interaction between the disputants. Sometimes a 'mediator' may have this effect without even being called in or taking any active part whatsoever. The fact that he is a potential intervenor is sufficient. To describe this phenomenon Barkun has coined the phrase 'Implicit Mediation'.[24]

Essentially what we mean here is that the mediative function is separated from the person of the mediator. The situation changes from dyadic to triadic without the actual physical presence of the third party. The fact that the disputants have to consider the possible reactions of the third party to what they might do causes them to modify their actions. For instance, the possibility of external sanctions or disapproval may have an effect on the certainty with which a party holds its position. Attitudes and expectations may then be modified.

Levine states that in some primitive socities the decision makers before committing themselves to military action must consider a) lineage relations, b) supernatural sanctions and c) spatial distance, all of which are nothing to do with the chances of winning.[25] Frequently the third party is some impersonal entity such as the law.

Today we see possible reactions of neutral states or the world in general influencing the actions of the Great Powers. Witness the speculation on whether Russia would risk invading Czechoslovakia at the expense of the adverse reaction which would be generated in certain other countries. Lerche thinks that when the international order is relatively stable and there is general satisfaction with the arrangement of things, potential aggressors are more likely to encounter adverse opinion. It is less likely to be effective in times of social change, ideological unrest and insecurity.[26]

Implicit mediation is of course much more limited than explicit mediation. Conflicts are not so much resolved by this method as restricted. The disputants may not make such great demands as they would have done had the mediator not been there. It tends to stop conflicts emerging rather than resolve existing ones.

In implicit mediation the potential intervener operates as a conflict resolving or preventing mechanism. In so far as the potential ally may force the opponent to make concessions or surrender, he too may cause a decline in the state of conflict. On the other hand he may enable the member of the dyad whose side he is on to make greater demands, thereby intensifying the conflict. A potential third party may cause an intensification of conflict, if consideration of the third party causes attitudes to harden and demands to be upheld strongly because of the loss of face resulting from concessions. Another situation where a state of conflict may be instigated or intensified by a potential third party is that involving blackmail.

2.11 BLACKMAIL

The only literature in which blackmail has appeared has been that produced by fiction writers. The plot in such works usually revolves round the dilemma created by the blackmail threat. This term is used in several ways so we must be clear in what sense we are using it.

The essence of blackmail is that one person, the victim, suddenly receives some communication from another, the blackmailer, saying that he has some information, usually documented, which will harmfully alter the victim's relationship to a third party, the audience. The victim is told he can prevent the blackmailer from divulging such information to the third party by following a prescribed course of action, usually the payment of money.

So the blackmailer tries to influence the actions of the victim by threatening great future harm if the desired actions are not carried out. The harm comes not from the blackmailer however but the third party. The blackmailer derives his power from the existence of the third party. The victim must of course believe that the third party is an interested party.

The dyadic interaction may arise out of the blackmail threat itself. The third party is then a passive instigator of the state of conflict. Alternatively the threat may be used during an existing interaction process in order to improve the position of the blackmailer. The third party in blackmail may thus influence the process in a similar way to the potential ally. Indeed the threat to call an ally could be regarded as blackmail of a sort. But a subtle difference is that the third party in blackmail is not necessarily in any way connected with the blackmailer.

In practice blackmail is most often based on personal indiscretions that the victim has committed at some time — some illegal, immoral or highly unconventional behaviour. But this is not the only case e.g. an employee may solicit special favours from the company in return for not divulging information to a competitor.

What forms the basis of the blackmail threat is the importance the victim places on the information. The consequences of the exposure of this information may be difficult to assess and leaving the potential harm to conjecture probably serves to potentiate the penalties beyond actuality. Feelings of guilt may intensify the conjectured severity of the harm.

The third party may retaliate by punishing the victim in some way. But there is also the possibility of an alteration in the role relationship between the two. The victim may lose face, his power and status may fall.

As mentioned, the blackmailer has great power by virtue of the third party. Without the third party his demands would have no force. But because the third party exists, the blackmailer has everything to gain and nothing to lose. He can make his choice after and contingent upon the victim's choice and he can communicate his intentions and choice contingencies to the victim. His power is of a coercive nature.

Blackmail is usually seen as an illegitimate rather than legitimate activity. In most cases it is a criminal offence. But in some arenas it is viewed as a legitimate activity. For international spies it is one of the normatively acceptable means of influence.

2.12 RELATIONSHIPS BETWEEN VARIOUS TYPES OF THIRD PARTY

We have said that when a dyadic interaction exists the parties find themselves in some state which may be one of complete conflict, complete co-operation or a mixture of the two. The latter is most common in the real world. The dyadic interaction process, or sequence of decisions and their resulting outcomes, varies depending on the rules of the game. Thus it may be a bargaining process, a competitive process, a fight or a completely co-operative process. It has been argued that because the parties in any situation respect certain rules of conduct and because this represents a co-operative aspect of behaviour, no situation is one of complete conflict. However, we have defined conflict in terms of goal states and not in terms of the rules of the game. The third party may instigate any of the said processes and intervene in all except competition. This is because competition is the only process which cannot exist without a third party.

In order to compare the various types of third party first consider a particular situation. Suppose two parties, A and B, are both making claims on some resource X which no one at present owns and which is divisible if necessary. Both would like to possess the whole of X and so the situation has an element of conflict. But as X is divisible, possible compromise outcomes are available. Possible outcomes can be represented diagramatically as in fig. ix.

Fig. ix.

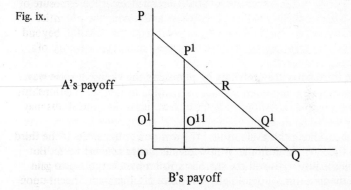

A's payoff

B's payoff

On this diagram the utilities or payoffs to the players from various outcomes are represented on the axes. For simplicity we assume that the sum of their utilities is a constant so that the straight line PQ covers all points which correspond to a complete division of X. The area between this line and the axes covers all points corresponding to an incomplete division of X. Any point outside this area is not a feasible outcome. The origin, O, represents the status quo or point at which the players will remain if they do not reach an agreement and X remains intact. Point P corresponds to the outcome 'A gets the whole of X and B gets nothing'. At Q these payoffs are interchanged. B will desire an

55

outcome or solution point as far to the right as possible while A desires
one as high as possible on the diagram.

Suppose the parties decide to resolve this conflict by bargaining and
suppose B makes a concession i.e. agrees to give up a part of his claim
ceding a small part of X to A. B's best possible outcome moves to
Q^1 and the new status quo point is O^1. If A then makes a concession
to B, A's best outcome or greatest demand has fallen to P^1 and the new
status quo point is O^{11}. This process goes on, the status quo point
moving in a north easterly direction until it reaches some point R on
the line PQ. This represents the final settlement.

It is the business of the mediator to facilitate the reaching of this
point R. He may do this by persuading A and B to reduce their
demands, emphasising the costs of not reaching a settlement. Or he may
persuade the players to change their evaluations of certain outcomes.
This is made clear in the following diagrams.

Fig. x. (a)　　　　　　　　(b)

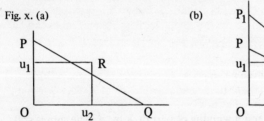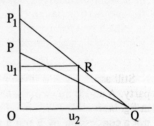

In fig. x. (a) A and B are making compatible demands, which result
in the non feasible solution, R. Were such an outcome possible the
payoffs would be u_1 and u_2 respectively. Now suppose the third party
causes A to change his evaluations. The utility frontier shifts to the line
$P_1 Q$ in fig. x. (b) and though A now gets a smaller amount of X than
before his utility u_1 is still the same and R is now a feasible outcome.

The mediator may operate on both parties in this way. The ally of B
however only tries to make A change his evaluations in the direction
indicated. Extra costs are imposed on A so that the same utility is
obtained from making a lower demand. The threat to call an ally or the
blackmail threat from B operate similarly, and if B takes a hostage of A
a similar thing may happen.

The payoff to A from any outcome will often be influenced by what
payoff he believes B would derive from that outcome. If B can make it
appear that he receives less than he really does, A will make a lower
demand. B may use the delegate for this purpose. The effect can be
described by the same diagram.

So far the influence of the third party has been directed at achieving a solution point R. The divider or exploiting third party on the other hand tries either to make such a solution impossible or to delay the reaching of a solution. He wants to keep the point R as far outside the feasible region as possible and therefore wishes to make the players make greater demands (or fewer concessions). He can achieve this by causing their evaluation of a given outcome to change in a downward direction, then, assuming they wish to achieve a certain payoff, they must make a greater demand. Suppose the demands were such that a solution would have been reached at R (fig. xi.). The third party causes the expected payoffs to fall so that the utility frontier falls and R is no longer a solution.

Fig. xi.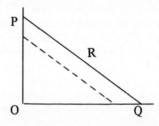

Still assuming X is divisible, suppose it is possessed by some third party. A and B now *compete* to increase their share of X. The diagram in fig. ix. is still applicable, but now a move from O to O^1 represents not a concession by B but a winning of part of X by A. The aim is still to arrive at some point R but the third party himself decides on where R shall be.

Returning to the bargaining process we recall that the mediator himself cannot decide on R; only the disputants can do this, though he may persuade them to accept some R which he suggests. The arbitrator or the law could however impose some R on the disputants and their actions change from those appropriate to bargaining to those appropriate to convincing the third party that their claim is just. Thus the bargaining and the competitive processes are seen to merge, and with them the roles of the third party.

If X is indivisible only three solutions are possible — those at O, P and Q. So long as O is a possibility there is a co-operative solution but the costs of remaining at O may be high and once a decision is taken to move away from it, fighting may take place. This is not to deny that fighting might result even when X is divisible. Nor is it to deny that a bargain could be struck when X is indivisible. But it is a far more difficult bargaining process, for one side must step down completely. Tactics of the mediator may be to persuade the parties to remain at O, emphasising the possible high costs of moving away from it. The effect of this would be to move P and Q towards the origin. Another tactic may be to bring in some other resource, W, and, assuming A gets the whole of X, persuading A to make some compensation payment to B in terms of W so that B's total payoff is not one of complete loss.

While the mediator's task is more difficult in this situation (unless he can impose a solution), that of the exploiting third party should be easier. His business is to emphasise the costs of remaining at O and to persuade each party that they have a good chance of winning if they do fight.

A similar case under competition is that where the third party must decide completely in favour of A or B.

We can also use the matrix representation to illustrate the third party's influence. Consider the members of the dyad, A and B, and an interaction described by the Prisoner's Dilemma game. Fig. xii. (a) shows a particular game and xii. (b) the general case where T > R > P > S.

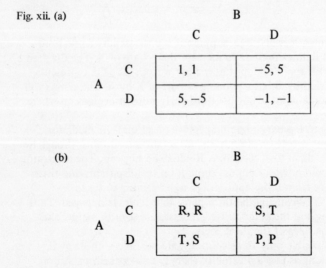

Fig. xii. (a)

(b)

The dominance of the "defective" choices makes for the outcome (P, P). We assume the mediator's payoff is greatest in the upper left hand cell, where A and B both behave co-operatively. He must try to make them change their evaluations so that the co-operative strategy is more attractive. Thus he will try to decrease the values of T and P and increase those of R and S. The exploitive third party on the other hand desires the outcome (P, P) so will concentrate mainly on increasing the value of T, the temptation to defect.

The ally of B or blackmail threat made by B, serves to put an extra cost on A for certain decisions. The matrix may change to

B

		C	D
A	C	1, 1	−5, 5
	D	0, −5	−6, −1

Fig. xiii.

in which A's co-operative choice is dominant so that B can make a large gain by defecting, without fear of A also defecting. The payoff structure is altered and as a result A's behaviour changes in a way which favours B.

Competition could be represented in a similar way with the choices interpreted in the appropriate manner. D might mean 'advertise' and C might mean 'don't advertise'. If only one firm advertises he captures a large share of the market so that the other must advertise to counteract this. The advertising of both tends to cancel out and both end up worse off.

Delegation is represented by a rather different game presented by Schelling. In this game B makes the first move and A knows what this is before he makes his own choice. In fig. xiv. (a) B will play α_2 because he knows that A will then have to play α_2. But suppose A can surrender his move to a third party, C, who gets the payoffs in brackets in fig. xiv (b).

Fig. xiv. (a)

B

		β_1	β_2
A	α_1	5, 3	0, 2
	α_2	0, 4	1, 5

Fig. xiv. (b)

B

		β_1	β_2
C	α_1	(2), 3	(1), 2
	α_2	(1), 4	(0), 5

If B believes he is playing against C he will play β_1 because he knows C will then play α_1. This means in effect that A is playing α_1 and getting a payoff of 5. B has reacted differently because he did not know the true identity of C.[27]

Notes

1. Thomas C. Schelling, *The Strategy of Conflict* (Cambridge, Mass.: Harvard Univ. Press, 1960), p. 144.
2. Section 2.10 above.
3. Wilhelm Aubert, "Competition and Dissensus: Two Types of Conflict and Conflict Resolution", *Journal of Conflict Resolution* Vol. 7, No. 1 (March 1963), 26–42.
4. See Raymond W. Mack and Richard C. Snyder, "The Analysis of Social Conflict – towards an Overview and Synthesis", *Journal of Conflict Resolution* Vol. 1, No. 2 (June 1957), 212–248.
5. Kurt H. Wolff (translator and editor), *The Sociology of Georg Simmel* (Glencoe: The Free Press, 1950).
6. Miron Rush, *Political Succession in the U.S.S.R.*, (New York; Columbia University Press, 1965).
7. Wilhelm Aubert, "Competition and Dissensus: Two Types of Conflict and Conflict Resolution", *Journal of Conflict Resolution* Vol. 7, No. 1 (March 1963), 25–42.
8. Martin Shubik, *Readings in Game Theory and Political Behaviour* (Doublesday: Garden City, 1954).
9. Georg Simmel, *Conflict and the Web of Group Affiliation.* trans. by Kurt H. Wolff and Reinhard Bendix (Glencoe, Illinois: Free Press, 1955) pp. 97–98.
10. Ibid. pp. 397–98.
11. Lewis A. Coser, *The Function of Social Conflict* (Glencoe, Illionois: The Free Press, 1956) p. 94.
12. Wilhelm Aubert, "Courts and Conflict Resolution", *Journal of Conflict Resolution,* Vol. XI, No. 1 (March 1967), 40–51.
13. Oran Young, *The Intermediaries: Third Party Intervention in International Crises* (Princeton N.J.: Princeton Univ. Press, 1967).
14. Wilhelm Aubert, "Courts and Conflict Resolution", *Journal of Conflict Resolution,* Vol. XI, No. 1 (March, 1967) 40–51.
15. Johan Galtung, "Institutionalised Conflict Resolution: A Theoretical Paradigm", *Journal of Conflict Resolution,* Vol. IX, No. 4 (December, 1965), 348–96.

16. Lewis A. Coser, *The Functions of Social Conflict* (Glencoe, Illinois: Free Press, 1956), p. 59.
17. Raymond W. Mack and Richard C. Snyder, "The Analysis of Social Conflict Towards an Overview and Synthesis", *Journal of Conflict Resolution,* Vol. I, No. 2 (June 1957), 212–248.
18. K. J. Holsti, "Resolving International Conflicts: A Taxonomy of Behaviour and Some Figures of Procedures", *Journal of Conflict Resolution,* Vol. X, No. 3 (September, 1966), 272–296.
19. Wilhelm Aubert, "Courts and Conflict Resolution", *Journal of Conflict Rsolution,* Vol. XI, No. 1 (March, 1967), 40–51.
20. George Liska, *Nations in Alliance: The Limits of Interdependence* (Baltimore: The Johns Hopkins Press, 1962).
21. Thomas C. Schelling, *The Strategy of Conflict* (Cambridge, Mass.: Harvard Univ. Press, 1960), p. 239.
22. Morton Deutsch, "Reducing the Reciprocal Fear of Surprise Attack", in Wright, Evans and Deutsch (eds), *Preventing World War III: Some Proposals* (New York, Simon and Schuster, 1962).
23. Thomas C. Schelling, *The Strategy of Conflict* (Cambridge, Mass.: Harvard Univ. Press, 1960), p. 142.
24. M. Barkun, "Conflict Resolution through Implicit Mediation" *Journal of Conflict Resolution,* Vol. VIII, No. 2, (June, 1964), 121–130.
25. R. Levine, "Anthropology and the Study of Conflict", *Journal of Conflict Resolution,* Vol. V, No. 1, (March, 1961), 3–15.
26. Charles O. Lerche, *Principles of International Politics,* (New York: Oxford Univ. Press, 1956), p. 217.
27. Thomas C. Schelling; *The Strategy of Conflict* (Cambridge, Mass.: Harvard University Press, 1960), p. 143.

CHAPTER 3

THEORY AND EXPERIMENT: A SURVEY

3.1 INTRODUCTION

In this chapter we survey the accomplished theoretical and experimental work directly concerned with the triad. The work came initially from two fields — sociology and mathematics. The sociological contribution came chiefly from the Swiss sociologist Georg Simmel, whose ideas have been elaborated by his followers. There is also a contribution from the mathematical sociologists with the idea of structural balance theory. From mathematics we can gather a great deal of information on triads from three-person games and their solutions. This work was pioneered by Von Neumann and Morgenstern.[1] There are in fact several different suggestions for solutions to three-person games, some of them very complicated and couched in terms of higher mathematics. We shall deal only with the simpler ideas because it is felt that the others are, at least at the moment, only exercises for the mathematicians. Another interesting idea, coming from the field of probability theory, is that of the three-man duel.

Leading on from Simmel, and with some of the mathematicians' ideas in mind, Mills[2], Caplow[3], and others began to formulate ideas about the stability of various triads with different 'power structures', (i.e. patterns of relative power of the different members), though the ideas of what constituted 'power' have varied somewhat. Vinacke[4] *et al.* have since undertaken a long series of experimental games, using triads of students as their subjects. Computer simulations of triadic situations have also been attempted.

Other authors such as Riker[5] and Gamson[6] have advanced different theories of coalition formation, whilst others such as Chertkoff[7] have compared the merits of these and performed further experiments. There is also a body of significant work relating to the concept of 'Balance of Power'. Though not always concerned strictly with the triad, the triad is often used to illustrate some of its points, and Zinnes[8] in particular has attempted to relate these ideas to those of Riker and others.

So the study of the triad has spread from the work of the pure sociologists and game theorists to the realm of the behavioural scientists and political scientists.

The triad is the lowest group, in terms of numbers, in which coalition formation is possible. It is not surprising therefore that the bulk of work on the triad has concerned itself with this phenomenon. As the term 'coalition' will be used extensively from now on, it is worth spending a short section discussing the definition of this word.

3.2   THE DEFINITION OF COALITION

In chapter 2 we used the term 'alliance' to describe the case of two parties combining to interact with a third. The term coalition might have been used here but this term has a somewhat broader usage. Sociologists refer to a coalition of two people; political scientists to a coalition of two political parties and sometimes to a coalition of two nations. Often the latter is referred to as an alliance but from now on we shall adopt the term coalition throughout.

Gamson defines coalitions as "temporary means-oriented alliances among individuals or groups which differ in goals. There is generally little value consensus in a coalition and the stability of a coalition requires tacit neutrality of the coalition on matters which go beyond immediate prerogatives."[9] This definition is rather unsatisfactory and needs some elaboration.

In dealing with the triad the coalitions we meet are of two persons, i.e. are dyadic groups. Already we have noted that two parties may interact over several different issues. When we talk about coalition we must be clear to which issues we are referring. Sometimes issues are completely independent and decisions taken with respect to one do not affect those decisions taken with respect to the other. But the reverse may be true and in this case we have to consider all issues together, as one large game. The decision to form a coalition may refer to a single issue or to a large number of issues combined in this way.

The formation of a coalition is a co-operative act. But the term is reserved for only those co-operative acts to which a third party is relevant. The members of the dyad decide to co-ordinate their actions in their interaction with the third party.

Thibaut and Kelly recognise the importance of mentioning the third party in the definition and they define a coalition as existing when "two or more persons act jointly to affect the outcomes of one or more other persons". They list three factors promotive to a coalition between A and B:

1) Correspondence of outcomes
2) C, the third party, has some control over these outcomes
3) By joint action they can mobilise greater power to counteract C.[10]

Our definition of a two-person coalition is:

"A dyad becomes a coalition with respect to some issue if its members co-ordinate their decisions in their interaction with a third party on this issue in order to improve their outcomes".

A coalition once formed will be considered to be the stronger, the larger the payoffs at stake. Thus a strong coalition may arise because its members interact with a third either on some single issue which involves a large payoff, or on a large number of smaller issues whose combined payoff is large.

While the formation of a coalition is a co-operative act, it does not follow that there is no conflict in the dyad. There may well be latent conflict insofar as certain issues are put aside while the issue involving the third party is fought out. Thus east and west combined in World War II, temporarily forgetting their ideological conflict. There may also be conflict with respect to the issue itself. The dyad may act together to gain something from the third party, but there may be a conflict over the division of that something once it is obtained.

The decision to form a coalition is a collective, not an individual decision. Each member must consider the issues at stake, the rewards which will be obtained from some and the costs which will accrue from others, if he forms the coalition. No one will join a coalition if he believes he will be better off alone. If the rewards expected from the co-operative behaviour on some issues exceed the expected costs of compromise on other issues, for both parties involved, the coalition will form. The larger the net rewards, the stronger we expect the coalition to be.

The life of the coalition depends on how long it takes to decide the issue but, insofar as expectations of rewards and costs change over time, the coalition may collapse before the issue is decided. Once the issue involving the third party reaches a point where the third party is no longer relevant, the dyad can no longer be called a coalition, whether it continues to behave co-operatively or not on this and other issues.

64

3.3 SOCIOLOGICAL THEORY ON THE TRIAD

In dealing with the triad arising out of the addition of a third party to a dyad we encountered some of the ideas of Simmel. Simmel goes on to say that what may be thought of as the normal triad, where the relations of A, B and C to each other are based upon equality in all respects and in which the power and influence of each member is equal, is extremely rare in practice. The chances of finding a triad with significant interactions and an identical degree of social distance between A, B and C must be very low indeed.

What usually happens is that two members become more intimate with each other than with the third, who then becomes isolated. Occasionally one member emerges as the leader and the other two become followers. This may lead to strong unification of the pair either because their interests converge at a single point, the leader, or because they may be forced to strengthen their unity in order to oppose more effectively the controlling power to which they are subordinate. History affords many examples where the death of a common superior has lead to the disruption of a political unity. More frequently however, two members of the triad become allies, relegating the third to an inferior rank.

Thus reconstruction on the two-to-one basis almost always takes place. Sometimes the underpriviledged member engages in a struggle with the pair, trying to enforce a division in their unity similar to the principle of divide-and-rule.

At the time of Simmel's writings no experiments had taken place to investigate these propositions but Simmel illustrated them by reference to the history of triumvirates. He pointed out that when administrative or governmental affairs are entrusted to three officials with equal rights, it is at the same time necessary to specify and to limit the functions of each as over against those of the others. Even then the preponderant power has often slipped into the hands of two of them. Witness the U.S. constitution regarding the 'separation of powers'. Therefore the triad must have an artificial differentiation of function if complete discord is not to ensue. In short, it marks the beginning of organization.

Sometimes the isolate in the triad may cease his interaction with the pair and seek a new partner outside. The triad is then transmuted into a double pair. Occasionally the isolate is at an advantage in being isolated. For one thing he may be freer. He may in such cases have an interest in the survival of the triad and at the same time his presence causes greater unification between the pair. Tension tending to separate the marital pair is not infrequently lessened by their child.

Thibaut and Kelley have made some interesting contributions to the theory of the triad.[11] They ask, "What makes the triad a viable group?"

which to use our terminology is equivalent to, "Given a triad with inter-actions between its members, what keeps these interactions at a significant level?" How is it that any particular member such as A can be better off in the A-B-C relationship than in other relationships? Consider the dyads A-B and A-C as alternatives. A is better off in the triad if his rewards are higher than elsewhere in relation to the costs he incurs.

Thus two persons may be able to cut A's costs when one alone cannot do so. The adolescent girl, confused about sex, may be willing to go on a date with two boys but not with one. If A produces some-thing which can be simultaneously enjoyed by two people instead of one, at little or no extra cost to A, the total value of his product is increased. A father may take two children on a picnic with little more effort than taking one. Again, the products of B and C may be of little value to A, taken alone, but together they may be greatly amplified. Finally we may get sequential patterns of interdependence — A may have a product of value only to B, B has one of value only to C and C has one of value only to A. Thus we get a circular trade pattern. A is dependent on C but has nothing to offer C in return. There exists however an intermediary, B, who is somehow able to transform A's product into something of value to C.

Here we see examples of triads which are not likely to split into a coalition plus an isolate. The reason for this is that there is a high correspondence of outcomes or coincidence of interests for all those members. In other cases there may be only a partial or low correspon-dence of outcomes and sometimes the high correspondence only exists for a subset of members. It is in the latter case where coalitions are likely to form.

The other contribution which we shall consider in this section is the theory known broadly as Structural Balance.[12] It provides a useful descriptive model of various triads and makes predictions about their stability.

The relationship between each pair within the triad may be considered as one of attraction, which may be positive or negative. We may think of the former as corresponding to co-operative behaviour and the latter to non-co-operative behaviour. Any dyad can be described as ++ (reciprocal positive), +− (mixed), or −− (reciprocal negative). Members of the first type tend to associate freely and communicate with each other with relatively few restraints, behaving cordially towards each other i.e. they indulge in co-operative actions. Members of −− dyads tend to do none of these things but behave in a conflictful way. The behaviour of +− dyads is restrained and tends to resemble the latter.

The theory of balance says that the more nearly A's attraction towards B and B's attraction towards A are the same, the more stable the dyadic level of attraction. If positive actions of A tend to be rewarded with positive actions from B, and vice versa, the dyad tends to remain stable at the ++ level. Aversion (negative attraction) that is reciprocated in kind tends also to result in stable dyads, because each member is negatively rewarded and thus motivated to avoid assocation and cordial behaviour. The more they avoid each other the less opportunity they have to modify their hostile attitude.

Mixed dyads tend on the other hand to be unstable and short lived. They move to either of the other types depending on how overtly one member shows his cordiality and the other his hostility. So as the interaction process takes place, a state where both parties co-operate or both don't co-operate may be long lasting whereas a state where one co-operates and the other does not will be short-lived.

There are thus four possible behaviour patterns as the triadic interaction process takes place. These are depicted in fig. xv. The first, (a), is balanced because each dyad is of the stable ++ type.
(b), however, is unbalanced because each member of the triad is positively attracted to another who does not share his attitude towards the third.

(c) is balanced, describing the case of the coalition A-B and isolate C. The final type, where all members behave unco-operatively, is unbalanced because while any pair has a hostile relationship both parties share their dislike for the third. This makes this particular type unstable and demonstrates that there can never be a complete opposition of interests in the triad.

Fig. xv.

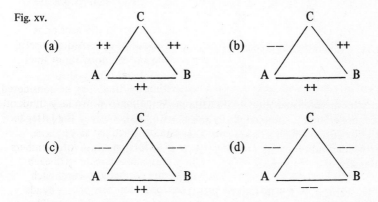

All this means that as the triadic interaction process takes place, the behaviour patterns most likely to be found at any time are (a) or (c).

(b) and (d) are possible but would always tend to one of the other types.

The above describes the state of relations existing in the triad at any point in time. The model can also be used to represent particular actions. To do this it makes use of the directed graph. A solid line represents a positive act, a dotted line a negative act. The arrow head represents the direction of the action. A ——→ B indicates that A makes a positive advance towards B. As a simple example consider the case of a man (M) quarrelling with his wife (W) and a stranger intervening, shown in fig. xvi.

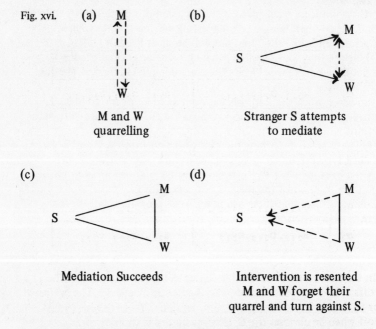

Fig. xvi.   (a)   (b)

M and W   Stranger S attempts
quarrelling   to mediate

(c)   (d)

Mediation Succeeds   Intervention is resented
                                      M and W forget their
                                      quarrel and turn against S.

Structural balance models are little more than descriptive tools. To be more complete there ought to be some representation of the neutral relationship in which acts are neither strictly positive nor negative. A serious limitation of the model is that it gives no indication of the intensity of a relationship.

3.4   THREE-PERSON GAME THEORY

The two-person game has been used to represent the interaction between the members of a dyad. We have seen that the third party can influence the payoffs in the matrix, but so far have given no represen-

tation to his own payoffs. These payoffs, as noted earlier, may be in somewhat different units from those made to the dyad, partly because the third party sometimes occupies a special position. While we might want to represent the third party's payoffs in such cases we will certainly want to do so in cases where all three parties stand in similar positions, such as three parties bargaining over the division of something.

We could extend the matrix representation of the interaction to three dimensions by using a cube with three payoffs in each cell. Alternatively we can use two matrices as follows:

Fig. xvii.

C_1 B

	β_1	β_2
α_1	$a_{111}, b_{111}, c_{111}$	$a_{121}, b_{121}, c_{121}$
α_2	$a_{211}, b_{211}, c_{211}$	$a_{221}, b_{221}, c_{221}$

A

C_2 B

	β_1	β_2
α_1	$a_{112}, b_{112}, c_{112}$	$a_{122}, b_{122}, c_{122}$
α_2	$a_{212}, b_{212}, c_{212}$	$a_{222}, b_{222}, c_{222}$

A

In the first matrix C makes his choice γ_1, in the second γ_2. The payoffs a, b, c are those made to A, B and C respectively. The suffixes refer to the choices of the players, in the same order. Thus a_{212} is A's payoff when he chooses α_2, B, chooses β_1 and C chooses γ_2.

A simple matrix representation of mediation is as follows:

Fig. xviii. C_1 B

	β_1	β_2
α_1	1, 1, 2	$-5, 5, -1$
α_2	$5, -5, -1$	$-1, -1, -2$

A

Fig. xviii. (cont.)

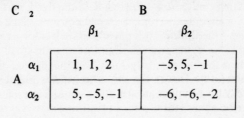

C $_2$ B

	β_1	β_2
α_1	1, 1, 2	−5, 5, −1
α_2	5, −5, −1	−6, −6, −2

The A-B interaction in the first matrix is of the prisoner's dilemma type and C gets his bets payoff from their joint co-operation and his worst from their joint defection. C can force this co-operation by playing or threatening to play γ_2. The interaction moves to the second matrix where a large cost is imposed on A and B if they both defect. But no extra cost is imposed on C. The third party has an especially powerful position here. Now let us turn to some situations where all three parties are in similar positions with respect to the issue at stake.

Fig. xix.

4, 4, 4	0, 0, 0
0, 0, 0	0, 0, 0

0, 0, 0	0, 0, 0
0, 0, 0	−4, −4, −4

Fig. xix. represents a case of complete co-operation. There is a perfect correspondence of outcomes insofar as all parties get their best payoffs in the same cell. The mixed motive game is represented by an extension of the prisoner's dilemma game in fig. xx.

Fig. xx.

1, 1, 1	−2, 3, −2
3, −2, −2	2, −2, 2

Fig. xx. (cont.)

−2, −2, 3	2, 2, −2
−2, 2, 2	−1, −1, −1

In two-person Game Theory the zero-sum game is one of complete conflict; one player's winnings are the other's loss. There can be no exact three-person equivalent of this. In the three-person zero-sum game either two players must win or two must lose. There will therefore always be some correspondence of outcomes for two players. If this correspondence is great enough we may expect a coalition in order to maximise rewards or minimise costs. The degree of correspondence of outcomes between the various players depends on the structure of the game so that even if there is a high correspondence, coalitions are not guaranteed to form.

In the following game for instance, the outcomes of A and B correspond with each other to a much greater degree than with those of C, but there is still a tendency for them to make their second (defecting) choice.

Fig. xxi.

2, 2, −4	0, 3, −3
3, 0, −3	−2, −2, 4

1, 1, −2	0, 1, −1
1, 0, −1	−1, −1, 2

It should be noted that these partial correspondences of outcomes can occur also in non-zero sum games, though here we may also get a complete correspondence and such an outcome may be preferred by all three players.

Coming to Game Theory itself, while the problem of two-person Game Theory is only to select a strategy, in three-person Game Theory there is the added problem of selecting a partner. The bulk of three-person and indeed n-person Game Theory is concerned with the theory of decisions with respect to coalition formation. For this reason the matrix representation is not often used. It is usually assumed that two opposing coalitions will form, one of which will win, and such coalitions will form as a result of negotiations and agreements on the division of the payoff.

In chapter 1 in dealing with two person Game Theory we saw that while zero-sum games have a mathematical solution i.e. there is a definite strategy which players should adopt in order to maximise their payoff, most non-zero sum games have no such solution. What is called a solution to the three-person game is a rather different thing from the solution to the two-person game. It usually takes the form of a list of the feasible coalitions and the division of the payoff between the players as a result of this. But rarely is a single coalition predicted and there are often many payoff structures corresponding to the same coalition.

In the classic Game Theory it is generally assumed that side payments are possible. This involves the notion of transferable utility, so it is assumed that utility can be translated into some common unit such as money. The theory then goes as follows.

Suppose a coalition, S, forms and receives a payment V(S). The function V is known as the *characteristic function* of the game. Such functions can be divided into two classes. In some games no coalition may be more effective than its members acting alone i.e.

$$V (AB) = V (A) + V (B).$$

If this is the case the game is called an *inessential game* and there is no point in a coalition forming. Other games, where there is something to be gained by the formation of a coalition, are called *essential games*.

We write down the individual payments to the players as a vector (x_1, x_2, x_3) known as an *imputation*. Different imputations relate either to different coalitions or to different payoff structures for the same coalition. It is the task of the theory to decide which vector is applicable in the equilibrium state or outcome.

The usual assumption of rationality i.e. that players act to maximise their payoffs, is made. Secondly, Pareto optimality is assumed i.e. whatever the outcome, the total payoff is divided up in some way so that none of it is wasted.

The Von Neumann-Morgenstern definition of a solution is based on the characteristic function and imputations. The set of all imputations for three-person games is a convex subset in three dimensions so if there are two distinct imputations there are infinitely many. An inessential game has but one imputation (V (A), V (B), V (C)); an essential game has many depending on the extent to which payoffs are divisible.

An imputation (y_1, y_2, y_3) will be preferred to an imputation

72

(x_1, x_2, x_3) by player i if $y_i > x_i$. The first imputation is said to *dominate* the second with respect to coalition S if

$$y_i > x_i \text{ for all i in S and } V(S) \geqslant \sum_{\substack{\text{all i in} \\ S}} y_i$$

The situation is more complicated however when we consider the dominance relation in general. Consider for instance the game in which

$$V(A) = V(B) = V(C) = 0$$
$$V(AB) = V(BC) = V(AC) = 1$$
$$V(ABC) = 1$$

If no coalition forms everyone gets nothing but any coalition or a triple alliance can get a payoff of 1. Consider the imputations:

$$(½, ½, 0), \ (0, ½, ½), \ (½, 0, ½) \ \ldots\ldots\ldots\ldots^*$$

and suppose AB forms with the first imputation. C may offer to form BC with the imputation $(0, ¾, ¼)$ which dominates the first imputation with respect to B and C. A could however offer AC with the imputation $(½, 0, ½)$ which dominates $(0, ¾, ¼)$ with respect to A and C. It is easily shown that any imputation other than those in * is dominated by one of those in * and no imputation dominates all those in *.

The set of imputations, *, is called the solution of the game. Thus the solution purports merely to set some limit on the number of admissable imputations.

All three-person zero-sum games have such a solution but often it consists of an infinite number of permutations and often there is more than one solution. Even in the above game the solution is not unique. If we choose c to be a fixed number in the range $0 \leqslant c < ½$ and let x_1 and x_2 be chosen so that neither is negative and $x_1 + x_2 + c = 1$, then the set of imputations (x_1, x_2, c) where x_1 and x_2 vary, forms a solution for each value of c. Von Neumann and Morgenstern suggest that whichever solution is accepted depends on the "standards of behaviour" ruling in society e.g. A and B may feel morally obliged to give some payment c to C.

But aside from these "standards of behaviour" are there game-theroetic requirements which impose a greater stability on one solution than on another? The problem is to define sufficient restraints so that only one coalition is left and some authors have attempted to do this.

Vickrey has defined what he calls a strong solution, i.e. one which has an inherent stability not possessed by other solutions and so might be expected to occur rather than one of the weaker solutions. In the above example, player B would end up worse off if he accepted C's offer of (0, ¾, ¼) and A then made a counter offer to C. It would be difficult for B to get away from (½, 0, ½) since the other players have now seen what happens to someone who accepts a better offer. Also, even if B makes a successful proposal, he must accept something less than his original ½. This solution * is said to be strong, and in general a solution is strong if the sequence (a) an imputation in the solution, (b) a change to a non-conforming (i.e. not in the solution) imputation, (c) a return to an imputation in the solution, always means that at least one player participating in the original deviation, ultimately suffers a net loss. All solutions of the type (x_1, x_2, c) are easily shown to be weak.[13]

Luce has developed the idea of *Psi-stability*. Basically the idea is that for a given imputation and coalition structure τ there is a class of coalitions $\psi(\tau)$ capable of disrupting τ. The original imputation and τ are not ψ —stable if and only if there exists a coalition S in $\psi(\tau)$ whose members can so co-ordinate their choices of mixed strategies that each improves by the defection from τ when the remaining players hold fixed their original strategies. Psi-stable pairs are not usually unique and in the three-person game any two-person coalition is ψ -stable so the concept is not of much value here.[14]

When we dealt with the two-person game we considered the value of the game to the players themselves. Shapley has attempted to do this for the n-person game in order to help determine relative bargaining positions. His general formula is

$$\emptyset_i (V) = \Sigma \ \gamma \ (s) \ \Big\{ V \ (S) - V \ (S-i) \Big\}$$

The term in brackets represents the incremental value added to the coalition by player i. s is the number of players in the coalition S and

$$\gamma \ n(s) = (s-1)! \ (n-2)! \ / \ n!$$

n being the total number of players. Summation is over all possible coalitions in which i can participate. All coalitions are considered equally likely.[15]

Shapley and Shubik have developed a power index for each player, based on the number of times he can turn a coalition from a losing one into a winning one. This will be dealt with in Chapter 4.

As Riker has said, scientific expectation is that, by studying the quasi-political interaction of games, where the variation among the institutional, psychological and ideological components of behaviour are minimised, one will be able to understand more profoundly the basic political activities of bargaining, forming coalitions and choosing strategies. The mathematically deduced solutions of games and strategies are not really useful unless we know how far they do describe actual behaviour and we can only discover this by experimentation.[16]

3.5   SOME AREAS OF GAMING

A considerable amount of work on gaming has been accomplished by the psychologists and behavioural scientists and some of it relates to the predictions of Game Theory. Not much however has been aimed specifically at a verification of game theoretical concepts. Game Theory is a normative theory, prescribing strategies for rational players. To some extent we can experiment to see if players do act in the way which Game Theory prescribes.

An experiment by Lieberman is interesting. He used two zero-sum games, the first of which had a specific solution, i.e. just one coalition was predicted. The characteristic function was:

If coalition AB formed A received 4, B received 2 and C received −6.

"   "   AC   "   "   "   4, "   "   −6 "   "   "   2.

"   "   BC   "   "   "   −6, "   "   3 "   "   "   3.

The solution is that BC should form, the third imputation dominating for both B and C.

The second game had no precise prescription for each player. If AB formed the coalition received 10 from player C; if AC formed it received 8 from B and if BC formed it received 6 from A. The Von Neumann-Morgenstern solution for this game is

$$(6, 4, -10), \ (6, -8, 2), \ (-6, 4, 2)$$

Each game was played forty times by sixteen triads of students. Each player had to choose one of the others and reciprocal choices became coalitions. In the second game the coalition members had to then decide on the division of the payoff. All communication was by writing.

In the first game BC occurred seventy per cent of the time whilst unstable coalitions (i.e. varying from trial to trial) occurred in the second, with BC occurring most often. However, a large minority of triads in game one did not adopt the Von Neumann-Morgenstern solution and in the second game players often employed an intuitive notion of trust realising the advantage of a stable coalition. About sixty per cent of the time there was equal division of the payoff in the second game.[17]

Riker has performed an experiment using the non-zero sum game with characteristic function:

$$V(A) = V(B) = V(C) = V(ABC) = 0$$

$$V(AB) = 4, \qquad V(AC) = 5, \qquad V(BC) = 6$$

The Von Neumann-Morgenstern solution of this is

$$(1.5, 2.5, 0), \ (1.5, 0, 3.5), \ (0, 2.5, 3.5) \ldots\ldots\ldots\ldots T$$

In the experiment Riker took some trouble to select subjects in several different ways. The first group consisted of twenty-eight businessmen, randomly selected from a wide variety of occupations. The second group was composed of randomly selected students and the third was a group of students who had answered an advertisement for such players. Subjects were allowed to confer twice in pairs after which each was asked if they had formed a coalition and with what division of payoffs. If two answers agreed, these players were paid. Stakes were set so that players could receive a maximum of about $4. Care was taken to see that players in any triad had not met before but they were encouraged to discuss the game between sessions, since it was a complex game and it was thought that this was necessary to obtain sophisticated play.

None of the first group recognised the significance of the set T and none gave the set T as answer when asked what they thought the division of payoff for each coalition should be. A few members of the other groups grasped its significance from the start and most knew it by the end as a result of discussion. While the stake was the chief incentive for the first two groups other factors were important for the third. Probably they showed a greater interest in the game itself, since they had volunteered to take part.

The overall results showed that triads rarely arrived at a division in the set T, but rather divisions which varied randomly about divisions in T. The average amounts won were almost exactly the quotas i.e. 1.5, 2.5 and 3.5 in all groups. Clearly the set T acted as a constraint. Maschler obtained a similar result in an experiment which he performed.[18] Possibly these results differ from those of Lieberman because of the stakes involved and the structure of communications. Perhaps Lieberman's subjects did not have enough time to recognise the complexity of the mathematical solution and under the circumstances followed the most obvious path of equal division.

So according to Riker's results, T constrains the players whether or not they recognise it. But why do deviations from T take place? Riker suggests, and backs up his suggestions with statistics, that players shaved off their expectations from the quotas in order to buy the allegiance of a potential ally. Such a strategy was adopted as a consequence of the local institutions of this particular game; the mathematical solution was modified.[19]

In Game Theory and in the above experiments it was assumed that a coalition would form as a result of negotiations. Sometimes the latter are not possible, in which case we are dealing with a 'non-negotiable' game. The prisoner's dilemma is the classic example of this type and Rapoport has published the results of one experiment on the three-person game.[20]

In this experiment, which used sixteen triads of students, the players sat in separate booths and in front of them were the payoff matrices for eight different games. At fifteen-second intervals a number (generated randomly), designating which game was to be played, was indicated, and the players had to press one of a pair of buttons marked R or L. R meant co-operation in some games and defection in others. About 300–500 trials took place followed by a break, followed by more trials making 1,200 in all. Winnings and losses for individual trials as well as cumulative winnings were displayed for each player.

It was found that after the break, in which communication was allowed, the percentage of co-operative choices greatly increased and the CCC outcome or triple alliance 'against the house' tended to form and remain stable. As conditions had changed after the break, results from subsequent trials were discarded in what follows.

It was assumed that there was some index for each game such that the frequency of co-operative choices would be a linear function of it. The best-fitting index was one based on a comparison of expected gain to self and others in the same outcome cell (regardless of whether they made the same or opposite choices). Such an index emphasises the competitive (or conflict) aspect of the game.

Having obtained the index for the games played its validity was tested over other games. Six triads played 800 trials without a break. It was found that as games became more competitive the regression line kinked and took a smaller slope (fig. xxii).

Fig. xxii.

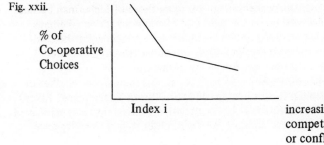

% of Co-operative Choices

Index i

increasing competitiveness or conflict

This was interpreted as being due to an increase in co-operative choices by one player, after being discouraged by repetitive losses through unanimous choices of D, attempting to communicate a willingness to co-operate. But since the others are rewarded if one player alone plays C, non-compliance with this invitation is re-inforced and after 20—30 plays of the co-operative choice the first goes back to defection.

A third experiment, identical with the second save that matrices were not displayed in order to bring out the learning aspect of group behaviour, showed that ignorance of the payoff matrix elicited a higher level of co-operation. Here the individual is probably more concerned with the success or failure of his own individual previous play than with the strategy of other players. The percentage of co-operative choices didn't appear to vary much with different payoffs — the regression line based on the index was almost horizontal.

In a fourth experiment triads played 400 trials of one game followed by 400 of another. The percentage of co-operative choices here was higher than in any of the other three experiments, probably due to the learning effect.

With increasing use of the computer in the social sciences it is not surprising that some work on the simulation of three-person games has been started. Hernifer and Wolpert have begun an interesting study in this field.[21]

They were concerned with the inter-nation stalemate situation in which it becomes impossible or difficult to communicate meaningful threats between major powers. Sometimes a minor power, in coalition with one of the major powers, may undertake such a communication. Firstly they considered a two person prisoner's dilemma game which had been going for some time and had 'locked in' on the CC response. The third player was added as an ally of one of the others.

In the first experiment the payoffs were contrived so that B and C (the coalition) were not harmed by one another's defection, but A could be severely penalised for co-operating without corresponding harm to the coalition member who co-operated while the other did not. Typical matrices of this type are shown in fig. xxiii.

The model used for the simulation was a version of the Bush-Mosteller linear learning model and started by giving each player a probability of playing co-operatively which was modified as a result of the payoff at each trial. A positive payoff raised the probability, a negative one lowered it.

The learning rate, or rate of change of this probability, was assumed to be proportional to the payoff involved. The rates were normalised with a parameter k which was interpreted as a measure of

Fig. xxiii.

C $_1$ B

                β_1 β_2

	β_1	β_2
α_1	1, 1, 1	−20, 20, 0
α_2	20, −20, −10	10, 0, −10

(A labels the rows)

C $_2$ B

                β_1 β_2

	β_1	β_2
α_1	−10, 0, 10	−30, 20, 10
α_2	20, −20, 0	−1, −1, −1

(A labels the rows)

the relation of the value of money to the player. The initial probabilities were set at 0.5.

Simulations took place varying the payoff structures and k parameter. Co-operation increased as the value of P (the punishment for triple defections) increased, but player A's degree of co-operation increased far more slowly than did B's or C's. Increasing the value of R (the reward for triple co-operation) also increased the co-operative responses.

Because of the comparative rarity of trilateral co-operation it is in the interests of A to continue defecting unless the penalty for triple defection becomes very great. A's choice is more responsive to previous outcomes because his payoffs are of a relatively greater magnitude. B and C learn more slowly and are not so easily induced to shift to defection after being duped. Player A typically accumulated a large positive payoff, B and C building up deficits.

This shows that A can benefit considerably at the expense of B by involving B's ally in a struggle in which there is no collusion. The tacit agreement by B and C not to benefit by one another's improper choices actually does considerable harm to the long run interests of both. It would pay B and C to work towards raising common reward or common penalty.

In the second experiment two two-person games, A v C and A v B were played in this order. The BC alliance was apparent in that player B reacted not only to his own plays and payoffs but also to those of C. Player A on the other hand played each game independently and C played the A-C game without reference to the other.

As the penalty for double defection in the A-C game increased, all players increased co-operation. But when this penalty was raised in the A-B game there was only a moderate increase in the co-operative play by A, a small decline by B and a large decline by C. Increasing R increased co-operation greatly, especially when R was increased in the A-C game.

This game is more favourable to the alliance. The departure from the triple blind choice so as to permit B to observe the impact of C's play in the A-C game gives B the opportunity to retaliate against A. In terms of winnings B fared somewhat better than C and considerably better than A. An exception to this occurs when the penalty for double defection in the A-C game is increased. C is then able to dupe A in the A-C game and A cannot retaliate because of the large loss incurred in the A-B game if he does so.

Results so far from these simulations should only be regarded as tentative but much more work can be expected here.

3.6   LATER SOCIOLOGICAL THEORY AND THE FIRST EXPERIMENTS

The first attempt to investigate some of Simmel's propositions was undertaken by Mills at Harvard University in 1953.[22] The project examined three questions:

a) Does segregation into a pair and isolate generally take place in a triad?
b) To what extent are relationships in the triad interdependent?
c) When does interdependence develop into a rigid power structure and when are relationships in a state of fluctuation?

48 triads of students were each given a number of pictures and asked to create a story around them, upon which they all agreed. Each act was scored according to Bales method of interaction process analysis.[23] Acts relevant primarily to the group problem are called 'contributions', positive acts directed specifically to other group members are called acts of 'support' and negative acts directed to other members are called acts of 'non-support'. The data therefore was a list of the number of contributions made by each member and the exchange of support and non-support responses between members.

Members of each triad were ranked in order of contributions made and matrices of rates of support between members were drawn up. (The rate of support of B by A is the percentage of B's contributions supported by A.)

The relative number of contributions together with the total support received were taken as being indicative of a member's power. If these were both high, that member was in a strong position. Many different measures of power have been used in different experiments and later we shall discuss these measures in a separate section.

For any pair of members, the magnitudes of their rates of support for each other were taken as manifestations of the nature of the relationship existing within that pair.

From the 48 matrices, a single matrix giving the median rates of support was computed from the distribution in each cell. This showed that the highest rates of support were those exchanged between the two most active members and that the rates were almost equal. The cell distributions were almost identical and differed from those in all other cells. This gives some evidence in favour of Simmel's idea of the pair and isolate.

Referring to the two most active members in each individual triad, Mills called the relationship between them *solidary* if the support rates both exceeded the respective medians; *conflicting* if both rates were below the medians; *dominant* if the more active member's was below and the other's above; and *contending* if the more active member's was above the median and the other's below.

Statistical tests showed that in the solidary type there was association: the least active member tended to oppose the pair and the pair tended to reciprocate the opposition. Support to and from the isolate was lower here than anywhere else. In the conflicting pattern the isolate's position was indeterminate. He tended to fare better than when facing the solidary pattern but no better than when facing the other two types. So it is difficult to conclude anything about Simmel's idea of Tertius Gaudens (see section 2.4 above).

Considering the rank ordering of contributions over time it was found that activity positions were most stable in the solidary pattern and least stable in the conflicting pattern. In the other two the position of the most active member was more or less stable but the others were not.

Analysis of support rates over time showed that fluctuations in activity positions were related either to a low rate or loss of support and that stability was associated with gain, the striking exception being the isolate in the solidary pattern, who remained in a fixed position whilst losing support.

Regarding the stability of the four patterns themselves the solidary one was the single stable pattern with ten of the thirteen of this kind remaining this way. Next most stable was the conflicting type whilst the other two tended to shift towards this type.

Mills drew the following conclusions:
1) Where the coalition forms, its intensity increases because there is a

common object of opposition for each member – the isolate.
2) Tertius Gaudens is not a general tendency but the principle is involved in another way. Consider one member of the coalition – he benefits from the conflict between the other member and the isolate.

It should be stressed, as Mills did, that these results were obtained under a particular set of circumstances and the same conclusions may not necessarily be drawn under different conditions. The triads used were short-lived, of one particular age group, sex and academic standard, and were engaged on one specific task only.

Thibaut and Kelly commented on this experiment.[24] They suggested that the four patterns observed may arise initially because, owing to random fluctuations, it just so happens that two members sometimes get on well, see eye to eye or their outcomes correspond to a noticably higher degree than those of any other pair. They may have similar values, similar problem-solving strategies etc. Then if we apply some of the reasoning behind the structural theory of balance (positive acts are rewarding, negative acts punishing and each type has a tendency to invoke a similar reply), we see that Mills' data on the stability of the patterns lends support to this theory.

As Mills' conclusions could only be applied to the particular ad hoc triads under certain conditions, Strodbeck investigated the family as a three person group to see if similar conclusions could be reached.[25] The family is, of course, not an ad hoc group. It is one which has been in constant interaction for some time. It would seem that Simmel's segregation hypothesis may not hold here or at least a permanent coalition would not form. No member can easily withdraw from this triad and in many ways they have each other's interests at heart.

Each family member filled in a questionnaire, and nine questions where two members agreed on an answer and the third disagreed were selected for debate. The isolate was a different member for three questions each. They were then asked to talk the question over and if possible, come up with an agreed answer.

The families were second generation, half Jews and half Italians, with equal numbers of high, medium and low sociometric status. All the children were boys, 14 – 16 years old. Again Bales' method of scoring was used and individual as well as median matrices of rates of support were drawn up. Support rates in the median matrix between the two most active members were higher, but not significantly higher, than those between others. The levels of support were significantly lower than those obtained by Mills and the isolate was not in his worst position when there was a solidary relationship between the pair.

While Mills had measured power by participation rates only, Strodtbeck attempted an arbitrary measure by giving two points for each decision made and dividing them up on the basis of who persuaded whom. Again the lowest ranking member, in terms of points, was not significantly worse off in the solidary type. Strodtbeck did agree with Mills that the solidary pattern was the most stable of the four.

It appears that the most important difference between the populations studied by Mills and Strodtbeck is the ad hoc nature of the first and permanence of the second. There is also the possibility that the difference in task influences the disparity. The families had nine different tasks and the position of isolate was rotated. This may well have influenced the stability of the relationships.

Mills undertook further experiments in order to test the persistence and interdependence of the structure of the relationships and to specify the conditions under which the structure is more persistent and under which it tends to dissolve.[26] In the first series of experiments twelve triads, each composed of two trained collaborators and one naive subject, a student, were used. Each triad had to reach a decision on a hypothetical military court case. As discussion proceeded, one of the collaborators began to side with the subject, the other arguing against him. The resulting coalition pattern was allowed to develop until it seemed to have reached a permanent form. Then the isolate collaborator began to strengthen his argument and the other collaborator gradually switched his allegiance. In the final stage the collaborators maintained their alliance, letting the subject initiate whatever strategy he wished but rejecting all overtures for acceptance unless the subject said he had changed his opinion to one of agreement with them.

The hypothesis behind the experiment was that the coalition structure would reconstitute itself following the changes of roles because of the strong structural forces operating in the triad. The subject would not be expected to alter his opinion after the switch to conform to the majority. This assumes that the pressure towards isolation is stronger than the pressure to conform to the majority, which, as Asch has demonstrated, exists in a small group situation.[27]

Again behaviour was scored according to Bales' method. The subject's attitude toward self and others as well as motivational changes were also measured by various sociometric techniques.

It was found that regardless of the direction of change in the position of the coalition, behavioural roles of the subjects when isolate correspond in detail as did their roles when parties to the coalition. These results gave support to the hypothesis that the structural fact of two members being in coalition against the third is more important in determining behaviour in the group than temporal change itself or previous position in the group.

Of the thirty subjects in the deprivation sequence only sixteen maintained their original opinion. So as far as opinion goes there is no strong tendency towards isolation. Attitude tests showed the subjects still tended to choose their former ally as a friend, even after the switch, and perceived themselves as being regarded as a friend by the former ally.

Mills' overall conclusion was that the coalition pattern is a fully independent structure only in respect to behaviour. These structural tendencies are likely to impinge on different individuals in different ways.

The second experiment aimed at testing the effect of the subject's status position and certain personality variables in pushing him towards the role of isolate or pressing him into submission. Three hypotheses were suggested. The coalition is more likely to persist:
a) when the isolate is of higher status relative to the others.
b) when the isolate has a low need for acceptance of others.
c) when the isolate has a strong need for self-enhancement.

Results showed that high status was not associated with resistance to the coalition but, on the contrary, the low-status isolate offered more resistance. Nor did the prediction hold for need dependence. There was no significant difference between the strongly dependent and less dependent isolate. Self-enhancement was more important for high status members than for low. On the basis of these findings Mills offered two propositions:
1) That members of the coalition being willing, the structure is more likely to dissolve when the isolate is of relatively high status and has a relatively low need for self-enhancement.
2) The structure is most apt to persist, even become increasingly rigid, when the isolate has a strong need for self-enhancement.

As a tentative hypothesis he suggested that the level of anxiety generated by isolation may affect the coalition structure i.e. the latter is more likely to persist the higher the anxiety. He concluded with a general hypothesis formally stated as:

"In a role structure of some stability, the structure of personal, emotional attachments (positive or negative) is stronger than the structure of common values or beliefs that are relevant to the purpose purpose of the groups, and these structures are stronger than the pattern of manifest interaction between members. Further, when the structure is by some means changed, readjustments are made with differential facility in three aspects of a role, such that there is a greater lag in adjusting personal emotional attachments than in adjusting values and beliefs, and a greater lag in adjusting values and beliefs than in adjusting manifest behaviour towards others within the structure."

While Strodtbeck had used the family as a permanent triad and compared his results with Mills' ad hoc triads, Torrance did a similar experiment using temporary and permanent three-man combat crews.[28] These crews consisted of pilot, navigator and gunner, a recognised hierarchical decision-making structure. The permanent groups had been together for several months. The temporary groups were formed by re-grouping the same type of personnel so that none from the same permanent crew were together.

Each triad was given four decision-making problems, varying in nature and difficulty. These were a simple arithmetic problem, estimating a number of dots, creating a story round pictures, and a survival situation where the crew could designate one member to a position where he would possibly have to give up his life. Bales' method was again used.

Results from the first problem showed that in permanent groups the higher the status of the member, the less frequently he failed to influence the others to accept his answers if there was disagreement. In the temporary crews this effect was diminished, all members exerting more influence.

In the second problem it was assumed that the person whose estimate was nearest the final decision had exerted most influence. In both types of triad it was found that the higher the status the greater the number of times a member influenced, whether the answer was a good estimate or a poor one.

The measure of influence in the third problem was created by comparing the member's individual stories with the crew's story agreed upon and listing the salient points common to both. In both types again influence was correlated with status.

In the final problem influence was measured by the number of contributions. Of the permanent crews 93.7 per cent showed concern for keeping their crew together whilst only 71.8 per cent of the temporary crews did this.

From questionnaires and interaction analysis it appeared that certain types of interaction tended to characterise occupants of different positions. Navigators made more effort to influence but felt they had little influence. Gunners made little attempt to influence and felt they influenced the decision very little.

One final study which took place in the early fifties and is relevant for inclusion here, was undertaken by Hoffman and others.[29] These authors investigated the subject's evaluation of his ability in the light of comparisons made between his own performance and that of others whom he considered comparable. The triad was used as the reference group.

This experiment differed from those above in that it had a concrete motivational aspect — players had to maximise a number of points. Payoffs could only be had by forming coalitions of two and the payoff for any coalition was the same, so Game Theory would predict each coalition to occur equally often. The author's hypothesis was, however, that there are several additional motivations at work and by considering these we can predict which particular coalition will form.

The individual may be concerned about his comparability with others in the group, because this is indicative of his status relative to them. But the others in the group must be comparable i.e. they must be considered his equals. When this is so we have what the authors call 'peer' conditions as against 'non-peer' when the others are regarded as being definitely superior or inferior. Another important variable is the importance of the task. Increasing the importance is likely to increase the individual's concern about status differences.

Two similar experiments were undertaken each using twenty-eight triads of male students. The conditions peer or non-peer, high or low task importance, gave four replications. One member of each triad was a paid participant, a stranger to the others, trained beforehand in the role he was to play. The players were told that the purpose of the experiment was to gather data on a new intelligence test. The conditions of high and low task importance were created by the contents of a written test and by the instructions given to the subjects about the validity of the test. The 'peer' or 'non-peer' conditions were created in part by instructions and in part by the actions of the paid participant.

After the written test the players took part in a bargaining game. Each had a number of triangular shapes and was instructed to make a square. It was possible, but difficult, for an individual to do this, but two members acting together could make a larger square and get more points for it. If two squares of equal size formed, no one got any points. If any person formed an individual square on the first trial he got a bonus of twelve points. The paid participant always did this, thereby gaining an initial points advantage. The paid participant's bargaining behaviour was predetermined over the remaining four trials.

Data from a questionnaire revealed that manipulation of the experimental conditions was successful. Results from the experiment showed the paid participant receiving more points under the condition of low task importance than under high task importance and more under non-peer conditions than under peer conditions. In fact he always received less than the number expected by chance over trials two to five. His failure was due a) to his inability to form a fair share ($^2/_3$) of terminal coalitions (i.e. those in being at the end of a trial) even though he was willing to offer as many as seven out of the eight points available, to his partner, and b) to the fact that even where he was a coalition member his share of the points was less than half.

Thus coalitions tended to form against the player who had the initial advantage and the strength of this tendency was greatest when players perceived themselves as equals and the task as being important. One further finding was that under peer conditions the subjects tended to compete against the paid participant and split their winnings equally, whilst under the non-peer conditions they competed against each other, only 34 per cent of the coalitions involving equal division. Also if the paid participant succeeded in taking part in a terminal coalition he had to pay more points to his partner in the peer relationship than in the non-peer, and more in the high task importance case than in the low.

In summary, if the subjects perceived the paid participant as a person of comparable status, his initial points advantage seemed to be interpreted as a loss in status to them and this loss appeared greater the more important they believed the task to be. They tended therefore to form a stable coalition against him. Such coalitions were less likely if he was perceived as being non-comparable in status because then the loss of status was smaller. Instead the subjects then tended to compete against each other, the paid participant becoming the medium by which changes in status could be achieved.

3.7   CAPLOW'S THEORY AND SUBSEQUENT EXPERIMENTS

The above experiments all involved some notion of relative power. In those by Mills and Strodtbeck this was indicated by the players' contributions to the problem and was therefore derived from the experiment itself. Hoffman created status differentials by means of experimental manipulations, and Torrance used triads with a recognised hierarchical structure of decision making. In no case was an attempt made to quantify power, merely an ordering of the three individuals took place.

Caplow did not attempt to quantify power either, but he considered six different power relationships between members of the triad, using equalities and inequalities.[30] Caplow's idea is that the formation of a coalition "depends upon the initial distribution of power, and, other things being equal, may be predicted under certain assumptions when the initial distribution is known". Caplow was concerned with the sociological triad in which the "typical gain consists of domination over other triad members".

He began by making four assumptions:

"1. Members of a triad may differ in strength. A stronger member can control a weaker member and will seek to do so.
2. Each member of the triad seeks control over the others. Control over two others is preferred to control over one other. Control over one other is preferred to control over none.
3. The strength of the coalition is equal to the strength of its two members.
4. The formation of coalitions takes place in an existing triad, so there is a pre-coalition condition in every triad. Any attempt by a stronger member to coerce a weaker member in the pre-coalition condition will provoke the formation of a coalition to oppose the coercion".

From now on we will use larger case letters to represent players and small case letters to represent their power (or resources). Caplow's six power structures were:

Type I. $a = b = c$ (i.e. all equal in power).

All coalitions are equally likely here, members trying to enter a coalition in which they are equal to their ally and stronger, by virtue of the coalition, than the isolate.

Type II. $a > b$, $b = c$, $a < (b + c)$

If b forms a coalition with A he will be stronger than C by virtue of the coalition, but weaker than A inside the coalition. C is in a similar position. If B and C combine they are stronger than A and equal within the coalition, so this coalition seems most likely.

Type III. $a < b$, $b = c$

A can strengthen his position by joining B or C who both welcome him as an ally. B and C cannot improve their pre-coalition positions by joining forces. Thus $\overline{AB}$ and $\overline{AC}$ are the probable coalitions.[31]

Type IV. $a > (b + c)$, $b = c$

B and C have no reason to join forces and A being stronger anyway, has no reason either, so no coalition is likely here.

Type V. $a > b > c$, $a < (b + c)$

A seeks to join either B or C, C seeks to join either A or B. But B has no incentive to join A, and has a very strong incentive to join C. Thus $\overline{BC}$ or $\overline{AC}$ may form.

Type VI. $a > b > c$, $a > (b + c)$

This is similar to Type IV. with the one difference that in IV both B and C may try to join A whilst here only C could improve his position by doing so.

If we look at all these predictions it becomes apparent that the weakest member is often favoured insofar as he is included in most coalitions. Though his position within the coalition may be weak, he at least has the security of being included.

The first test of these predictions was made by Vinacke and Arkoff at the University of Hawaii in 1957.[32] On the one hand, Game Theory, assuming play was determined by rational analysis of the final outcome, i.e. winning, and the player acted with sole aim of maximising, would make certain predictions about coalition formation. Caplow on the other hand, assuming play was determined by the initial conditions, i.e. how players interpret the position of themselves and others, would make, in most cases, a different prediction.

In Types IV. and VI. only the strong member can possible win but in other Types any pair can beat the isolate so that really all three members are in equivalent positions regardless of their power distributions. Game Theory therefore predicts that all coalitions are equally likely, or that each may be expected to occur one-third of the time, in such Types. Caplow regards the initially perceived relation of each member to the others as overriding these considerations.

The experiment used thirty triads of male students. A modified pachisi board was used and the players ran a 'race' over 67 spaces, the first home being the winner and receiving 100 points. If a coalition won, the prize was shared according to its members' wishes. Each player was given a weight and every time a die was cast he moved a number of spaces equal to the product of his weight and the die score. If a coalition formed both members had a weight equal to the sum of their individual weights and both moved together. Coalitions, once they had formed, lasted until the end of that particular game. The weights used corresponded in their orderings to the six power structures formulated by Caplow. Each triad played three series of games, there being one of each power structure in each series. Thus all played eighteen games. The order of the different types was varied in a Latin Square design and weights were allocated randomly to the players for each game. The weights used and the predictions of Caplow and Game Theory are summarised in Table I.

Results[33] showed that in Type I all coalitions occurred a large number of times though $\overline{AC}$ was significantly under-represented. In Type II $\overline{BC}$ formed significantly more often than the others. In Type III $\overline{AC}$ and $\overline{BC}$ occurred more often than $\overline{BC}$, though $\overline{AC}$ occurred relatively more frequently than $\overline{AB}$. Only twenty-eight out of a possible ninety alliances occurred in Type IV and only thirty in Type VI. $\overline{BC}$ occurred most often in Type V with $\overline{AC}$ next. On the whole the results agreed quite well with Caplow's predictions.

Table I. *Coalition Predictions by Caplow and Game Theory.*

Type	Weights			Prediction by Game Theory	Prediction by Caplow
	a	b	c		
I	1	1	1	Any	Any
II	3	2	2	Any	$\overline{BC}$
III	1	2	2	Any	$\overline{AB}$ or $\overline{AC}$
IV	3	1	1	None	None
V	4	3	2	Any	$\overline{AC}$ or $\overline{BC}$
VI	4	2	1	None	None

Consideration of which member initiated an alliance showed that all did so approximately equally in Type I and III but in the other Types B and C did so significantly more times than A. It was also evident that the division of points within the coalition closely followed the perceived power patterns.

It is possible that the Game Theory predictions could not be fulfilled until some learning had taken place so the authors looked at the coalitions formed over the three series of games. There was no significant difference between the first and third series for Types I, II, III and V. The players did however learn when a coalition was necessary and when it was futile, shown by a drop in the incidence of coalitions for Types IV and VI.

The evidence was that all triads at least some of the time and most triads most of the time, adopted the strategy based on manipulations of the initial conditions.

What may be considered a test of Caplow's theory was a study of fifty sibling triads undertaken by Gerstl.[34] Power was assumed to be ranked according to age and the distribution followed Type V. Twenty-three triads were found to contain coalitions verified by the separate reports of all three members but contrary to expectation fifteen were $\overline{AB}$, seven $\overline{BC}$ and only one $\overline{AC}$. It appeared that the coalitions were based on similarity of age, sex and interest rather than balance of strength in the triad. The study demonstrates how differently these more permanent triads may react from the ad hoc triads which come together in the laboratory for a single experiment. For the latter the experimental conditions are their raison d'être and other considerations are secondary. But for the triads which have existed for some time

90

many more issues may be important and may contribute to coalition formation.

Kelley and Arrowood questioned Vinacke's use of weights as measures of power.[35] In the Type VI game with weights 4, 2 and 1 the player with the highest weight has power in the sense that he can win regardless of what the others do. But in Type V games the player with the '4' has no more power in this sense than the others, if all recognise that any coalition can win. Vinacke and Arkoff's results showed that their subjects treated the '4' in Type V as if he had real power.

Kelley and Arrowood believed Vinacke's experiment was too complex and confusing to the subjects, especially in the way it mixed up the different games. Consequently the subjects erroneously equated weights with real power. These authors therefore undertook a simpler experiment to see if subjects showed a better understanding and acted more in accord with a rational analysis of the situation.

Thirty triads of male students were used and the procedure followed that of Vinacke and Arkoff save that only power structure Type V was used and the number of trials varied from ten to seventy. The subjects were told to maximise their payoffs, regardless of other players.

The distribution of coalitions was similar to that obtained by Vinacke and Arkoff but biassed a little more towards the chance distribution predicted by Game Theory. There was no significant change over time. A questionnaire administered afterwards showed that all but fourteen subjects had at some time in the experiment believed that '4' was the most powerful but only twenty two never realised the fallacy of this. Asked what led to their belief in 4's power the greatest number referred to the fact that he would win if no coalition formed.

In a second experiment the same authors sought to test Caplow's predictions under conditions where power differences were real rather than illusory. In Vinacke's experiment with the Type V power structure a player who failed to get in a coalition received a zero payoff. Kelley and Arrowood gave each player a specific alternative payoff which he received if not in the coalition. The person with a higher alternative payoff has greater power in that he is less dependent on getting into a coalition, and during the bargaining phase he can hold out for a greater share since he has less to lose if no agreement is reached. The latter fact makes him less desirable as a coalition partner. We expect therefore that the poorer his alternative the more likely is he to be included in a coalition. (All this assumes that the size of the prize is invariant to who is in the coalition.)

Fifteen triads were used and each player given a weight — 4, 2 or 0, the weight representing the number of points he obtained by playing alone. A coalition could get ten points and prospective members had one minute to decide on the division of these points. Before each trial the players privately indicated a prospective partner and reciprocal choices became coalitions. If the coalition members could not agree on a division, they received only their weight in points. Each triad completed twenty trials and again players had to maximise their payoffs regardless of others.

The weights used are comparable with Vinacke and Arkoff's 4, 3 and 2 insofar as in the absence of coalitions the player with greatest weight wins and any coalition can beat the isolate. The 0-2, 0-4 and 2-4 coalitions were therefore regarded as equivalent to the 2-3, 2-4 and 3-4 coalitions respectively.

The results showed that the distribution of coalitions was very closely in line with that in Vinacke and Arkoff's experiment, especially as time went on. The tendency to divide points in proportion to weights also persisted.

While Kelley and Arrowood provided further data on the Type V power structure, Strycher and Psathas did more work on the Type III structure.[36] They were also concerned with Simmel's theory of Tertius Gaudens. We recall that Simmel said the weak man could profit far out of proportion to his intrinsic power by aligning with one of the two more powerful members. This effect is greatest if there is contention between the latter two because the third party then holds a balance of power. The present authors wished to see whether variations in the initial strength of the weak man relative to the others made a difference in coalition outcomes.

Five hypotheses were advanced, dealing exclusively with the Type III triad:

1. Weak-strong coalition will occur with a frequency greater than chance.
2. In such coalitions the weaker member will get less than half the prize.
3. Increases in the weight of the weak man will result in a) more coalitions including the weak man, b) a larger proportion of the prize going to the weak man.
4. Contention between the strong members will lead to a larger proportion of the prize going to the weak man.
5. Contention between the weak man and one of the strong men will lead to a smaller proportion of the prize going to the weak man.

The first three are based on Caplow's theory and the last two on Simmel's theory.

Twelve triads of male students played twelve games each in a Latin Square design with the variables, contention between the strong members, contention between one strong and the weak member either present or not and under one of three weight variations. The strong members always had weight 6 whilst that of the weak member was either 1, 3 or 5. Coalitions were forced to form by having players re-play games in which they did not form.

Considering the games without contention between the strong members, i.e. those that did not force the weak-strong coalition, the number of coalitions including the weak man was exactly as predicted by chance so that there was no evidence for the first hypothesis. The second hypothesis was generally upheld but the weak man's weight made no difference to the frequency with which he entered coalitions, constituting negative evidence for the first part of the third hypothesis. There was however considerable evidence for the second part and for the fourth hypothesis. The conclusion reached on the fifth was that the absence of constraint on the weak man operated to his benefit only when there was contention between the strong members. It seemed that an increase in the relative weight was important for the division of the prize but not for gaining acess to coalitions.

Caplow himself had something to say about Vinacke and Arkoff's findings when he further extended his theory in 1959.[37] Firstly he added two more fundamental Types based on power orderings:

Type VII $\qquad$ $a > b > c, \qquad a = (b + c)$

Type VIII $\qquad$ $a = (b + c), \qquad b = c$

In these Types no effective coalition of B and C is strategically possible. $\overline{BC}$ can block the dominance of A but cannot control the situation. The probable coalitions are $\overline{AB}$ or $\overline{AC}$ in both Types.

Caplow went on to elaborate three different situations in which coalitions may occur and in which different sets of strategies govern their formation. These are:

1. *Continuous.* "Here the object of a coalition is to control the joint activity of the triad and to seek control over rewards which are found within the situation itself." Caplow's assumptions set forth earlier are applicable in this case.

2. *Episodic.* "The membership of the triad is stable and the contest for power continues over an extended time, but the object of the coalition is to secure an advantage in episodic distributions of reward which occur periodically and under predetermined conditions." For this situation assumption 2 is changed to: "Each member of the triad seeks a position of advantage with respect to each distribution of reward. A larger share of reward is preferred to a smaller share, any share is preferred to no share." In this situation coalitions will always form

except in Types IV and VI. There will also, says Caplow, be a tendency for coalition to be limited to a particular episode and to be more changeable than in the continuous situation.

3. *Terminal.* "The coalition is directed towards a single redistribution of power — terminal, either because it dissolves the triad or because it leads to a state of equilibrium which precludes further re-distribution". Assumption 2 is here modified to: "Each member of the triad seeks to destroy the others and add their strengths to his own. A large increase of strength is preferred to a small increase, a small increase is preferred to no increase, no increase is preferred to a loss and a loss of strength is preferred to complete destruction". In the terminal situation coalitions are only possible between equals or potential equals, otherwise the stronger member will absorb the other.

Caplow's predictions for all eight Types of power structure are set out in Table II.

Table II: *Caplow's Predictions of Coalitions in Three Situations.*

Type	Continuous	Episodic	Terminal
I	Any	Any	Any
II	$\overline{BC}$	Any	$\overline{BC}$
III	$\overline{AB}$ or $\overline{AC}$	Any	$\overline{BC}$
IV	None	None	None
V	$\overline{BC}$ or $\overline{AC}$	Any	None
VI	None	None	None
VII	$\overline{AB}$ or $\overline{AC}$	$\overline{AB}$ or $\overline{AC}$	$\overline{BC}$
VIII	$\overline{AB}$ or $\overline{AC}$	$\overline{AB}$ or $\overline{AC}$	$\overline{BC}$

It will be noticed that the prediction for the episodic situation are the same as those made by Game Theory.

Caplow interpreted Vinacke and Arkoff's results as follows. Even though the experimenters intended the game as an episodic situation, the players, being given weights, believed these to be an integral part of the game and interpreted the situation as a continuous one. If they had treated the situation as episodic it would have rendered their weights meaningless. Given this, Caplow says their behaviour was quite rational.

A further attempt to test Caplow's theory was made by Chertkoff in 1966.[38] He was concerned with the Type V structure and particularly with reference to a political convention. He argued that the man with most votes at the U.S. party convention is the one most likely to win the national election and he will be most likely therefore be the preferred choice of those wishing to form an alliance.

In this experiment the probability of future success was manipulated in a simulated political convention situation. It was hypothesised that if the candidate with most votes had the greatest probability of success in the future election, he would be preferred as a coalition partner by those with fewer votes. As the one with most votes would have greater bargaining power it was also expected that he would obtain a greater share of the reward.

The ninety votes in the convention were always divided so that A had forty, B had thirty and C had twenty. 24 triads played under one of four conditions. In three of these B and C each had a 50% chance of being elected while A's chance was either 50%, 70% or 90%. The probability variable was omitted in the fourth condition. It was assumed that if a candidate was nominated and elected he would have 100 jobs to dispense with as President.

Two players had to form a coalition to nominate a candidate i.e. to get the necessary forty-six votes. They also had to agree on who to nominate and how to divide the jobs. Players indicated in writing with whom they would like to negotiate, and reciprocal choices met and conferred for two minutes to decide who to nominate and how to divide the jobs. This being settled, the candidate nominated drew a slip to determine whether or not he had won. If he won, the coalition won the 100 jobs. All triads played a series of three conventions.

Results supported the first hypothesis. B and C tended to prefer A as partner increasingly as A's probability of success increased. Under the fourth coalition $\overline{BC}$ was found to occur more often so this was in accord with Vinacke and Arkoff's findings. But there was some decline in the incidence of $\overline{BC}$ after the first convention − a phenomenon similar to that noted by Kelley and Arrowood.

The frequencies of the various coalitions did not differ significantly from chance values under any of the first three conditions though there was a high incidence of those involving A when his probability of success was at its highest. A tended to receive more jobs as his probability of success increased, though the difference was only significant for alliances with C. The coalition partner possessing most votes usually became the candidate.

95

Overall the main hypothesis received somewhat stronger support from the results on coalition partner preferences than from the data on coalitions actually formed.

In a later article Chertkoff suggested a revision of Caplow's Theory in the light of results obtained by Vinacke and Arkoff, Kelley and Arrowood and himself.[39] It will be recalled that while Caplow predicted $\overline{BC}$ and $\overline{AC}$ as being equally likely in Type V, these experimenters found that $\overline{BC}$ occurred more frequently than either $\overline{AB}$ or $\overline{AC}$. Chertkoff devised a method whereby $\overline{BC}$ would be predicted to occur most frequently.

When choices were reciprocal Caplow assumed coalitions would form. Consider fig. xxiii. which shows the proportion of time each member directs his choice at the others in Type V.

Fig. xxiii.

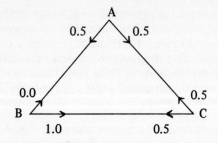

If we multiply the proportions with which reciprocal choices are made, the frequency of occurrence of each coalition is:

$$\overline{BC} = 1.00 \times 0.50 = 0.50 \text{ or } 50\% \text{ of the time}$$
$$\overline{AC} = 0.25 \text{ or } 25\% \text{ of the time}$$
$$\overline{AB} = 0.00$$

No coalitions are assumed to form in the remaining 25% of the time. But suppose that players were allowed to choose again in such cases. Then these 25% would be split up into 0.50 of $\overline{BC}$, 0.25 of $\overline{AC}$ and 0.25 of no coalition. If this process went on indefinitely the ratio of $\overline{BC}$ to $\overline{AC}$ coalitions would remain at about 2 : 1. In the Vinacke and Arkoff experiment the frequencies were: $\overline{AB}$, 9; $\overline{AC}$, 20; $\overline{BC}$, 59; and no coalition, 2.

After his initial experiment, Vinacke along with other experimenters, investigated other factors which may influence coalition formation. The first study was aimed at comparing the play of male and female triads under two different conditions.[40]

They used two sets of thirty male student triads and two sets of thirty female student triads. One set of each played under conditions exactly as before (designated 'Game by Game' play) while the others were supplied in addition with a record sheet displaying their cumulative scores as the session progressed.

As regards coalition formation there were not significant differences in the incidences of each between males and females under the Cumulative Scores condition and only one or two significant differences under the Game by Game condition, the males appearing to play in accordance with initial patterns of strength. Both sexes tended to follow the general strategy reported for the earlier experiment.

Considering the incidence of no coalition and triple alliances, the female triads allied less often as pairs against an isolate and formed triple alliances more often than males. Both tendencies were much reduced under the Cumulative Scores condition. Another difference was that females, more often than males, formed alliances in the Types IV and VI games. In Types I, II, III and V, males more frequently established alliances on a disproportionate basis, the difference being most marked under the Game by Game conditions. Males engaged more frequently in extended bargaining under this condition but there was no significant difference between the sexes in this respect under the other condition.

In general the introduction of the Cumulative Score tended to make the females behave more like the males whilst it did not change the male performance appreciably. The author suggested that the females are less concerned about winning and more concerned with arriving at a fair and friendly solution. Thus they adopt tactics such as forming triple alliances with equal division of points and strong members often give up points voluntarily to weak members.

Following this study, the question arises, "What happens in mixed sex triads?" Bond and Vinacke undertook an investigation to answer this question.[41]

In such experiments, on top of the weight structure we have a majority-minority factor to consider. Two members of the triad have something in common — their sex — whilst the other is different.

Thirty triads of students, fifteen with two males and fifteen with two females, were used. Each triad played twelve games, two of each Type, in the same pre-arranged order which placed the more competitive Types towards the beginning and end of the sequence in the expectation that this would maximise bargaining. The games were played exactly as before under the Cumulative Scores condition.

Regarding the Cumulative Score, this study as the one before it, showed that the two members who got behind on points tended to ally against the leader, regardless of their strengths. In other words relative standing became important in addition to relative strengths. The present experiment showed however that in groups with a female majority such an alliance only took place when those behind were weak members. Both sexes, when in the majority tended to ally against the minority but it was especially typical of males to ally when strong and females to ally when weak.

When in a minority, females tended to form alliances with a male when it was not necessary in order to win. But under similar circumstances the male minority refused to ally. Females tended to do better in terms of points gained, especially when in the minority.

The authors explained all these results in terms of strategies adopted. They called the male strategy *exploitative* — the males always competing to advance his own interests and endeavouring to use the female to his own advantage. The female *accommodative* strategy is characterised by a sense of fairness and sympathy for the weak.

In a paper published in 1963, Vinacke examined coalition formation under four incentive conditions.[42] Thirty triads of each sex played each Type six times under one of these conditions. The latter were Game by Game, Cumulative Scores, Delayed Payoff (where a cumulative score was kept and translated into money at the end) and Immediate Payoff (where a payoff of ten cents was made to the winner after each game). In the Delayed Payoff variation an additional ten dollar bonus was paid to that player out of the ninety of each sex who acquired the highest individual score. Thus there was competition not only within triads but between triads.

Results showed little difference in the incidence of two-person coalitions among the incentive conditions save for a somewhat lower overall incidence under the last two. Triple alliances were more common amongst females than amongst males but the occurrence of these amongst men increased when there was a monetary reward. Sometimes it occurred under the third condition when one member was given all the points in an attempt to secure the ten dollar bonus for that triad. It may be that the males became more accommodative where monetary payment was concerned or it may be that because competition had increased, two-person deals had become more difficult.

In general male-female differences loomed larger than incentive differences and it appeared that the condition under which the games were played resulted in a particular variation in the style of play rather than a fundamental change of strategy. The monetary reward seemed to complicate the problem of winning rather than change the strategy itself, doing so to a lesser extent for the female. There was a markedly lower degree of accommodative play under Cumulative Scores, suggesting that the presence of more tangible objectives than mere competition are essential to females. On the other hand, financial reward seemed to increase their desire to share it.

A somewhat different study by Harford and Cheney also compared the play of males and females in a game.[43] This study followed an earlier one by Harford, Solomon and Cheney which examined the effects of the presence of punitive power in a bargaining game with female triads.[44] Signalling devices in the form of written messages were available to the players, thereby separating the means of influencing other players via threats, promises or information-sharing from the actual use of punishments. Results of this experiment showed that the amount of loss incurred by the players increased as the number of players armed with punitive power increased.

Harford and Cheney attempted to test the hypothesis that increasing the number of players armed with punitive power would reduce the levels of co-operation for both male and female triads. It was also hypothesised that females would choose a co-operative strategy more frequently than would males.

Six triads of each sex played under one of four conditions where none, one, two or all three members of the triad had punitive power. Players were each given two differently coloured chips from which they had to choose. The chips were such that only two players could match their colours at the same time and thereby win twenty-five cents on a single trial. Written messages were allowed. Punitive power consisted of the possession of a black chip which could be played once during the game at which point the game ended and that player got twenty five cents. But if two players played black chips simultaneously, the game ended and neither received a bonus. A game could last up to ten trials.

An examination of total payoffs showed that there was increasing loss with increasing punitive power for both sexes but losses for males were significantly greater than losses for females. Males used their punitive power about four times as often as females. 'Co-operative Triads' where dyads alternated winnings rather than a single coalition forming for all ten trials occurred in fifteen of the female triads but in only seven of the male triads.

An earlier study by Vinacke and Cheney considered the effect of personality variables on the players.[45] The variables considered were "achievement", described as a desire to overcome obstacles, exercise power and to strive to do something as well as and as quickly as possible, and "nurturance", defined as a need to nourish, aid or protect the helpless, to express sympathy and to be associated with traits of generosity, sympathy and tolerance towards others. These variables correspond roughly to the exploitative and accommodative strategies mentioned above. But the subjects here were all males.

In each of twenty triads there was one subject who was high in one of each of these variables, the third being about midway on both scores and serving as a control. Games of Types I, II, V and VI were played three times each. As in the other experiments, coalitions formed in accordance with initial strengths. Motivational differences seemed to have little effect indicating that perceived difference in power is a very compelling determinant of behaviour. Subjects high in achievement tended to be the initiators of coalitions and tended on the whole to benefit more than the others.

Vinacke and others further investigated the points raised by Kelley and Arrowood, in a study published in 1966.[46] Would knowledge of the true power relationship produce the strategies prescribed by Game Theory?

Firstly the authors pointed out that the Kelley and Arrowood experiment, involving a long series of trials of the same game, could be prone to a possibility of a fixed routine developing with a consequent loss of interest. Players may then simply mix up coalitions in order to alleviate boredom. Another possibility in Kelley and Arrowood's experiment was that players kept an informal cumulative score, thereby giving rise to coalitions against the leader on points.

Thirty-five male and thirty-four female triads played six successive games of Types I, II, V and VI, the order being randomised. Two sessions of play took place and during the break information about the two possible strategies was given to one, two or all three members of the triad. But no suggestion that either strategy was to be preferred was made.

Results clearly showed that special information did not result in chance occurrence of all coalitions. Weak coalitions were preferred to a high degree in both sessions for both sexes. The only significant tendency was for fewer weak coalitions towards the end of the second session in male triads with all members informed.

Responses to a questionnaire showed that informed subjects clearly had a better understanding that the player with '4' in Type V was not really the strongest with respect to his ability to win. Even most of the uniformed members tended to arrive at this view.

Results also showed that the greater the number of members of the triad who expressed a motivation to win, the smaller the proportion of weak coalitions. There was also a tendency for those who showed good understanding to express more frequently a desire to win. So the formation of weak coalitions, it was suggested, may be a function of the desire to win rather than of the understanding of the power situation.

All of the above experiments and theory will be further discussed and assessed in the final section of this chapter.

3.8   OTHER THEORIES OF COALITION FORMATION

Apart from classical Game Theory and Caplow's theory, the best known theories of coalition formation are those devised by Gamson[47] and Riker[48].

Gamson argues that when several individuals are required to make a decision there exists a weight associated with each participant, such that some critical quantity of these weights is necessary for the decision to be made. The weights are called resources. The rules of the game include specification of the resources relevant to the decision and the amount of resources necessary to control the decision, though an amount less than the formal amount may be sufficient to control the decision for all practical purposes.

A *winning coalition* is one with sufficient resources to control the decision and a *minimal winning coalition* is defined as a winning coalition such that the defection of any one member will make it no longer winning. The *cheapest winning coalition* is that minimal winning coalition with total resources nearest to the decision point.

The general hypothesis is:

"Any participant will expect others to demand from a coalition a share of the payoff proportional to the amount of resources which they contribute to a coalition".

If the payoff is constant to all coalitions a player will maximise his own payoff by maximising his share of resources in the coalition, which he will do, according to Gamson, by maximising the ratio $\frac{\text{Own Resources}}{\text{Total Resources}}$. Thus he will favour the cheapest winning coalition.

If we look at Caplow's six power structure Types (Types VII and VIII do not apply since Gamson is only interested in cases where no member is essential to a winning coalition) and assume the decision point is a simple majority of resources and winning coalitions all have the same payoff, we can use Gamson's theory to predict coalitions in these cases.

Only in Type V do Gamson's predictions differ from those of Caplow. Gamson predicts only $\overline{BC}$ here while Caplow predicted $\overline{BC}$ or $\overline{AC}$. It will be recalled that Vinacke and Arkoff found that $\overline{BC}$ occurred three times as often as $\overline{AC}$.

The theory is based on what has been called the *parity norm*, which

101

is the belief by the players that one ought to get from an agreement an amount proportional to what one brings into it. The weights or resources suggest what these amounts are.

Riker's theory is rather similar to that of Gamson but Riker builds on the concepts of Game Theory. He deals only with zero-sum games in which side-payments are permitted. His theory is characterised by the *size principle* which states:

> "In social situations similar to n-person zero-sum games with side-payments, participants create coalitions just as large as they believe will ensure winning and no larger".

Riker quotes some evidence for the size principle from the fields of politics but stresses that in the real world lack of information means that the minimum size is usually a subjective estimate.[49] He further hypothesises that the greater the incompleteness of information, the larger will be the coalition which the coalition makers seek.

In the model the rule of decision is "that a coalition with weight m where $m > \frac{1}{2} \sum_{i=1}^{n} w_i$, where w_i is the weight of player i, can act for or impose its will on the body as a whole".[50] The term proto-coalition refers to a coalition in the making which hasn't yet achieved a weight m, and the players are designated as leaders or followers according to whether they offer or receive side-payments.

In the building of the coalition Riker assumes that there are certain general strategic considerations which can be made. Players are interested in their chances of winning, and consideration of the size principle "may place severe restrictions on admissible coalitions and thereby greatly influence the chance that a particular proto-coalition will become part of a winning coalition".

Five situations are distinguished. Those with

1. *A uniquely preferable winning coalition* which is a coalition which has a greater value than any other possible and is one in which all the participating proto-coalitions can satisfy their initial expectations.
2. *A uniquely favoured proto-coalition*, X, is one such that (i) any winning coalition containing it is more valuable than one not containing it and (ii) if more than one proto-coalition satisfies (i), then there is at least one winning coalition containing X and none of the others that satisfy condition (i).
3. *A uniquely essential proto-coalition*, which is one which appears in all winning coalitions when no other proto-coalition is so favoured.
4. *A unique coalition*, which is a winning coalition in the final stage such that only one combination of proto-coalitions in the previous

stage can produce such a coalition.

5. *A strategically weak proto-coalition*, which is one that cannot by reason of a given partition in the penultimate stage, become part of the most valuable winning coalition.

The three members of the triad A, B and C may be considered as proto-coalitions. Suppose the ordering of weights is $w(A) > w(B) > w(C)$ and suppose $m > w(A)$. If $m = \frac{n+1}{2}$ or $\frac{n+1}{2}$ where $n = \Sigma w$, any coalition can win. Suppose the values of these coalitions are

$$v(\overline{BC}) = a = -v(A)$$
$$v(\overline{AC}) = b = -v(B)$$
$$v(\overline{AB}) = c = -v(C)$$

where $a > b \geq c$.

Obviously $\overline{BC}$ has the greatest value but can B and C both satisfy their initial expectations? The most B can get from $\overline{AB}$ is c when A gets nothing. The imputation for an alliance of B and C is then $(-a, c, a-c)$. C's initial expectation is calculated similarly — in alliance with B he can initially expect an amount b and the imputation for $\overline{BC}$ would be $(-a, a-b, b)$. If $c < (a-b)$ both B and C can obtain the payoffs they desire. $\overline{BC}$ is then a uniquely preferable coalition. Table III sets out other cases.

Caplow's Types IV and VI are irrelevant here if $m = \frac{n+1}{2}$ or $\frac{n}{2} + 1$; but if $m > \frac{n+1}{2}$ or $m > \frac{n}{2} + 1$, Types IV and VI are equivalent to row 1, column 3 or 4 or rows 1 and 2, column 3.

If m is larger than a bare majority, Types VII and VIII are equivalent respectively to row 1, columns 3 and 4 and row 2, column 3.

Type I is equivalent to row 4; Type II is equivalent to row 2, column 2; Type III is equivalent to row 3; and Type V is equivalent to row 1 columns 1 and 2.

Predictions are the same as those made by Caplow except for Type V. Because Caplow does not differentiate amongst payoffs, he does not distinguish column 1 from column 2. Hence he regards $\overline{BC}$ and $\overline{AC}$ as equally likely. He fails to observe the unique position of C. Gamson also fails to make this observation.

Again we note the striking fact that there is a relative absence of advantage for the largest or weightiest proto-coalition, A.

Mazur has developed a theory of coalition formation behaviour that is not based on any rational maximisation principle.[51] He makes use of

Table III. Riker's Predictions for Coalitions in the Triad.

	Column			
	$w(\overline{AB}) > w(\overline{AC}) > w(\overline{BC}) \geq m$		$m > w(\overline{BC})$ or $w(\overline{AC})$	
Row	**1**	**2**	**3**	**4**
	$c \leq (a-b)$ or $b \leq \frac{a}{2}$	$c > (a-b)$ or $b > \frac{a}{2}$	$w(\overline{AC}) \geq m$	$m > w\,(\overline{AC})$
1 $w(A) > w(B) > w(C)$	ⓒ B	ⓒ	Ⓐ C	Ⓐ Ⓑ *
2 $w(A) > w(B) = w(C)$	B. C	–	Ⓐ	///
3 $w(A) = w(B) > w(C)$	ⓒ		///	///
4 $w(A) = w(B) = w(C)$	–		///	///

ⓒ indicates a uniquely favoured proto-coalition

* indicates a unique coalition

Ⓐ indicates a uniquely essential proto-coalition

BC indicates a uniquely preferable winning coalition

– indicates no sort of uniqueness

/// indicates that the combination of conditions is impossible structural balance theory. The model specified a subset of the conceivable coalition situations which are unlikely, and predicts that the coalition will be one of the subset of coalitions which are not unlikely.

Unbalanced situations are rejected as well as those which are *identity inconsistent,* which is defined as follows:

"In the triad A, B, C if (i) A and B are close with respect to C and (ii) A and B have a negative relationship and (iii) at least one other line in the balance diagram is negative, then the triad is identity inconsistent".

This model is probably of more use when dealing with groups higher than the triad.

Cross suggests that the same competitive forces that constrain market behaviour have an equally important role in the determination of coalitions.[52] The search for the best alliance is no different in principle from the search for the lowest price. He assumes players are motivated by a desire to maximise the value (to themselves) of their membership. Each individual wishes to join the coalition that would give him the most, given the demands of the necessary allies. However, for different individuals, the coalition giving the maximum may be different, suggesting that competition may arise for "scarce" members.

Cross argues that there will be a set of coalition configurations that can be called stable insofar as deviations from one of these configurations will set up competitive forces tending to restore it (or some other stable configuration). The set of all the stable configurations constitutes the solution. The theory makes use of the diagram in fig. xxiv.

Fig. xxiv.

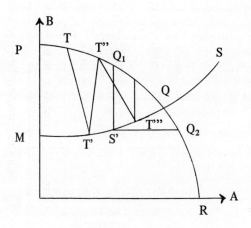

105

The curve PQR represents various divisions of the payoff to $\overline{AB}$. MQS represents the combination of returns to A and B which would leave C indifferent to coalition $\overline{AC}$ or $\overline{BC}$. The payoff to C falls as we go up the curve, reaching zero at S. It is determined implicitly, whilst the payoffs to A and B can be read off the graph.

If the coalition $\overline{AB}$ has formed with some division at T, C can make a better offer, say T', to A. B can respond to this alliance by making an offer to A or C, but we expect him to make it to A since B himself gets more from the $\overline{AB}$ coalition. C may then make a new offer to A and in this way we move through the points T, T', T'', T''' to converge at Q. Since there is a unique intersection the model implies that the division of payoff is completely determined. This is because it assumes that if any player left out of the coalition asks for a lower payoff than that at Q, such a reduction will lead to competition for this player and restore his higher payoff. But there is complete uncertainty as to which of the three coalitions will form.

Suppose now that point S falls below the curve PQR, say at S'. The coalition formation process would stop here because C can no longer exert any influence beyond this point. We now know for certain which coalition will form i.e. $\overline{AB}$ but we don't know the division of payoff, which could be anywhere between Q_1 and Q_2.

3.9 THE THREE-PERSON DUEL

The three-man duel, or "truel" as it has been called by Shubik, represents another interesting sort of three-person game and provides another instance of the weakest member of the triad enjoying a position of strength. Whilst the ordinary duel approximates a zero-sum game, (since conflict of interest is maximal), in the truel any damage inflicted by one party on the second will incidentally benefit the third.

The idea is that each player shoots in turn, having one shot each and the order being randomised. Each has a certain rating or probability of making a hit. Suppose for example these are A = 0.8, B = 0.7, C = 0.6 and suppose the order of firing is A, B, C. If more than one player survives, the prize is divided in proportion to the ratings.

Rationally, A should fire at B since B represents the greatest threat to his life. B's chance of survival is

$$1 - \text{(probability that A hits)} = 0.2.$$

If alive, B must fire at C, since C has a shot to come. C's chance of survival is then

$$1 - \text{(B's chance of survival)} \times \text{(probability that B hits)} = 0.86.$$

If C survives he should shoot at A whether or not B lives, because A will take a greater share of the prize. A's chance of survival is

1 − (C's chance of survival) × (probability that C hits) = 0.484.

So C has the greatest chance of survival. The reason is that there is no possibility of a coalition. The strong are forced to eliminate the strong in order to maximise their own chances of survival. The conclusion is the same no matter what the order of firing.

It should be noted that there are cases where the disparity in relative strengths is great enough to ensure the strongest of the best chance of survival, even when the reasoning is as above. But it does not pay to be only slightly stronger than the others since it will invite action against oneself.

Willis and Long have run an experiment in this field in the form of a simulation of an internation truel.[53] They employed triads of university students, each player representing a nuclear power. Each had the choice of three moves at each trial: (a) do nothing, (b) attack the first of the others (c) attack the second of the others. If an attack was made it was certain to succeed. If a player was attacked he was eliminated from the game but allowed to make one further decision on the next trial. Three replications of a two by two by two orthogonal design were run. The variables were (i) knowledge of the source of attack, (ii) knowledge of the number of trials, and (iii) the sex of the subjects. Experiments were run over fifty trials or until two players had been eliminated. The experimenters announced the outcomes after each trial.

The results were briefly as follows. Of the twelve groups with the source known there were attacks in seven whilst attacks occurred in eleven of the twelve triads with source unknown. Initial attacks were invariably followed up by at least one and more often two or three counterattacks. Over three-quarters of the initial victims responded by counterattacking and there were thirty-nine attacks altogether in the source-unknown case as against twenty in the source-known case. There were thirty two attacks when the number of trials was unknown and twenty-seven when known. Males made thirty five attacks altogether and females made twenty four.

If attacks took place at all, nine out of ten times they occurred in the first five trials. In fifteen out of the twenty four triads there were no survivors, in six there were three survivors, in three there was one survivor and in none were there two survivors. The latter again illustrates the impossibility of coalition formation in this situation. The absence of communication will of course influence this but even if it is allowed there is still the problem of trust. This is one situation where the two-one split is very difficult.

107

The authors advanced three hypotheses on the basis of these results:
1. A policy of non-aggression is more effective than one of aggression and is therefore more likely to be adopted on all sides under conditions favouring veridicality.
2. The occurrence of but a single attack is a highly improbable event.
3. The basic strategic decision to aggress or not to aggress is made early, so that the probability of an act of aggression decreases rapidly as time goes on.

The basic dilemma confronting all is that if no one else is going to attack, it is foolish to attack, but if someone else is going to attack it may be foolish to let him attack first.

3.10 COMMENTS AND CONCLUSIONS

Of all three-person situations, those in which coalition formation is a possibility are undoubtedly of the greatest interest. We can consider three types of triadic situations:
1. That described by the pure co-ordination game where there exists a solution which maximises the return to all players so there is no reason for anyone to be excluded.
2. The situation of pure conflict where no player can gain more in coalition than acting alone. It should be noted that whilst all two-person zero-sum games represent conditions of pure conflict, some three-person zero-sum games make it possible for a subset of players to combine and gain at the expense of the third.
3. The mixed-motive situation where no outcome maximises the return to all players but an element of co-ordination exists in that two players can improve their payoffs by combining. This is the type found in most real life situations.

Simmel hypothesised that most triads would split up into a dyad plus an isolate. Given that this is true the question arises "How does the split occur or what is the basis for the resulting coalition?" While theoreticians could advance various theories on coalition formation and attempt to predict coalitions under certain rules, the experimenters could set up situations in which a split was either forced to occur or was pretty certain to occur because of the rules of the game, in order to test these theories.

Two other ideas of Simmel could also be investigated. These were *tertius gaudens,* the third party benefiting from conflict in the dyad, and the idea of the weakest member of the triad benefiting out of proportion to his intrinsic strength.

Most theories attempt to tell us which coalition will form and with what division of the prize. Gamson distinguishes four types of theory:
a) *Minimum resource theory* which is derived from the assumption

that players seek to maximise their share of the payoff and hold a belief in the parity norm. Under the latter, they believe that the player with greatest weight or resources should get the greatest share but players prefer to unite with someone with a lower parity price. Caplow's theory would come under this heading, though he does not attempt any measure of the payoff. Gamson and Riker are more explicit about this and also about the relative strengths of members of the triad.

b) *Minimum power theory* which assumes that coalitions are determined by relative power rather than resources. This is an outgrowth from Game Theory and includes such things as the Shapley value.

c) *Anticompetitive theory* based on Vinacke and others' results with female triads. It assumes coalitions will form along the path of least resistance in bargaining. These will be between those partners for whom there exists the most obvious and unambiguous solution to the problem of dividing the payoff. The more openly a player seeks to get as much as he can the less likely is he to be preferred as partner.

d) *Utter confusion theory* which says that coalition formation is entirely at random.[54]

No theory has received complete support from experimental results. There is some evidence for each of them.

The experiments by Mills and Strodtbeck aimed at testing Simmel's hypothesis on the split. Mills found evidence in favour of this. When a "solidary" coalition formed the third party grew increasingly isolated. The coalition here appears to form between the strongest members of the triad, but the measure of strength is itself dependent on the existence of the coalition i.e. the players grow in strength because of the reinforcement process which takes place because they are in agreement. Strodtbeck's results were less encouraging. His experiment differed in that there was something of a coalition at the outset, i.e. two family members agreed on an answer whilst the third disagreed with them. The subsequent discussion pitted the resources of the isolate against the coalition in a battle of influence.

Possibly the differences in results can be explained as follows. Mill's triads were ad hoc and we may think of initial relationships within each dyad as being basically hostile. Referring to structural balance theory such a triad is unbalanced, but can become balanced by the formation of a positive bond between two members in the way that Thibaut and Kelley suggested. The process is perhaps intensified by the common opposition to the isolate. Strodtbeck's families began with strong positive bonds linking all three and the coalition only existed with respect to one small issue amongst the many issues of longer duration which would confront such a triad. Thus there may be found no strong tendency for negative bonds to intensify. Indeed Mills has demonstrated in his second experiment that other factors such as emotional attachments can temper somewhat the tendency to split into a coalition and isolate. Torrance demonstrated that there may be a recognised and accepted structure of decision making which again inhibits this tendency.

We have said that coalitions form with respect to an issue in order that players can maximise their payoffs. Where other issues interfere with the one in question they may impose sufficient costs to prevent a coalition forming. To investigate coalition formation with respect to a particular issue it is therefore necessary to set up a situation where none of these factors can interfere. Insofar as Mills used ad hoc triads such a situation was created. The payoff in this instance was of a purely psychological kind resulting from the influence the players had on the situation. Though the payoffs were of a similar nature, insofar as they were not ad hoc triads, other factors could interfere in the experiments carried out by Strodtbeck and Torrance.

No evidence was found for tertius gaudens unless we accept Mill's alternative interpretation (page 67). Stryker and Psathas did however find some evidence for this in that the third party's share of the payoff in coalitions tended to rise when there was dissension between the others.

Like Mills, Vinacke and the experimenters associated with him have used ad hoc triads so that coalitions formed on the issue in question and were not affected by other issues. These experiments have aimed at testing not whether coalitions form but rather which coalitions form and what the criteria for these are. Even here factors not strictly concerned with the issue (such as the tendency for members of the same sex to ally in mixed triads) may interfere.

These experiments have certainly given much support to the minimum resource theory and have thus constituted evidence against the minimum power theory. There are however a number of experiments which have turned out the other way so no firm conclusions can be drawn. Caplow's theory fell down on the Type V prediction and Gamson's is not entirely satisfactory here. Chertkoff's revision of Caplow's theory may be useful, especially as it is based on a consideration of initial contacts made by players, a thing which most experimenters have neglected. Chertkoff found that virtually all reciprocal contacts resulted in coalitions. Phillips and Nitz suggest that the contact phase may be the most important.[55] In an experiment similar to Chertkoff's they asked players whom they would contact first in various situations where the number of votes pledged to each varied. Results were again in line with minimum resource theory.

Just why players form coalitions in accordance with this theory is not fully understood. Even where they understand the relative power positions they still tend to form weak coalitions in the Type V game for example. There is evidence from the division of prizes that they do hold a belief in the parity norm though the evidence is less extreme than the parity price would suggest. But the players are faced with the problem of winning and must decide with whom to form a coalition. Even if they know that any coalition can win they must somehow make a choice. The man with the '4' may become the isolate because he has a certain saliency. He is the one who would win if no coalition formed.

It is dangerous however to assume that because a given outcome resulted, the assumed process of decision making was responsible for it. As Stryker and Psathas point out, such inference is very risky unless one outcome alone is logically and empirically possible when and only when a given process operates.

More data concerning the process as well as the outcome is needed. Stryker and Psathas have moved in this direction by observing the bargaining process. They noticed that initial offers were often accepted without the third party entering into the bargaining process at all. Sometimes players tossed a die to decide which coalition would form.

Experimental results have not lent much support to Game Theory predictions. However Riker and Maschler, in what were quite sophisticated experiments, have shown that the Game Theory solution does appear to have some relevance as far as average payoffs are concerned.

The evidence for anticompetitive theory comes from Vinacke's results using female subjects. But what may often seem to be anti-competitive behaviour may arise from entirely different motivation. The subject may focus on the entire experiment rather than an individual trial and even the most selfish and exploitative player may find his best long run strategy involves deliberate restraint in seeking immediate advantage. Lieberman noted that sometimes players forego immediate larger gains in the hope of establishing a long run relationship of trust with a partner. As Vinacke demonstrated under the Cumulative Scores condition, a player who does well too soon may motivate a coalition of the others against himself.

There is some evidence for the fourth theory e.g. subjects tossing a die, but as Gamson points out, there may well be other evidence which the experimenters have not published because they obtained such uninteresting results.

Obviously a large number of factors influence coalition formation even in these comparatively simple experimental situations. The subjects here, faced with a single task or issue and interacting on this alone, must use some criteria to decide with whom to ally. When either partner is equally good as far as payoff is concerned they must look for something which makes one player stand out either as friend or foe. This may be the weight given to the player, the relative standing of the player on points or perhaps some entirely extraneous factor such as the colour of his hair.

There are many difficulties in running experiments of these types. In Vinacke's experiment for instance, if one mixes up games it may lead to confusion so that the players do not really understand the situation at all. On the other hand, playing the same game over and over again may lead to boredom and the players may change their strategies for the sake of novelty. Chertkoff has suggested that the problem may be overcome by giving a player a fixed power position but playing each game with two different people.

The experiments usually deal in small amounts of money, points or prizes. None have paid really large sums and it is possible that players would react differently if they did so. Experiments are often non-realistic as situations and regarded merely as a game. Subjects rarely seem to get involved in these situations as they would in real life, notes Rapoport. Above all, as frequently stressed, any conclusions drawn can only refer at best to the populations which have been tested by the experiment.

It has often been noted how the triad favours the weak over the strong. The weak player can more frequently get into a coalition even though his position therein may be somewhat weaker than that of his partner. Most of the games considered made the same payoff to all coalitions. Now if coalition effectiveness depends on who is in the coalition the weak player may not enjoy such a position of strength. Chertkoff has begun some work along these lines and it will be interesting to see the results of further studies.

The other areas of experimental work are less developed. Computer simulations will undoubtedly become very important but do suffer from the great disadvantage of ruling out negotiations. It would be interesting to see more work done on the truel. Willis and Long's experiment did not involve any prize for the players, and so there was no concrete motivation. The experiment could also be run with various probabilities of an attack succeeding.

Notes

1. John Von Neumann and Oskar Morgenstern, *The Theory of Games and Economic Behaviour* (Princeton, N.J.: Princeton Univ. Press, 1947).
2. Theodore M. Mills, "Power Relations in Three-person Groups", *American Sociological Review,* 18 (1953), 351–357.

3. Theodore Caplow, "A Theory of Coalitions in the Triad", *American Sociological Review*, 21 (1956), 489–493.
4. W. Edgar Vinacke and Abe Arkoff, "An Experimental Study of Coalitions in the Triad", *American Sociological Review*, 22 (1957), 406–414. Also see later footnotes.
5. William H. Riker, *The Theory of Political Coalitions* (New Haven: Yale Univ. Press, 1963).
6. William A. Gamson, "A Theory of Coalition Formation", *American Sociological Review*, 26, 3 (1961) 373–382.
7. Jerome Chertkoff, "A Revision of Caplow's Coalition Theory", *Journal of Experimental and Social Psychology*, 3 (1967), 172–177.
8. Dina A. Zinnes, "An Analytic Study of the Balance of Power Theories", *Journal of Peace Research*, 3 (1967), 270–287.
9. William A. Gamson, "A Theory of Coalition Formation", *American Sociological Review*, 26, 3 (1961), 373–382.
10. John W. Thibaut and Harold H. Kelley, *The Social Psychology of Groups* (New York: John Wiley and Sons, Inc., 1959), p. 205.
11. Ibid. pp. 196–198.
12. See for instance, T. M. Newcomb, R. H. Turner and P. E. Converse, *Social Psychology* (London: Tavistock Publications Ltd, 1952).
13. Vickrey, William, *Strong and Weak Solutions in the Theory of Games.* (Department of Economics, Columbia University, 1953 [dittoed]).
14. R. Duncan Luce and Howard Raiffa, *Games and Decisions* (New York: Wiley, 1957), p. 176.
15. L. S. Shapley, "A Value for N-Person Games", *Annals of Mathematics Studies*, 28 (1953), 307–317.
16. William H. Riker, "Bargaining in a Three-person Game", *American Political Science Review*, Vol. LXI, No. 3, (1967), 642–656.
17. Bernhardt Lieberman, "Experimental Studies of Conflict in Some Two and Three Person Games" in J. H. Criswell et. al (eds.), *Mathematical Methods in Small Group Processes* (Stanford: Stanford Univ. Press, 1962).
18. Michael Maschler, *Playing an n-Person Game: An Experiment,* (Princeton University, Econometric Research Program, Research Memorandum No. 73, 1 February, 1965).
19. William H. Riker, "Bargaining in a Three Person Game", *American Political Science Review*, Vol. LXI, No. 3 (1967), 642–656.
20. Anatol Rapoport, Albert Chammah, John Dwyer and John Cyr, "Three-Person Non-zero-sum Non-negotiable Games", *Behavioural Science*, 7 (1962), 38–58.
21. J. Hernifer and J. Wolpert, "Coalition Structures in Three-person Non-zero-sum Games", (Preliminary Draft), *Peace Research Society Meeting*, The Hague, August 1967.
22. Theodore M. Mills, "Power Relations in Three-Person Groups", *American Sociological Review*, 18 (1953), 351–357.
23. R. F. Bales, *Interaction Process Analysis* (Cambridge, Mass.: Addison-Wesley, 1950).
24. John W. Thibaut and Harold H. Kelley, *The Social Psychology of Groups* (New York; John Wiley & Sons, Inc., 1959), p. 211.
25. Fred L. Strodtbeck, "The Family as a Three Person Group", *American Sociological Review*, 19 (February 1954), 23–29.
26. Theodore M. Mills, "The Coalition Pattern in Three Person Groups", *American Sociological Review*, 19 (December 1954), 657–667.

27. S. E. Asch, "Studies of Independence and Conformity: I. A Minority of One Against a Unanimous Majority", *Psychological Monographs,* 70 No. 9, (Whole No. 416), 1956.
28. E. Paul Torrance, "Some Consequences of Power Differences on Decision Making in Permanent and Temporary Three-Man Groups", in A. Paul Hare, Edgar F. Borgatta, Robert F. Bales (Eds.), *Small Groups: Studies in Social Interaction* (New York: Alfred K. Knopf, 1955), 488–489.
29. Paul J. Hoffman, Leon Festinger and Douglas H. Lawrence, "Tendencies Towards Group Comparability in Competitive Bargaining", *Human Relations,* 7 (1954), 141–159.
30. Theodore A. Caplow, "A Theory of Coalition in the Triad", *American Sociological Review,* 21 (1956), 489–493.
31. The notation IJ will henceforth be used for a coalition between I and J.
32. W. Edgar Vinacke and Abe Arkoff, "An Experimental Study of Coalitions in the Triad", *American Sociological Review,* 22 (1957), 406–414.
33. Summarised in Appendix I.
34. Joel E. Gerstl, "Coalitions in the Sibling Triad", Mimeograph (Minneapolis: University of Minnesota, Department of Sociology, 1956).
35. H. H. Kelley and A. J. Arrowood, "Coalitions in the Triad: Critique and Experiment", *Sociometry,* 23 (1960), 231–244.
36. Sheldon Stryker and George Psathas, "Research on Coalition in the Triad: Findings, Problems and Strategy", *Sociometry,* 23 (1960), 217–230.
37. Theodore M. Caplow, "Further Development of a Theory of Coalitions in the Triad", *American Journal of Sociology,* 64 (1959), 488–493.
38. Jerome Chertkoff, "The Effect of Probability of Future Success on Coalition Formation", *Journal of Experimental Social Psychology,* 23 (July, 1966), 265–277.
39. Jermoe Chertkoff, "Further Development of the Theory of Coalitions in the Triad", *American Journal of Sociology,* 64 (1959), 488–493.
40. W. Edgar Vinacke, "Sex Roles in a Three-person Game", *Sociometry,* 22 (1959), 343–360.
41. J. R. Bond and W. E. Vinacke, "Coalitions in Mixed Sex Triads", *Sociometry,* 24 (1961), 61–75.
42. W. Edgar Vinacke, "Power, Strategy and Formation of Coalitions in Triads under Four Incentive Conditions", *Office of Naval Research,* Nont 3748 (02), (1963), Technical Report No. 1.
43. Thomas Harford and John Cheney, "The Effects of Proliferating Punitive Power in a Bargaining Game with Male and Female Triads", Mimeograph. (V.A. Outpatient Clinic, Boston, Mass., 1968).
44. T. Harford, L. Solomon and J. Cheney, "The Effects of Proliferating Punitive Power in a Three-person Bargaining Game", *Journal of Personal Social Psychology.*
45. M. V. Cheney and W. Edgar Vinacke, "Achievement and Nurturance in Triads Varying in Power Distribution", *Journal of Abnormal Social Psychology,* 46 (1957), 277–286.
46. W. Edgar Vinacke et al, "The Effect of Information about Strategy in a Three-person Game", *Behavioural Science,* II (1966), 180–189.
47. William A. Gamson, "A Theory of Coalition Formation", *American Sociological Review,* Vol. 26, No. 3 (1961), 373–82.
48. William H. Riker, *The Theory of Political Coalitions* (New Haven: Yale University Press, 1963).
49. Ibid., p. 47.

50. For any reader unfamiliar with the use of the symbol Σ, $\sum_{i=1}^{n} w_i$ is the sum of each w_i, from the 1st weight to the nth weight.
51. Allan Mazur, "A Nonrational Approach to Theories of Conflict and Coalitions", *Journal of Conflict Resolution,* Vol. XII, No. 2 (1968), 196–205.
52. John G. Cross, "Some Theoretic Characteristics of Economic and Political Coalitions", *Journal of Conflict Resolution,* Vol. XI, No. 2 (1967), 184–195.
53. Richard H. Willis and Norman J. Long, "An Experimental Simulation of an Internation Truel", *Behavioural Science,* 12 (1967), 24–31.
54. William A. Gamson (Ed.)., *Power and Discontent* (Dorsey: Illinois, 1968).
55. James L. Phillips and Lawrence Nitz, "Social Contacts in a Three-Person Political Convention Situation", *Journal of Conflict Resolution,* XII, 2 (1968), 206–213.

CHAPTER 4

POWER, STABILITY, AND SOME HYPOTHETICAL GAMES

4.1 INTRODUCTION

By so arranging the rules of their games, most of the experimenters considered in chapter 3 more or less forced coalitions to form. The situations were usually such that coalitions had to form if players were to maximise or win and the question was "Which coalition?" rather than "Will a coalition form?".

The experiments referred to zero-sum situations in the sense that only the winner received a final payoff, the losers getting nothing. Note that this is not zero-sum in the traditional Game Theory sense where one player's winnings are another's loss. Rather it is used in the weaker sense of there being a winner and a loser. Coalitions which formed and were effective were always winning coalitions i.e. coalitions only formed in order to win and no one could improve his payoff by forming a non-winning coalition. Further, any winning coalition received, in most cases, the same payoff. The payoff to individual members could however vary for membership in different coalitions.

When speaking about the tendency for the triad to split into a dyad and isolate we have often referred to its stability. This term needs some investigation. To test this tendency we must devise games in which coalitions are possible but are not forced to form. It is up to the players to decide. To investigate the criteria on which these coalitions are decided it is necessary to make the game as simple as possible, eliminating all interfering issues. The rules of the game could be changed to see what effects these had on coalition formation.

From the previous chapter it is obvious that power is an important variable (though by no means the only one) in determining which coalition will form. But this term has been used rather loosely and like stability needs investigating further.

Time is an important variable in most real world situations. Caplow recognised this with his continuous, terminal and episodic types. The way in which payments are made over time will doubtless influence coalition formation.

This chapter begins with sections on stability and on power. From this we lead on to the notion of Balance of Power and the relation of such theories to theories of coalition formation. This enables us to see better some of the inadequacies of the accomplished gaming and to suggest further possible research. Some alternative games are suggested and an analytic model of these is presented in an attempt to predict coalitions given certain rules and rational behaviour.

4.2 STABILITY

The dictionary defines stability as "firmness of position" or "continuance without change". A system is stable therefore if it is enduring or permanent.

To decide when a triad is stable we must answer the question, "When is a triad not a triad?" In other words if we start with three separate entities or decision makers, under what conditions do we cease to have three? The answer is that we cease to have three either a) when the interaction ceases altogether because the issue is settled or b) when two parties combine and act as one with respect to the third. In the second case the triadic interaction process becomes a dyadic interaction process.

But in asking about the stability of the triad we must be referring to stability with respect to the issue in question. It could happen that a triad was stable with respect to one issue and at the same time was unstable with respect to another issue. As we said earlier, sometimes it may be possible to combine smaller issues into one larger issue. Sometimes we are forced to do this because issues are so inter-related. So it should always be remembered which issue we are referring to.

To any particular issues there may be a large number of decisions. Now two parties may combine to make one decision and then cease to act together even though the issue is not settled. If it happens that after such a decision the triadic interaction process resumes, we cannot say such a triad is unstable. If on the other hand the triadic interaction process ceases with this decision the triad is said to be unstable. The dyad may continue to interact with the isolate for some time and many further decisions may be made. But if there is never a return to the triadic interaction process i.e. if there remains in effect only two decision makers, the triad is unstable.

If the triadic interaction process exists at the completion of the issue even though coalitions may have formed and disintegrated as the issue was fought out, we shall say that such a triad is stable. Sometimes the issue is finally decided between the coalition and the isolate, sometimes the isolate ceases to be an effective decision maker before the completion so that the issue is finally decided between the coalition members themselves, now no longer considered a coalition. It is hoped that these points are clearly summarised in fig. xxv.

4.3 POWER

This word has been used extensively in what has gone before but it has not been properly defined. As it is so important a variable in coalition formation and indeed in most aspects of life, it is now necessary to consider a definition.

As Dahl says, power is a relation among people, groups or nations.[1] Most authors seem to agree that A has power over B if he can make B do something he would not otherwise do. This however refers only to the influence on the behaviour of another. As we said in chapter 1 influence is based on the ability to affect another's payoff. Whether or not behaviour is changed as a result of this is another question. The ability to affect payoffs is the basis of the power relationship.

So far we have used the term influence very broadly to refer to any possible way of affecting payoffs. Now we wish to use it in a narrower sense to refer to one particular way.

In chapter 2 we noticed that the arbitrator for example is in a position much stronger than that of the mediator. The mediator can only change the disputants' payoffs by persuading them to alter their evaluations of certain outcomes. This method of affecting payoffs we are going to term influence in the narrow sense. The payoffs in terms of real resources are not changed but the utilities of various payoffs are changed. This influence is then purely psychological.

Kaplan distinguishes power from influence in saying that "influence becomes power whenever the effect on policy is enforced by relatively severe sanctions".[2] This statement seems to imply that power is coercive or always enforces a cost on another. This is not necessarily the case for power may also be exerted where one party promises some reward for another if he complies with the wishes of the first.

We shall say that party A has power over another, B, if he can control B's payoffs in some way by taking certain actions. He will not necessarily control the behaviour of B. This implies that A can change B's payoffs in terms of real resources, but in so far as the extent of this

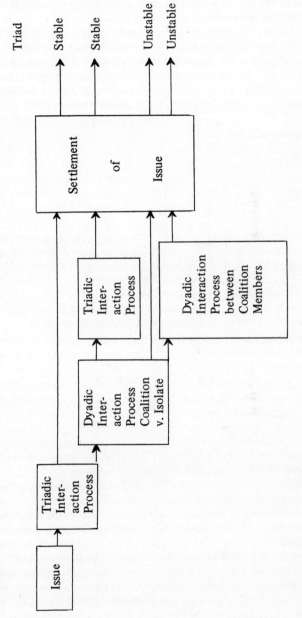

Fig. xxv.

119

change depends on B's perception of what A can do a psychological component is still involved.

In the power relationship A can make threats or promises of certain payoffs to B if B does or does not comply with A's wishes. B still has some choices in the matter — he can still control his own payoffs to some extent. If this choice disappears however, so that A can impose some payoff on B, the relationship is said to be one of authority.

Influence, power and authority can be compared using matrices.

Fig. xxvi.

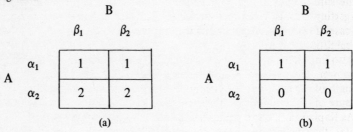

(a)   (b)

In the first matrix, which shows only A's payoffs A will play α_2 but B wishes him to play α_1. He does so by persuading A that the matrix is that in fig. xxvi(b). In this case B exerts influence over A.

In fig. xxvii. B has power over A.

Fig. xxvii.

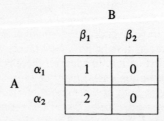

By threatening to play β_2 if A plays α_2, B may succeed in changing A's choice to α_1. If B has authority over A, A's choice α_2 is removed altogether.

Power and authority are then based on the notion of control of another's outcomes in the sense of being able to take actions which definitely alter the other's payoffs. One or two further points should be noted. Firstly, while such control may be available to a player it does not follow that it will be used. Threats will not necessarily be

120

made and if they are they will not necessarily be carried out. Secondly power may sometimes be exerted only incidentally — one player may alter another's payoff without meaning to do so. Finally, a player A may possess power without knowing it if another, B, believes that A will take a certain action, though in fact A has no such intention.

Obviously there are degrees of control and statements such as "X has more power than Y" are far from uncommon. But how does one go about measuring power? Occasionally statistics are available where a long series of similar actions have been taken. Thus Dahl has attempted to measure the power of Congressmen by measuring the probability of a bill getting through given their backing.[3] But such cases are rare and in the case of once and for all events it is impossible to estimate probabilities.

Also important in the power relationship is the cost to A of exerting the power. The costs to B of refusing A's demands measure the strength of B's incentive for yielding to A and may thus give some measure of the strength of A's power over B.

As Kaplan says, other things being equal, A's power over B is greater, the smaller the cost of A's power and greater the strength of A's power. But to combine the costs of both parties into a single index of power is a very difficult problem. Even if this problem were overcome there is the added problem of comparing the powers of different individuals, due to the psychological factors involved.

In considering the power of nations perhaps we could measure power by considering resources possessed. Military equipment or G.N.P. are possibilities. But there are difficulties in making these measurements. If we consider their monetary value for instance there are problems due to technology. If one country spends half as much as another on aircraft it does not follow that it can have half as many planes of the same quality as those of the first nation. In addition there is the subjective element to consider. One nation's assessment of another's power is very much based on perceptions both of the amount of resources and the nation's skill in using them effectively. Power and resources may not therefore be well correlated. A party good at bluffing may in fact have more power than one with more resources. Further the structure of the situation or game itself may well favour one player, giving him a greater control over the other's payoffs — and this may be in no way related to resources possessed.

In the games considered in chapter 3 players were often given weights which were supposed to represent power. It was often said for instance the the player with weight '4' in the Type V game of the Vinacke and Arkoff experiments was perceived as being the most powerful. Undoubtedly the players in these games had a certain amount of control over each other's payoffs and in Types IV and VI the player with greatest weight certainly had the greatest power since the other players had no control over his payoff. But in the situations involving other resource orderings how much control did the players have? In speaking of control here we must remember we are referring to potential power — what a player might do, not what he actually does. The power actually exerted can only be seen after decisions are taken i.e. after coalitions have formed in these cases. In order to see if Caplow's theory is really supported we must develop some measure of power and then see if players were maximising their use of power in forming the coalition they did. This will be attempted in chapters 5 and 6. At the moment we cannot accept these experiments as a test of Caplow's theory for the reasons which follow based on what we have said above.

Caplow, in his continuous situation, was concerned with the power relationship. While players seek control over the situation in order to secure the rewards accruing, their total payoff includes an element resulting from their control or power over other players, his theory went. Caplow attempted no measure of power but at the same time said that the power of a coalition was equal to the sum of the powers of its members. Even if we could say that A and B have equal power over C could we say that the coalition $\overline{AB}$ has twice as much power over C as either player acting alone? There is another dimension of power known as the 'scope' or range of stimuli which can be influenced by the party possessing power. Now if A has power over C with respect to a range of stimuli which are mutually exclusive from a range of stimuli where B has power over C, it might be meaningful to add power. But if they overlap the amount of power might be less than the sum. It is easy to add resources and it makes sense to say a number of resources are needed to control the situation or secure the reward, but if we insist that resources represent power we may find ourselves in difficulty.

We can then look upon the weights of players in these experiments as resources needed to control the situation. The most obvious example in practice is where they represent votes. So Vinacke and Arkoff's experiment is acceptable as a test of the theories of Gamson and Riker.

Assuming that weights represent resources and a certain number of them are needed to control the situation, Riker and Shapley developed a measure of power.[4] This is not strictly power in the sense of controlling another's payoff, rather it is a measure of the chances of influencing the situation.

Let us consider a triad with various weights and consider the 3! or 6 possible orderings of the members.[5] For any one ordering, as we add weights reading from left to right, at some point we reach a minimum winning coalition. The player at this point is said to be in a *pivotal* position. The index of power is then given by

$$\phi_w = \frac{p(w)}{n!}$$

where $p(w)$ is the number of times the player with weight w is in a pivotal position.

The authors also constructed a relationship between power and weight defining the power ratio as

$$\rho_w = \phi_w \div \frac{w}{\Sigma w}$$

where Σw is the sum of all weights in the system.

When weight and power are identical the power ratio is unity and if a player exerts an influence in greater proportion than his weight his power ratio exceeds unity and vice versa.

If we now consider the various weight structures used by Vinacke and Arkoff and suppose that m, the number of resources needed to control the situation, must exceed $\frac{\Sigma w}{2}$, we can construct Table IV.

This is interesting in that it demonstrates in the ρ values how the weakest player benefits out of proportion. But there is a drawback to this method. Consider for example Type V. The six possible orderings are

$$AB*C, \quad AC*B, \quad BC*A, \quad BA*C, \quad CB*A, \quad CA*B.$$

The pivotal member is indicated by an asterisk. The point is that all these orderings are considered equally likely. Now if we consider the coalition process starting with the initial contacts phase, we must assume that each player approaches each of the others with equal probability. This may not be the case. If one party has some saliency e.g. A is perceived as the one who wins in the absence of coalitions, the first most likely contact may be between the other two. So in Type V the orderings BCA and CBA may be more likely than the others.

4.4 BALANCE OF POWER

The concept 'Balance of Power' has been open to a wide variety of interpretations, but fortunately Zinnes has summarised these and sorted out the essential ideas.[6] While Balance of Power theories in general refer to the n-person situation, the triadic type has frequently been chosen as an example.

TABLE IV. *Power Ratios and Power Indices for Triad Members under Eight Orderings of Weights.*

Type	Weights Used (Numerical)	Numerical and in General ϕ_A	ϕ_B	ϕ_C	Numerical ρ_A	ρ_B	ρ_C	General ρ_A	ρ_B	ρ_C
I	1, 1, 1	$\frac{1}{3}$	$\frac{1}{3}$	$\frac{1}{3}$	1.00	1.00	1.00	1.00	1.00	1.00
II	3, 2, 2	$\frac{1}{3}$	$\frac{1}{3}$	$\frac{1}{3}$	0.78	1.17	1.17	$\frac{1}{3}\left(\frac{a+2b}{a}\right)$	$\frac{1}{3}\left(\frac{a+2b}{b}\right)$	$\frac{1}{3}\left(\frac{a+2b}{b}\right)$
III	2, 2, 1	$\frac{1}{3}$	$\frac{1}{3}$	$\frac{1}{3}$	0.83	0.83	1.67	$\frac{2}{3}+\frac{c}{3a}$	$\frac{2}{3}+\frac{c}{3a}$	$\frac{2}{3}+\frac{2a}{3c}$
IV	3, 1, 1	1	0	0	1.67	0.00	0.00	$1+\frac{2b}{a}$	0	0
V	4, 3, 2	$\frac{1}{3}$	$\frac{1}{3}$	$\frac{1}{3}$	0.75	1.00	1.50	$\frac{1}{3}\left(\frac{a+b+c}{a}\right)$	$\frac{1}{3}\left(\frac{a+b+c}{b}\right)$	$\frac{1}{3}\left(\frac{a+b+c}{c}\right)$
VI	4, 2, 1	1	0	0	1.75	0.00	0.00	$1+\frac{b+c}{a}$	0	0
VII	4, 3, 1	$\frac{2}{3}$	$\frac{1}{6}$	$\frac{1}{6}$	1.33	0.44	1.33	1.33	$\frac{1}{3}\frac{a}{b}$	$\frac{1}{3}\frac{a}{c}$
VIII	4, 2, 2	$\frac{2}{3}$	$\frac{1}{6}$	$\frac{1}{6}$	1.33	0.67	0.67	1.33	0.67	0.67

Theories of coalition formation have been concerned with predicting which coalition will form when several are possible. Balance of Power theorists on the other hand have concerned themselves with the systemic consequences of the formation of certain coalitions. In the first attempt to link the two fields of research Riker has related his own theory of coalition formation to the Balance of Power theory of Morton Kaplan.[7]

All Balance of Power Theories can be formulated in terms of an independent variable, Balance of Power, and a dependent variable, the systemic consequences of the balance which may be peace and/or preservation of the status quo.

Examining the various definitions of Balance of Power over the years Zinnes concludes that there has been a convergence of thought. Balance of Power refers to "an international system in which the distribution of power and coalition structure is such that no state or alliance of states is in a position to dominate the remaining members of the system". The defining characteristics rest therefore on the variables, distribution of power and alliance structure.

Zinnes constructs six different Balance of Power systems (and there are others too) which all satisfy the above definition. She assumes that power is additive and in view of what we said earlier this is difficult to accept if we use the traditional definintion of power. In fact as we are going to relate Balance of Power to Riker's theory we would prefer to use the term "Balance of Resources". We may then use the term power to refer to the strength of a player and assume complete information, so that the element of perception is ruled out and power is proportional to resources.

Kaplan's Balance of Power system is defined in terms of rules which the actors in the system must follow. While they are rules for an international balance they can of course be modified to fit any system of balance. The rules are

1. Act to increase capabilities but negotiate rather than fight.
2. Fight rather than pass up an opportunity to increase capabilities.
3. Stop fighting rather than eliminate an essential national actor.
4. Act to oppose any coalition or single actor which tends to assume a position of predominance with respect to the rest of the system.
5. Act to constrain actors who subscribe to supranational organizing principles.
6. Permit defeated or constrained essential national actors to re-enter the system as acceptable role partners or act to bring some previously inessential actor within the essential actor classification. Treat all essential actors as acceptable role partners'.[8]

125

Though couched in rather different terms from most traditional theories it is easily seen that rules 4 and 5 state the essential components referred to by Zinnes above. Rules 1 and 2 establish the existence of conflict in the system and 3 and 6 state that a certain minimum number of actors is required.

We recall that Riker was concerned only with the zero-sum situation. There could be only one winner in the sense of receiving some positive payoff. Assuming no party has more resources than the remaining parties' resources taken together, coalitions must form. Assuming division of payoff amongst members of the winning coalition to be proportional to resources possessed, he concludes that the size of the coalition will be minimal, or just big enough to win. Such a (pre-coalition) situation is unstable, he says, because it makes for decision rather than indecision.

Riker assumes that the Balance of Power theories presuppose a zero-sum situation. Kaplan's rules 1 and 2 imply this. Such a situation will lead to the formation of a winning coalition and destroy the stability of the system. The formation of this coalition of course violates rule 4 and so Riker concludes that the rules for a Balance of Power are internally inconsistent and can never guarantee stability.

The validity of this conclusion seems to rest on the answer to the question, "Is a Balance of Power situation a zero-sum situation?" Kaplan lays down his six rules without any order of priority. It may well be that rules 1 and 2 are followed but only within limits and those limits may be set by a consideration of rule 4. If rule 4 is observed extra costs may be imposed on the outcomes from forming coalitions. Thus coalitions become less attractive. Maximisation is only carried on up to a point. Rule 4 must not be violated. If such is the case the situation is no longer zero-sum in the above sense. All parties can get some positive reward from preserving the system.

This is not to say that the Balance of Power system is always stable, for if all states become involved in some zero-sum conflict, perceiving their national interests to be in jeopardy, a winning coalition may form and thus destroy the Balance of Power. Further, zero-sum conflicts may develop between some members of the system and yet the Balance of Power may be maintained because some members remain outside the conflict and have an interest in preserving the system.

4.5   A HYPOTHETICAL GAME

So far the experiments considered have portrayed zero-sum situations in so far as there was only one winner, either a single player or a coalition. The losing player never received a positive payoff. By the rules of these games the weights of the players were related to the issue

126

in such a way that either the player with greatest weight won automatically or weaker players could combine their weights in an effective coalition against him. Only triads with resource or weight orderings of Type IV or Type VI appeared to be stable and these were special insofar as the weaker players could not affect the payoffs of the strong one unless he chose to form a coalition with one of them, and there was no good reason for this. All other types were unstable since the triadic interaction ceased once a coalition had formed.

The following questions must now be answered.

1. Do coalitions tend to form in the non-zero-sum setting?
2. If they do form what conditions are conducive to this and what particular coalitions form?

As we have said earlier, the non-zero-sum situation is far more common in the real world so such an investigation is well justified.

Our answer to the first question must be 'yes'. The term non-zero-sum here refers to situations where there exist outcomes where all players can get a positive payoff, or all players can get a negative payoff i.e. where the interests of the players are not completely opposed. It is therefore consistent with the Game Theoretical sense of the term and as we saw, coalitions can form here if there is a partial correspondence of interests which for two players outweighs the outcome with complete correspondence. Note also that the setting of Mill's experiment was not necessarily zero-sum and yet coalitions formed. But we can still ask which particular coalition will form and whether the triad under these conditions is more or less stable than under the zero-sum rule.

Our job is now to devise a game to portray the non-zero-sum case, and in order to make a fair comparison it must be amenable to a change of rules to make it a zero-sum situation.

Power we have seen is an important factor but we have not yet established its relationship with resources or weights. One way round this problem is to build a rule into the game which gives the players some measure of power which is related to their resources. Players could still be given weights and these could follow Caplow's orderings.

The time factor could also be brought into the game. In the real world we expect decision makers to look into the future when making a decision i.e. they have a time horizon or certain period of future time over which they consider the impact of their decision. Such a consideration will influence their current actions. We can build this factor into the game by making it of uncertain duration. We could divide the game into a number of trials and possible operate some random device to decide whether the next trial would take place. A further note on time horizons is given in Appendix III.

127

It depends of course on the particular situation but it is certainly not always the case the any coalition would get the same payoff. The coalitions considered by Gamson and Riker always received the same payoff (though the value of different coalitions to the same player could vary). This is a crucial factor in determining their predictions. Because of their assumed belief in the parity norm, players maximised their individual payoffs by forming weak coalitions. In the real world certain coalitions may get greater payoffs in total, if the players in them have greater resources. Even if a belief in the parity norm is still present, players may now prefer strong coalitions. This possibility should also be considered in experimental games.

Firstly we may ask if the Vinacke and Arkoff game can be altered in order to make it a non-zero-sum game. It should be possible for even the losers to get some payoff. If the game has a definite terminus we could pay the winner 100 points and the losers a number of points proportional to how far they had travelled along the board when the winner arrived 'home'. This setting would be rather similar to Kelley and Arrowood's second game. The player with greater resources would stand to lose least by not getting into a coalition. Further, weak coalitions would be worthwhile even in Types IV and VI. So all triads would tend to be unstable under such rules.

As another alternative we could make the board of infinite length so the objective would be to get as far as possible in a given time. All players have a similar interest now and if other rules are as before the best strategy is a triple alliance. The game is one of pure co-operation and in such a game no coalition of two is to be preferred to an alliance of all, so the triad may be considered stable.

But most real-life situations involve elements of co-operation and conflict; so how do we bring in the latter? We may do this at the same time as we bring in the measure of real power. Suppose players can also gain points by eliminating other players i.e. going to 'war', or by appeasement payments. If we allow players with greater resources to eliminate those with fewer resources the element of conflict is introduced. It may be more profitable for a player to declare war or it may be more profitable to co-operate and form a coalition.

If a player goes to war he must incur some cost and make some gain. In the following game we shall assume that the gain is a shortrun or once-and-for-all thing, while the cost is a long-run one in so far as his weight or resources level is reduced for the rest of the game.

We shall first of all list the rules of this proposed game and then explain them in greater detail. We shall then present an analytic model of the situation in an attempt to discover the strategies of rational players. In giving the players real power we have changed the character of the game somewhat from the Vinacke and Arkoff original. So we must also re-consider the case where winning (i.e. the zero-sum case) is the only criterion in order to make a fair comparison with the non-zero sum case.

4.6 A THREE-PERSON GAME AND ANALYTIC MODEL
The rules of this game are
1. There are three players A, B and C with weights a, b and c which may follow any of Caplow's orderings.
2. The game is played over a number of trials and at each trial players receive a number of points equal to their weights.
3. A player I with a greater weight (i) can attack, or extract payments by threat from, a weaker player J with lower weight (j). The latter is eliminated from the game if attacked. The former receives a payoff $k(i - j)$ and a new weight $(i - j)$. k is a constant greater than unity.
4. The number of trials is unspecified and only after the players have made their decisions for a particular trial and the outcome is ascertained do they know whether or not the next trial will take place.
5. Coalitions may form, the weight of the coalition being equal to the sum of the weights of its members. A coalition is binding once formed, so long as the isolate remains in the game. If the isolate is eliminated the coalition lapses.
6. Division of weight within the coalition must be specified by the players and points are paid at each trial to individuals, rather than to the coalition as a whole. If the division is equal players must concur on any decision. If the division is unequal, the player with greater weight can make the decisions for the coalition.
7. The winner is that player or coalition of players with most points at the end of the game. The winner's points might then be translated into money payment.
8. Players must make all decisions on whether to attack or form coalitions at the first trial. Only if an attack takes place are new decisions allowed at the next trial.

For simplicity we shall adopt the ordering $a \geqslant b \geqslant c$. As we have dispensed with a definite terminus to the game we can also dispense with the die throwing of the original game.

We assume in rule 3 that war results in a long run cost in terms of reduced resources i.e. the points-generation rate or growth falls off. But there is the short run gain which varies inversely with the opponent's weight or resistance he offers and directly with the attacker's resources. The constant k must exceed unity for otherwise an attack would never be profitable.

129

Rule 4 takes account of the uncertainty of the future. Once a trial has taken place the experimenter operates a random device to determine whether the next trial will do so. So in making a decision players only know that the present trial is certain.

Coalitions could be allowed to form by means of negotiations but the exact set up for these is irrelevant at present.

In rule 6 we assume that resources are transferable. The coalition counts as one player as far as winning goes but payments are made to individuals in accordance with their own weight.

Rule 8 assumes that a player's time horizon is fixed so that he would have no reason to change his decision from trial to trial unless he attacked and was thereby confronted with new circumstances.

Additional rules are now needed to define the zero-sum or non-zero-sum conditions. We shall consider three alternative rules which will give three possible conditions of play.

9. Everyone is paid at the end of the game in a proportion to points earned providing they have not been eliminated earlier. The motive is thus to maximise points and the game is non-zero-sum.

10. Only the winner is paid and the prize does not depend on the number of points possessed. If a tie results the prize is divided. If a coalition wins the prize is divided equally between its members. The motive is simply to win and the game is zero-sum.

11. Only the winner is paid and payment is proportional to points possessed. The motive is now firstly to win and secondly to maximise. The game is again zero-sum.

In the following analysis, we shall assume that, if a coalition forms for the purpose of attack, its members must be equal in weight. The reason for this assumption is as follows. By rule 6, division of weight within a coalition must be specified by the members. Now a player would not agree to a coalition if he were to have less than half weight. For then the one with greater weight could make the decision to eliminate the third player, and then, being the stronger of the two remaining, could eliminate its former partner. Thus, if a coalition forms, its members will agree to divide weight equally.

Let t_i be player I's estimate of the number of trials to go after the present trial; i.e. t_i is his time horizon.

We shall now consider in turn the different coalitions which will result from structuring the game in accordance with one or other of the three rules 9, 10, and 11 stated above. For each rule, we shall take each of our eight Types in turn (a Type being defined according to the ordering relationships between the payoffs). The coalitions predicted are summarised in Table V on page 137.

A. Play under Rule 9.

Type I $(a = b = c)$

Any coalition may form to eliminate the third player. If all players have weight a the coalition members must believe that the payoff from attack exceeds the payoff from no attack i.e.

$$\left(\frac{2a-a}{2}\right)(k+t_i) > a(t_i+1) \qquad\qquad i = A, B, C$$

$$ak + at_i > 2at_i + 2a$$

or $\qquad t_i < k - 2$

i.e. their time horizon must be less than $k - 2$ trials.

Type II $(a > b, b = c, a < (b+c))$

Suppose B and C each have weight b. If A attacked B or C his new weight would be less than that of the isolate and he would himself become vulnerable to attack. We always assume that players are not so short-sighted that they believe the present trial will be the last one. So a player will never attack another if he is left in a vulnerable position.

A's attack being unlikely, there is no reason for $\overline{BC}$ to be provoked. Coalitions may only form therefore for the purpose of attack or threat.

If $\overline{AB}$ attacks C, A and B each get

$$(k+t_i)\frac{a}{2} \underline{\hspace{3cm}} (1) \qquad\qquad i = A, B$$

A should be indifferent between coalition with B or C.

If $\overline{BC}$ attacks A, B and C each get

$$\left(b - \frac{a}{2}\right)(k+t_i) \underline{\hspace{2cm}} (2) \qquad\qquad i = B, C$$

B prefers (1) to (2) if

$$\frac{a}{2} > b - \frac{a}{2}$$

i.e. if $a > b$ which is true.

Similarly C will prefer a coalition with A to a coalition with B. A prefers some coalition to no coalition if

$$(k+t_A)\frac{a}{2} > a(t_A + 1)$$

or $\qquad t_A < k - 2$

B and C may prefer $\overline{BC}$ to no coalition. They would do if

$$(b - \frac{a}{2})(k + t_i) > b(t_i + 1) \qquad\qquad i = B, C$$

i.e. if $t_i < \dfrac{k(2b - a) - 2b}{a}$

But if they attempted to form $\overline{BC}$, A could make either a better offer always preferring this to elimination. So if coalition form they will be either $\overline{AB}$ or $\overline{AC}$. Note that if C (say) is the isolate, it is pointless for him to offer some unequal coalition with one of the others for the reason mentioned above when we assumed unequal coalitions do not form.

Type III (a = b, b > c)

Suppose that A and B each have weight a. They cannot attack C individually since they would be vulnerable afterwards.

If $\overline{AB}$ formed and eliminated C, A and B would each get

$$(a - \frac{c}{2})(k + t_i) \;\text{——————}\; (1) \qquad\qquad i = A, B$$

If $\overline{AC}$ eliminated B, A and C each get

$$\frac{c}{2}(k + t_i) \;\text{——————}\; (2)$$

A prefers (1) to (2) if

$$a - \frac{c}{2} > \frac{c}{2}$$

or $a > c$ which is true.

Similarly B will prefer $\overline{AB}$ to $\overline{BC}$. $\overline{AB}$ will form if

$$(a - \frac{c}{2})(k + t_i) > (t_i + 1)a \qquad\qquad i = A, B$$

or $t_i < \dfrac{2a(k - 1) - ck}{c}$

The player with the shorter time horizon should be able to dictate whether the coalition forms, for if his partner's time horizon did not meet the above condition he would threaten to ally with C if the partner refused to form $\overline{AB}$.

132

Type IV $(a > b, b = c, a > (b + c))$

Suppose that B and C each have weight b.

A may attack B or C or both. He would attack B or C above if

$$(a - b) (k + t_A) > a (t_A + 1)$$

or $\quad t_A < \dfrac{(a - b) k - a}{b}$

If $\overline{BC}$ forms as a purely defensive measure, A is forced to attack both if he wishes to attack at all. This is profitable if

$$t_A < \dfrac{(a - 2b) k - a}{2b}$$

which means that his time horizcn must be somewhat shorter or for a given t_A there is a greater likelihood of A attacking if B and C remain alone. By combining they produce a deterrent effect. Faced with having to attack both, A may prefer a coalition with B or C to eliminate the other. This he would do if

$$(k + t_A) \dfrac{a}{2} > (a - 2b) (k + t_A)$$

or $\quad 4b > a$

which may or may not be true, but if A does desire a coalition he should always be able to obtain it by threatening attack.

A would prefer a coalition to no coalition if

$$t_A < (k - 2) \text{ as in Type II.}$$

We may consider A's decisions by looking at the time scale in fig. xxviii.

Fig. xxviii.

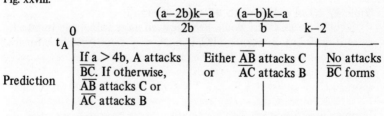

If we assume that $\overline{BC}$ will form in the absence of other coalitions the point $\dfrac{(a - b) k - a}{b}$ is effectively ruled out of our considerations.

The decision is always A's. He can always tempt B or C from the $\overline{BC}$

133

coalition with a better offer and if this fails he can threaten to eliminate the coalition.

So either there will be a defensive coalition $\overline{BC}$ or either of $\overline{AB}$ or $\overline{AC}$ will form to attack or threaten the isolate.

Type V $(a > b > c, a < (b + c))$

Neither A nor B can attack C without risking their own position. If $\overline{AB}$ attacks C, A and B each get

$$(\frac{a + b - c}{2}) \ (k + t_i) \ \text{———————} \ (1) \quad i = A, B$$

If $\overline{AC}$ attacks B, A and C each get

$$(\frac{a + c - b}{2}) \ (k + t_i) \ \text{———————} \ (2) \quad i = A, C$$

If $\overline{BC}$ attacks A, B and C each get

$$(\frac{b + c - a}{2}) \ (k + t_i) \ \text{———————} \ (3) \quad i = B, C$$

It is easily seen that A will prefer (1) to (2) and B will prefer (1) to (3). A prefers no coalition to (1) if

$$t_A \ > \ \frac{(a + b - c) \ k - 2a}{(a - b + c)}$$

i.e. if this were the case he would not offer to form $\overline{AB}$. But suppose that B happened to prefer $\overline{BC}$ to no coalition. If $\overline{BC}$ is going to form A must offer $\overline{AB}$ whether this inequality holds or not. A can always win but his decision may be forced in this case. If any coalition forms it will be $\overline{AB}$.

Type VI $(a > b > c, a > (b + c))$

B could attack C but would become even more vulnerable to attack by A if he did so. By forming $\overline{BC}$, B and C may deter A's attack for the reasons found under Type IV. The division of weight in $\overline{BC}$ may now be unequal since it is a defensive coalition and since A's attack on C is more likely than his attack on B. B may be able to demand more than his initial weight. Other considerations are as Type IV save that if A desires a coalition it will be with B only.

Type VII $(a > b > c, a = (b + c))$

Again it would seem pointless for B to attack C. If $\overline{BC}$ formed, no attacks could take place. The division of weight in $\overline{BC}$ may again be

134

unequal since C is more vulnerable. B may be able to demand even more here than in Type VI because if A attacks C, A could not afterwards attack B. So B's position is safe and C is in much greater need of the coalition.

A may wish to form $\overline{AB}$ and attack C. From such a deal B would get

$$(\frac{a + b - c}{2}) \ (k + t_B) \ \text{———————— (1)}$$

If he remained with C he would get

$$(b + pc) \ (t_B + 1) \ \text{———————— (2)}$$

where p is the proportion of C's weight 'paid' to B by C. (2) is preferred by B if

$$(b + pc) \ (t_B + 1) > (\frac{a + b - c}{2}) \ (k + t_B)$$

i.e.   if $p > \dfrac{b}{c} \dfrac{(k - 1)}{(t_B + 1)}$

The smaller is k and the larger is t_B the more likely is the right hand side to be less than unity and C therefore able to make the payment.

If B refused an offer by A, A may then make an offer to C. B, faced with elimination, would have to take up A's offer and as A would prefer $\overline{AB}$ to $\overline{AC}$, $\overline{AB}$ should form.

Type VIII $(a > b, \ b = c, \ a = b + c)$
Suppose that B and C each have weight b.

The defensive coalition $\overline{BC}$ may form with equal weights to protect both members from A's attack. A may offer a coalition to B or C which they would prefer to $\overline{BC}$ if

$$\frac{a}{2} \ (k + t_i) > b \ (t_i + 1) \qquad\qquad i = B, C$$

i.e. if $k > 1$ which is true.

If C say were the isolate he could offer an unequal coalition with B as in Type VII and B might benefit from this. But B would be foolish to accept, as it would provoke the coalition $\overline{AC}$. So the decision is again effectively left to A.

In the above considerations we have so far omitted the possibility of *appeasement payments* i.e. instead of eliminating the isolate, the coalition demands points from him by making threats of elimination. Provided these demands do not take the whole of the isolate's points these payments should be made since even the losers have an interest in remaining in this game.

The attacker could demand just a little more than the difference between what he could get from an attack to what he would get from no attack.

It is easily shown that appeasement payments may be possible in Type I. Suppose $\overline{AB}$ formed. It could demand from C at least

$$a(k + t_{AB}) - 2a(t_{AB} + 1)$$

$$= a(k - 2) - at$$

Assuming t trials take place after the present one, C has available a possible $a(t + 1)$ points so he can only make such a payment if

$$a(t + 1) > (k - 2)a - at$$

$$t \geqslant (k - 3)/2 \text{ which is less than } (k - 2)$$

But it was shown that for the attacking coalition to form in the first place $t_{AB} < k - 2$. So $\overline{AB}$ believes in some time horizon which may exceed that required for C to make the payments.

It can also be shown that appeasement payments may be possible in each of the other types. Consider, for example, Type II.

$\overline{AB}$ could demand at least

$$(k + t_{AB})a - (a + b)(t_{AB} + 1)$$

C has available $b(t + 1)$ points and can meet the demand if

$$b(t_{AB} + 1) > (k + t_{AB})a - (a + b)(t_{AB} + 1)$$

$$\text{i.e. if } t_{AB} > \frac{a(k - 1) - 2b}{2b} = t^*$$

But we know that $t_{AB} < k - 2$. Where does t^* fall with respect to $k - 2$? It falls below if

$$k - 2 > \frac{a(k - 1) - 2b}{2b}$$

$$\text{i.e. if } k > \frac{2b - a}{2b - a} \text{ which is true.}$$

But we do not know whether t_{AB} falls short of t^*. If it does, appeasement is not possible but if it falls between t^* and $k - 2$ appeasement is possible.

Even where it is possible however, appeasement payments may not be desirable because they involve payment over a long period of time, whereas from attack the players can get the bulk of their payoff in the more immediate future, which is less risky.

A further possibility is that a coalition may form even if its time horizon is longer than the critical value, in order to bluff the isolate into making payments. One would still however expect the same coalition as predicted above.

If coalitions do form the complete set of predictions for all three rules (9, 10 and 11) is summarised in Table V.

TABLE V. *Coalition Predictions under three Different Rules*

Type	Rule 9		Rule 10	Rule 11	
	Offensive	Defensive		Offensive	Defensive
I	Any		Any	Any	
II	$\overline{AB}$ or $\overline{AC}$		$\overline{BC}$	$\overline{AB}$ or $\overline{AC}$	
III	$\overline{AB}$		None	$\overline{BC}$	
IV	$\overline{AB}$ or $\overline{AC}$	$\overline{BC}$	None	$\overline{AB}$ or $\overline{AC}$	
V	$\overline{AB}$		$\overline{BC}$	$\overline{AB}$	
VI	$\overline{AB}$	$\overline{BC}$	None	$\overline{AB}$ or $\overline{AC}$	
VII	$\overline{AB}$	$\overline{BC}$	$\overline{BC}$	$\overline{AB}$	$\overline{BC}$
VIII	$\overline{AB}$ or $\overline{AC}$	$\overline{BC}$	$\overline{BC}$	$\overline{AB}$ or $\overline{AC}$	$\overline{BC}$

The defensive coalitions only form in the absence of offensive coalitions, so at least in Types IV, VI, VII and VIII some coalition will always form and the triad is unstable. In the other Types, coalitions are not bound to form but when appeasement is considered they seem to be highly likely since the players can resort to bluffing. So all Types appear to be unstable.

We note that such a game favours the stronger players. This is partly because the stronger players have the ability to force coalitions by means of threats, and partly because attacks on weaker players result in higher gains and lower costs than those from attacks on stronger players.

B. Play under Rule 10.

We now move on to consider the games played under Rule 10. This is the zero-sum game, only the winner being paid and this payment being independent of points. Again we take each Type in turn.

Type I. $(a = b = c)$

If all three remain in the game each will get one third of the prize. Any two have an interest therefore in forming a coalition and securing half the prize each. There would be no reason however to eliminate the isolate.

Type II $(a > b, \ b = c, \ a < (c + b))$

As A would win in the absence of coalitions, $\overline{BC}$ will be motivated and A will be unable to tempt either away from this coalition since points are irrelevant. Even if payments were made to coalition members in proportion to resources, as the prize value is constant, it would be of no advantage to A to bring a greater weight to the coalition. He could of course offer some division which would be attractive to B or C but they would be foolish to accept since the other may then make a better offer to A and so on.

Type III $(a = b, \ b > c)$

If no coalition forms, A and B share the prize. It would be futile for either to attack C and pointless to attempt a coalition with C since they would still only get half the prize. So no coalition is likely here.

Type IV $(a > b, \ b = c, \ a > (b + c))$

A wins and no coalitions or attacks are either necessary or effective.

Type V $(a > b > c, \ c < (b + c))$

Considerations are the same as those under Type II.

Type VI $(a > b > c, \ a > (b + c))$

Considerations are the same as those under Type IV.

Type VII $(a > b > c, \ a = (b + c))$

The coalition $\overline{BC}$ will be motivated if B and C are to get anything but A always gets at least half the prize. The division of resources in $\overline{BC}$, if the prize division depended on it, would most likely be equal since each member needs the coalition as much.

Type VIII $(a = (b + c), b = c)$

Considerations are the same as those under Type VII.

138

Attacks are unlikely in all situations under rule 10. There is no possibility of appeasement payments because points are irrelevant and no consideration of time horizon is necessary.

In summary the predictions are set out in Table V.

Types III, IV and VI are therefore stable under rule 10, whereas the other Types may be considered less stable than under rule 9 since coalitions should now definitely form and do not sometimes depend on bluffing. Weak coalitions tend to form here and so A's power in the form of ability to attack is of no use to him. But it is not his threats or possible attacks which provoke the coalition, rather it is the fact that he will win otherwise.

C. Play under rule 11.

Now we consider the games played under rule 11. Only the winner is paid and payment depends on points possessed. The first consideration is to secure a winning position and then to maximise payoffs.

Type I

Considerations are exactly the same as those under rule 9. Appeasement payments are however unlikely, as they are in all Types under rule 11, since no one has an interest in remaining in the game if excluded from a coalition.

Type II

Because they would otherwise lose, B and C will definitely be motivated to form a coalition $\overline{BC}$. This would almost certainly lead to A's proposing $\overline{AC}$ or $\overline{AB}$ and one of these should form. Whether or not it eliminates the isolate depends on the time horizon.

Suppose B preferred an aggressive $\overline{BC}$ to a peaceful $\overline{AB}$ proposed by A. If B refused, A may approach C and B must know that in the last resort A would prefer an aggressive coalition to none at all. So if C refused a peaceful $\overline{AC}$, A may settle for an aggressive $\overline{AC}$ and B would lose. C would always prefer the aggressive AC to the aggressive $\overline{BC}$ as proved under the analysis for rule 9. So in practice A's first offer should be accepted.

Type III

In the absence of coalitions A and B share the prize. If their time horizons are short enough they may form a coalition and attack C.

Type IV

Considerations are similar to those for rule 9 but the defensive $\overline{BC}$ is now pointless since B and C have no interest in remaining in the game.

139

Type V

$\overline{BC}$ must be motivated to form at the outset which will lead to A's proposing $\overline{AB}$. If B wishes to attack C he may now find it easier to persuade A since C is weaker than B and A prefers B as partner. So A's position is not quite so strong as in Type II.

Type VI

Considerations are identical to Type IV.

Type VII

$\overline{BC}$ will be motivated to form immediately and the resource distribution will probably be uneven, as under rule 9. Other considerations are the same as under rule 9.

Type VIII

Considerations are again as under rule 9.

We see then that the actual coalitions expected to form (set out in Table V) are almost always the same as those under rule 9. The exceptions are that defensive coalitions in Types IV and VI are pointless now so these Types are more stable than before. Appeasement is no longer feasible so Types I and III are more stable too. On the other hand Types II and V are probably less stable since strong coalitions are now definitely provoked because weak ones would form otherwise. Types VII and VIII are completely unstable under all conditions.

It appears that in this particular game different resource or weight structures are affected by the various conditions of play in different ways. The necessity of winning alone tends to provoke weak coalitions thus making for instability in those situations where such coalitions are capable of winning. Where this necessity is absent and the aim is merely to survive and maximise, strong coalitions tend to form and either attack or threaten the isolate so the triads are still rather unstable. Where the need to maximise meets the need to win the former motive tends to dictate which coalition will form.

Time horizons are an important determinant of stability only in those triads which are more stable under rule 11 than under rule 9, i.e. Types I, III, IV and VI. The desire to win tends to provoke coalitions irrespective of time horizons but where this desire is present and no weak coalition is provoked, the time horizon becomes the determining factor. It would also be the determining factor under rule 9, were appeasement not possible, but because players may resort to bluffing it is effectively ruled out. It is important in determining which particular coalition will form in those cases where defensive coalitions are feasible.

The individual player's power to attack is only important in provoking defensive coalitions and in some cases, deciding the resource distribution within the coalition. In so far as it provokes coalitions it is a further factor making for instability.

This model is of course of only limited value and its conclusions are only applicable to this particular game. But it does demonstrate that the non-zero-sum situation is not necessarily more stable than the zero-sum, where instability means the formation of some coalition. It also demonstrates that certain factors will operate in different ways under different rules affecting both the stability of the triad and the formation of a particular coalition. Further it shows that different power structures structures are affected in different ways by a change in the rules.

Variants of the game can be suggested — such as presenting war as a long run gain and a short run cost situation — and the model changed accordingly. In such a game we would have to decide how many resources a player must possess before he can incur the costs, so that his power may vary over time and the number of players with the ability to attack would vary. Not only the ordering of resources but also their absolute magnitude would become important in deciding stability.

It is not our intention to pursue this line of thought any further, partly because such games and models ought to be tested using real players and partly because we wish to concentrate on power as the main variable in determining stability.

Notes

1. Robert A. Dahl, "The Concept of Power", *Behavioural Science,* 2 (1957), 201–215.
2. A. Kaplan, "Power in Perspective" in R. L. Kahn and E. Boulding (Eds.), *Power and Conflict in Organizations* (London, Tavistock Publications 1964), pp. 11–12.
3. Robert A. Dahl, "The Concept of Power", *Behavioural Science,* 2 (1957), 201–215.
4. William H. Riker and Shapley "Weighted voting: A Mathematical Analysis for Instrumental Judgements", Rand 1965 *Meeting of American Society for Political and Legal Philosophy,* New York.
5. For any reader unfamiliar with this notation, 3! means 3 x 2 x 1.
6. Dina A. Zinnes, "An Analytic Study of the Balance of Power Theories", *Journal of Peace Research,* 3 (1967), 270–287.
7. William H. Riker, *The Theory of Political Coalitions,* (New Haven: Yale University Press, 1963), p. 161.
8. Morton A. Kaplan, *System and Process in International Politics* (New York: Johy Wiley & Sons Inc., 1957).

CHAPTER 5

MEASURES OF POWER AND CONFLICT

5.1 INTRODUCTION

It is now time to develop our own measure of power. In the last
chapter it was established that the basis of A's power over B is his
ability to control B's payoff to some extent. Involving the notion of
control, power is undoubtedly an extremely important factor in the real
world. All decision makers are continually striving to control their
environment in order to improve their own payoffs. Often this can only
be done by controlling the payoffs of others i.e. by exerting power over
them. This is the principle motive for the exertion of power, though
it should be remembered that sometimes power is exercised as an end in
itself. Here the player gets some psychological payoff from the action
itself. We shall neglect this for the time being.

Payoffs must be made in some kind of resources and these may be
real or psychological. Further, the payoffs to one player from one issue
may be made in several different resources and the payoffs to two
different players interacting over some issue, could be in different
resources. In developing our measure we shall overlook these complications but will give them more consideration in later sections. It is
assumed that just one type of resource is at stake and that this resource
is measured either in real terms or in psychological units which can be
translated into real ones such as money. Both players are paid in the
same resources.

Whilst power will be measured with respect to the control over the
payoffs of another in terms of some resource, the degree of this control,

indeed the fact that it exists at all, may depend on many other things. The structure of the game itself — its payoff structure and rules — is important in this respect and this itself may be determined by other resources possessed by the players, e.g. the resource at stake may be land and the players may decide to fight for it. The rules are then the rules applicable to that kind of fighting, and the military resources of the players will determine how much control each has over the amount of land the other gets. Similarly bargaining skill is a resource which will determine the control players have in the bargaining process.

It should be remembered that the amount of power a player is capable of exerting is not necessarily the same as the amount he does actually exert after decisions are taken. The later depends partly on his motives and partly on the other player's actions. It is also important to note that a player might maximise his own payoff without exerting the full extent of his control over another.

Fig. xxix.

B

	β_1	β_2
α_1	1, −2	2, 1
α_2	1, −2	2, 1

(A at left, rows α_1 and α_2)

In the above figure B has some control over A's payoff but if he attempts to reduce A's payoff he is no longer maximising his own payoff i.e. he incurs a cost. The costs of exercising control should indeed be taken into account and our measure of power will do this.

These considerations lead us on to the other measure, that of Conflict.[1] If one player cannot maximise his payoff without depriving another, a state of conflict may exist. If one player, A, exerts control over another, B, he may prevent B obtaining his maximum payoff. But if A can still obtain his maximum payoff, no conflict exists. The issue can be settled because A is all-powerful and can guarantee what he wants. However, if B can also exert some control over A's payoff a state of conflict does exist. So the relationship between conflict and power becomes apparent. Conflict exists because the players have control over each other's payoffs.

Our measure of Conflict will be related to our measure of power. There are good reasons for developing a measure of Conflict. Firstly, if the amount of Conflict in any game can be measured, all games can be such a comparison is the one with whom the interaction is taking place; so our system of reference is the dyad. Within that system, in view of what has been said, we assume that the players have some idea of their relative standing or *status* with respect to resources possessed. As an index of this status we take the ratio:

$$\text{Player A's status} = \frac{\text{A's stock of resources}}{\text{Total resources in the system}}$$

We are of course referring to the type of resource at stake in the interaction.

After payoffs have been made new status indices may be calculated, and by comparing the old with the new we can see whether a player has lost or gained. As all statuses in the system must sum to one, a player's loss is always another's gain so the outcomes in terms of status changes are always zero-sum. We postulate now that players are more concerned about the status change than about the absolute payoff (i.e. the original payoff in terms of resources) and it is the status change which determines their decisions. Our measures of power and conflict will therefore be in terms of status changes.

As we have said, the basis of power is the control of another party's payoff. To distinguish this from control of behaviour we shall from now on refer to it as *Fate Control* implying the control of another's fate or payoff in the terms specified. The term was used by Thibaut and Kelley.[5]

Fate Control in our context refers to the control over the status change of another party. As the situation is now zero-sum, if A uses his Fate Control to prevent B increasing his status A must be preventing a decrease in his own status i.e. A must be minimising his costs. So the measure will take account of costs in terms of resources at stake.

For all possible outcomes or sets of payoffs for the two players each must have at least one payoff which represents his best status change for the particular issue, i.e. his greatest increase or minimum decrease in status. It doesn't follow that such a change will be desired by the player but we shall assume that players are rational and attempt to obtain their best status change. We must note that the best status change does not necessarily correspond to the best payoff so in obtaining his best status change a player may not be maximising his payoff in absolute terms. This is because when he gets his greatest absolute payoff, his opponent may get a greater payoff which could result in a fall of status for the first. We shall assume that if the same status change could result from two different payoffs, a player would prefer the higher of these.

For all possible outcomes there will also be for each player a status

144

compared in this respect. Secondly, in three-person games we saw that the degree of correspondence of preferences between outcomes is important but this is difficult to measure. The Conflict measure will take account of this correspondence and may therefore serve as an explanatory variable in coalition formation and stability. Thirdly we can measure the amount of Conflict both before and after decisions have been taken and thus see the extent of the change in Conflict as the interaction process proceeds.

Section 5.2 will develop the measures themselves, and 5.3 will apply them to certain two-person interactions. In the remaining sections we consider some of the complications involved in using them. The measure of power will form the basis of our model for coalition prediction in chapter 6.

5.2 THE MEASURES

Let us make one or two observations which will assist us in building the measures of Conflict and power. Obviously the payoff is important but is the same payoff as important to one player as to another? It would seem reasonable to assume that if £2 were to be given to someone, it would be worth far more to someone who possessed only £5 than to someone who possessed £100. We invoke here the notion of diminishing marginal utility. By taking into account a player's existing stocks of the resources at stake we can get a better idea of how much a payoff is really worth. Converse has noted the lack of consideration given to stocks in most literature on bargaining games.[2]

But it is not only the player's own payoffs and stocks that are important. There is much evidence, both from real life and from experiments, that players tend to make comparisons with others and consider the payoffs and stocks. One may be far more displeased if one loses money whilst others gain, than if one loses whilst others also lose. Hoffman and others have offered experimental evidence that players do make comparisons with other players whom they consider relevant and their behaviour in interactions with these players is different from their behaviour in similar interactions with others.[3] Vinacke and others demonstrated that stocks are a relevant consideration in their experiments with Cumulative Scores. Coalitions tended to form against players with most points i.e. greatest resources.

Experiments by Minas and others have suggested that comparisons are made.[4] The belief in the parity norm, supported by the results of many of the experiments in chapter 3, also suggests the relevance of both one's own and one's opponents payoffs and stocks in decision making.

We shall assume for the moment that the only player relevant for change which he can guarantee for himself i.e. his opponent cannot force him to accept anything lower. The status change may or may not be his worst possible — it depends on the structure of the game. The structure of the game in fact determines what a player can get at best and what he can guarantee himself.

We now define A's Control over B, exerted by taking some decision, as:

(B's best status change had A not taken the decision *minus* B's guaranteed status change given that A takes the decision).

In other words it is a measure of the extent to which A can frustrate B in his attempt to secure his best status change. We note that the measure takes into account both the payoffs and structure of these as well as the stocks of the players. The structure may favour one player or the other so that sometimes a player high in resources will not have as much power as one low in resources. This illustrates our objection to equating power with resources.

Fate Control must always be non-negative. Its a minimum value of zero occurs when B in the above definition can guarantee his best status change. If A takes a decision and application of the above formula yields a negative value, it means that A is exerting no Fate Control, since B's guarantee once the decision is taken exceeds his best status change had the decision not been taken. For such cases we give Fate Control a zero value. Its maximum value is one — when for example B starts off with a status of one half and may either lose everything (his guarantee) or end up with all the resources in the system (his best).

So far the measure has referred to the amount of Fate Control a player can expect to exert if he wishes. After decisions are taken the amount he has actually used is given by

(B's best status change had A not taken the decision *minus* B's actual status change given that A takes the decision).

If his best status change represents the player's goal state one would expect there to be less Conflict the nearer to this goal state the player could get. Our proposed measure of Conflict is

(A's best status change *minus* A's guaranteed status change) x
(B's best status change *minus* B's guaranteed status change).

This measure has a maximum value of one and a minimum of zero. Further it is zero when only one player has no Fate Control, i.e. in the situation where though goal states are incompatible one player can attain his no matter what the other does so there is really no Conflict. We note also that Conflict will be greater, the larger the payoffs are

146

with respect to stocks. This we might intuitively expect.

The amount of Conflict can be represented diagramatically as in fig. xxx.

Fig. xxx.

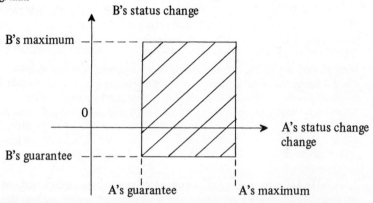

The shaded area represents the amount of Conflict. This particular example favours A since he can guarantee a positive change in status.

The maximum amount of Conflict occurs in those situations where both players can lose all they have to their opponent. Certain wars have this property and as we expect high values of Conflict for wars the measure is in this respect consistent with intuitive experience.

Like Fate Control the Conflict measure depends on the payoffs and their structure and the stocks of the players. It refers intitially to the situation before decisions are taken. After decisions are taken the amount of Conflict remaining may be different. It is defined as

(A's best status change *minus* A's actual status change) x (B's best status change *minus* B's actual status change).

This of course is equivalent to

(B's Fate Control exerted over A) x (A's Fate Control exerted over B).

This represents the *Residual Conflict* after a decision has been taken. Conflict has changed by an amount

Original Conflict *minus* Residual Conflict

Of course when an interaction or game finishes it is pointless to talk about the amount of Conflict because we assume players are no longer making their original demands. But we can look back on the situation, and by noting how far players failed to achieve their objectives we see how much Conflict remained at the end of the interaction.

In a game where many decisions are necessary over time the amount of Conflict will usually be changed after each decision. If the decision results in a payoff being made the players arrive at new statuses before the next decision and so the best and guaranteed status changes may be different for the next decision. Further, some decisions may alter the structure of the game, thereby possibly altering the best and guaranteed status changes without a change in stocks being made.

Finally we note that the Conflict measure can be extended for interactions involving more players. For the triad it would be[6]

$$|\,|_I \text{ (I's best status change } \textit{minus} \text{ I's guaranteed status change)}$$
$$\text{for I = A, B, C}$$

5.3 THE MEASURES APPLIED TO TWO-PERSON INTERACTIONS

A better understanding of the measures will be achieved if we now apply them to some interactions. We shall look at some matrix games and at a bargaining game.

Firstly let us consider a matrix game. We assume that the only possible outcomes are those displayed in the matrix and that the game must be played. Suppose the matrix is as in fig. xxxi.

Fig. xxxi.

		B	
		β_1	β_2
A	α_1	5, 5	5, 10
	α_2	10, 5	5, 5

Suppose the players A and B have stocks of 10 and 5 respectively. The initial status indices are therefore $\frac{2}{3}$ and $\frac{1}{3}$. We now construct a matrix showing the new statuses. Each cell shows the new status of A and B if that outcome results.

Fig. xxxii.

$$B$$

	β_1	β_2
A α_1	$\frac{3}{5}, \frac{2}{5}$	½, ½
A α_2	$\frac{2}{3}, \frac{1}{3}$	$\frac{3}{5}, \frac{2}{5}$

Finally we subtract $\frac{2}{3}$ from each of A's new statuses and $\frac{1}{3}$ from each of B's to arrive at a Matrix of Status Changes.

Fig. xxxiii.

$$B$$

	β_1	β_2
A α_1	$-\frac{1}{15}, \frac{1}{15}$	$-\frac{1}{6}, \frac{1}{6}$
A α_2	$0, 0$	$-\frac{1}{15}, \frac{1}{15}$

Note again that this is a zero-sum matrix. All games are reduced to zero-sum games by this method.

Inspection of fig. xxxiii. shows that A's best status change is 0 and B's is $\frac{1}{6}$. By playing α_1 A could experience a worst possible change of $-\frac{1}{6}$ and by playing α_2 his worst possible is $-\frac{1}{15}$. He can therefore guarantee a status change of $-\frac{1}{15}$. By similar reasoning it is seen that B can guarantee himself a status change of $\frac{1}{15}$.

A's Fate Control over B is therefore $\frac{1}{6} - \frac{1}{15} = 0.100$ and B's Fate Control over A is $0 - (-\frac{1}{15}) = 0.067$. The amount of Conflict is $(0.100) \times (0.067) = 0.0067$.

If both players choose their second strategy the outcome is in the lower right hand cell, Conflict remains at its former level and both players are using their Fate Control. If A chooses α_1 and B plays β_2, Conflict is reduced to zero, A now exerting no Fate Control. B exerts an amount $0 - (-\frac{1}{6}) = 0.167$. It will be noted that this exceeds the the amount he could expect to exert. This is because A is now accepting something less than he can guarantee himself and he could if he wished, reduce B's Fate Control by playing α_2. If both players played their first strategy the amount of Residual Conflict would be

$$(0 - (-\tfrac{1}{15}) \times (\tfrac{1}{6} - \tfrac{1}{15}) = 0.067$$

i.e. even though the outcome is in a different cell, Conflict is still at its original value, because the payoffs are the same.

In this particular game both players could at the same time exert the maximum amount of Fate Control they could expect to exert irrespective of the other's actions. This is not always the case. Consider the following Matrix of Status Changes.

Fig. xxxiv.

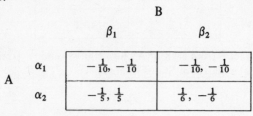

$$\text{A's Fate Control over B} = \tfrac{1}{5} - (-\tfrac{1}{10}) = 0.300$$

$$\text{B's Fate Control over A} = \tfrac{1}{6} - (-\tfrac{1}{10}) = 0.267$$

B exerts this amount if the outcome is in the upper right hand cell while A exerts this amount if the outcome is in the upper left hand cell. If the structure is altered however to that in fig. xxxv. both A's Fate Control and B's Fate Control can be exerted to the full amount if the outcome is in the upper left hand cell. This fact is reflected partly in the lower value of Conflict for this game i.e. 0.0267 as opposed to 0.0781 in the first game.

Fig. xxxv.

B

	β_1	β_2
α_1	$-\tfrac{1}{10}, \tfrac{1}{10}$	$\tfrac{1}{10}, -\tfrac{1}{10}$
α_2	$-\tfrac{1}{5}, \tfrac{1}{5}$	$\tfrac{1}{6}, -\tfrac{1}{6}$

(A on left)

It will be recalled from chapter 1 that Game Theory can offer a prescription to players of two-person zero-sum games. This is not of much use here however because (a) the prescription is only really useful if the same game is played many times over and (b) if the game is played many times over, in our case the matrix is not constant.

In Appendix III we consider four types of matrix games in algebraic form. But here we present numerical examples of these and Table VI below presents sample values of the Conflict index for these.

The four numerical examples are shown in figs xxxvi — xxxix.

Fig. xxxvi. Prisoner's Dilemma Game

B

2, 2	0, 3
3, 0	1, 1

A

Fig. xxxvii. Mixed-motive game without dominance

B

3, 0	0, 3
1, 2	2, 1

A

Fig. xxxviii. Co-operative game

B

0, 0	1, 2
2, 1	3, 3

A

Fig. xxxix. Zero-sum game

B

3, −3	−3, 3
−2, 2	0, 0

A

As far as possible the magnitudes of the payoffs in these games are kept roughly the same in order to render them more comparable. In the zero-sum game we must remember that a player cannot lose more than he possessed so if ever a player ends up with negative resources we call it zero in calculating the Conflict values.

With the exception of the Co-operative game, it can be seen from the table, that Conflict falls as total resources increase. In the Co-operative game Conflict falls up to a point, after which it rises, but this rise is very small and gradual. Conflict is generally much higher in the Zero-sum game and least in the Co-operative game. The others fall in between, the game without dominance having more Conflict, which is what we might expect.

The high values for zero-sum games conform with the notion that such games do represent situations of great conflict.

TABLE VI. *Conflict Indices for Four Games.*

Stocks of Resources of		Conflict Indices			
A	B	Prisoner's Dilemma	Mixed Motive without Dominance	Co-operative	Zero-Sum
1	1	0.090	0.160	0.010	0.500
2	2	0.048	0.082	0.005	0.500
3	3	0.028	0.050	0.003	0.417
4	4	0.019	0.033	0.002	0.234
2	1	0.062	0.111	0.006	0.667
3	1	0.045	0.082	0.004	0.563
4	1	0.034	0.063	0.002	0.360
5	1	0.028	0.050	0.000	0.250
6	1	0.023	0.040	0.001	0.184
1	2	0.062	0.111	0.006	0.667
1	3	0.045	0.082	0.004	0.250
1	4	0.034	0.063	0.002	0.160

Finally in this section we will consider a bargaining game. Here many more outcomes than the four in the above games are possible.

Consider two parties with resources a and b and an amount x of new resources to be divided amongst them. The status quo point or present status indices are $\dfrac{a}{(a+b)}$ and $\dfrac{b}{(a+b)}$ and each party can guarantee this point by making no agreement on the division. Each player's best new status accrues if he receives the whole of x. The best status change for A is $\dfrac{xb}{(a+b)\,(a+b+x)}$ and for B it is $\dfrac{xa}{(a+b)\,(a+b+x)}$. The guaranteed status change of each is zero. The conflict value is therefore

$$\frac{x^2 ab}{(a+b)^2\,(a+b+x)^2}$$

Note that for a constant total of resources possessed, Conflict has its greatest value when a = b.

If B concedes an amount t to A (t $<$ x) A's new status becomes $\dfrac{a+t}{a+b+t}$ and B's new status is $\dfrac{b}{a+b+t}$. A can still reach a possible status of $\dfrac{a+x}{a+b+x}$ but B's best has fallen to $\dfrac{b+x-t}{a+b+x}$. For the next round of bargaining A's best status change is $\dfrac{b\,(x-t)}{(a+b+x)\,(a+b+t)}$ and B's best is $\dfrac{(a+t)\,(x-t)}{(a+b+x)\,(a+b+t)}$. Each player can still guarantee a status change of zero i.e. the new status quo point.

The new Conflict value is

$$\frac{b\,(a+t)\,(x-t)^2}{(a+b+x)^2\,(a+b+t)^2}$$

If A now makes a concession, s, Conflict becomes

$$\frac{(b+s)\,(a+t)\,(x-t-s)^2}{(a+b+x)^2\,(a+b+t+s)^2}$$

at the next round.

Using this general formula, where s represents the sum of A's concessions and t the sum of B's concessions we may calculate the amount of Conflict at any stage of the bargaining process.

By making a concession a player is of course relaxing his Fate Control over his opponent. Before making the concession B's Fate Control over A was $xb/(a+b)\,(a+b+x)$. In the next round after the concession it was $b\,(x-t)/(a+b+x)\,(a+b+t)$. This is a decrease if

$$b\,(x-t)\,(a+b) < x\,b\,(a+b+t)$$

i.e. if $\qquad x < -a-b$

which is true. So by making a concession a player decreases the amount of Fate Control he can exert in the next round. It can also be shown that A's Fate Control will increase after B's concession if

$$t < \frac{bx - ab - a^2}{a + b}$$

It is conceivable that in the early stages of the process, one player's increase in Fate Control may outweigh the other's decrease and as Conflict is the product of Fate Controls here its value may increase. But eventually the decrease of one player outweighs the increase of the other and later that of both players declines.

Fig. xl. shows the diagrammatical representation of Conflict in the bargaining process. Its value is represented by the area of the rectangle. As concessions are made the rectangle moves inwards towards the origin.

Fig. xl.

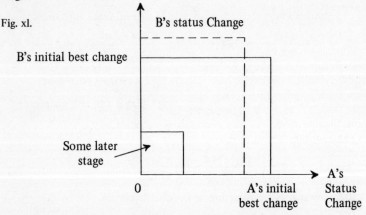

The dotted line represents the best status changes after the first concession. In this example A's Fate Control is increased by B's concession.

5.4   THE NATURE OF THE PAYOFFS

If could be said that the payoffs in any situation involve the notion of psychological payoffs. Even objective payoffs are somehow assessed by the player and rated on a psychological scale of payoffs. Our measure only deals with objective payoffs but based as it is on the status measure it does in effect convert them to a particular kind of psychological payoff. In effect we are postulating a particular utility function. It does take account of the phenomenon of diminishing

154

marginal utility, and so where the payoffs are made to both players in a single, similar, measurable objective resource, the measure can be utilized.

Often however situations do arise in which there is no objective payoff i.e. payoffs are in strictly psychological terms. Here it would be difficult to use the measure because firstly it would be a difficult task to assess the payoffs and secondly the notion of a stock of psychological resources is difficult to comprehend.

Often games involve payoffs in more than one resource. If we only consider one resource we do not get the full story, and this may explain why a player sometimes does not exert his Fate Control. If certain resources are neglected there may be costs which are not apparent in the matrix. It should also be noted that there are certain resources which though relevant do not imply a cost or a reward e.g. skill. Resources such as these influence the payoff structure and rules of the game. They may determine whether a game favours one side more than the other as well as the number of decisions available to the players.

If only one resource is relevant for calculations of rewards and costs, costs are automatically taken care of in the matrix i.e. in exerting his Fate Control a player is minimising his costs. The fact that power is multidimensional is reflected in situations where payoffs are made in more than one resource. A player may be exerting Fate Control with respect to one resource but at the same time may be dominated with respect to another. He must therefore weigh up the importance of each resource in deciding his action.

One way round this problem is to develop a single index by expressing all resources in similar units such as money. The resulting matrix of rewards and costs would then take account of all relevant resources. But the snag here is that often psychological components cannot be expressed in these units. This imposes a limitation on our measure, but it may help to explain the fact that players often do not exert the amount of Fate Control which they could do.

Sometimes the payoffs to one player are in resources different from those made to another player e.g. the mediator's payoff may be purely psychological while the disputants' payoffs are in real terms. Possibly we could translate these payoffs into similar terms but another possibility is that the player paid in different resources is not relevant for comparison. More will be said on this in the following section.

From now onwards we shall assume that all relevant costs and rewards are included in the payoff structure either because only one resource is at stake or because several resources have been measured in the same units and combined.

One other point should be noted in connection with payoffs. Sometimes they are made in new resources i.e. resources in addition to those possessed by the players. All competitive situations are of this type as are many bargaining problems. But often it is a re-distribution of existing resources over which the players interact. Wars are often of this type and in general these situations are zero-sum, though they do not necessarily involve the loss of the player's entire resources.

It is important to recognise these two situations because it often makes a great difference to the analysis, when three players are involved.

5.5 SYSTEMS OF REFERENCE

So far the system which players are assumed to refer to in calculating their status has been the dyad itself. It is likely however that in situations where players do make comparisons with others they exercise some discrimination in deciding who is comparable. The amateur golfer for example is more likely to compare his score with those of other members of his local golf club than with those of the top professionals. Similarly countries tend to compare themselves in living standards etc. with others which they consider near equals e.g., Ghana with Nigeria, India with Pakistan. Geographical proximity is one factor influencing who is selected but it is by no means the only one.

It does not follow however that interactions only take place between such parties. They may take place between parties which differ vastly in stocks possessed. Further even when the two parties to the interaction are comparable there may also be outsiders who are considered relevant for comparisons too. It is this case to which we turn first.

Suppose there is just one other party, outside of the interacting dyad, with whom they make comparisions in calculating their status i.e. they also take this third party into account. The effect of this, if the interaction involves a re-distribution of resources between members of the dyad is to change the magnitude of their statuses and Fate Control. But all outcomes are affected in a similar way and to the same extent, and so the decisions taken will be no different from those taken, had the third party not been considered. Had the interaction been over new resources a settlement would possible mean that the pair could also exert Fate Control over the third party. Both may gain at the third's expense. This has important consequences for mediation, as we shall see in chapter 7. The third party does not necessarily have any control over the absolute payoffs and is not necessarily believed to be capable of exerting any. But the fact that he is considered in status calculations places him in a position similar to that of the potential intervener of chapter 2.

Suppose now that the members of the interacting dyad differ widely in resources. Though they do not compare themselves with each other there may be extraneous parties with whom each identifies in terms of stocks of resources and status. Suppose both members compare themselves with outsiders (these of course being different outsiders for each member). The main difference from the strictly dyadic situation is that the Matrix of Status Changes may now be non-zero-sum.

Previously, in exerting Fate Control, players were protecting or improving their own position and so there was a resonable motive for its use. There may also be present a psychological payoff derived from the actual act of exerting power, but we have assumed that this is included in the payoff itself. In the Matrix of Status Changes one player's best outcome is always the other's worst (except in the trivial case where all cells in the matrix are identical). If the four cells of the matrix are ranked in order of preference for each player we find just three possible types.

a) Both players have a dominant strategy.

Fig. xli.

		B	
		β_1	β_2
A	α_1	3, 2	4, 1
	α_2	1, 4	2, 3

The 1, 2, 3 and 4 in this figure refer to the player's preference orderings of the cells, A's being given first.

Each player's best and guaranteed outcome result from playing the same strategy which means that both can at the same time exert the amount of Fate Control which they can reasonably expect to. In this particular matrix A is favoured insofar as he can guarantee his second preference whilst B can guarantee his third. But it doesn't follow that A is the better off because the magnitude of these payoffs are also important.

b) One player has a dominant strategy.

fig. xlii.

B

β_1　　　　　　β_2

A

	β_1	β_2
α_1	1, 4	4, 1
α_2	2, 3	3, 2

For B, β_2 is dominant and by playing it he exerts Fate Control over A. This means that A must play α_2, thereby exerting his Fate Control over B.

c) Neither has a dominant strategy.

Fig. xliii.

B

β_1　　　　　　β_2

A

	β_1	β_2
α_1	1, 4	4, 1
α_2	3, 2	2, 3

The players' best and guaranteed payoffs accrue from playing different strategies, which means there can be no stable outcome. Whatever cell results one player will always be motivated to move away in an attempt to increase his use of Fate Control.

Now when the players compare themselves with others outside their interaction the Matrix of Status Changes will no longer be zero-sum, and best outcomes can now coincide. The motive for using Fate Control is not now necessarily the betterment of one's own position, because the payoff structure may be such that one is better off if one doesn't use it. There are now in fact a possible twenty-one matrices based on cell orderings. Fate Control may be exerted purely incidentally because its use happens to coincide with a player's best payoff.

The players outside of the interaction have no control over the payoffs and so members of the dyad exercise Fate Control over them in aiming for their best absolute payoffs.

Still referring to this case, suppose now that one player's payoffs are so small compared with his total resources that his status changes are negligible. His status change may be regarded as zero for all outcomes. The only motive he has for exerting Fate Control is the purely psychological one of deriving utility from the act itself.

Finally suppose that a player has no one with whom to compare. He will still experience some kind of diminishing marginal utility and to take account of this instead of status change we could compute a measure

$$\frac{\text{Change in Resources}}{\text{Total New Resources}}$$

which we will call the *Resource Ratio*. It can be positive or negative, with a maximum value of one. We assume a player in such a position will attempt to maximise this ratio while his opponent's Fate Control over him is given by

(Best Resource Ratio *minus* Guaranteed Resource Ratio)

Again the matrix is non-zero-sum and the same considerations apply as in the above non-zero-sum case.

Whether players compare themselves with each other, with extraneous parties, or with no one esle, the same formula for the measure of Conflict may be used.

5.6 SCOPE AND LIMITATIONS OF THE MEASURES

Based as they are on status considerations, the measures only have relevance in situations where we believe such considerations are made. There is evidence both from the real world and from experiments that such situations are quite common, especially where the payoffs are strictly in psychological terms, though there are of course many situations where these status considerations are not made.

We have assumed that players have stocks of the resources at stake but this is not absolutely necessary. If they had no stocks, players would all begin with equal statuses which summed to unity. It is probably true however, that if the players had stocks they would be more likely to make comparisons.

The measure of status itself is probably the simplest possible measure we could have taken. We are not implying however that players in the real world make even such a simple calculation as this. More likely they have some very hazy notion of status due for one thing to the imperfect nature of information regarding the stocks and payoffs of other players. What we do hope is that our measure will act as a good substitute for what players really consider, i.e. if the latter could be quantified we hope it would be well correlated with our measure.

Regarding power, our measure takes any interaction and represents the payoffs in such a way that the interaction is seen in terms of the players' control over one another's outcomes. Because the situation is usually zero-sum, if a player is rational i.e. acts to improve or at least maintain his present status, he must use his control or exert his power over others. In practice a player may not have this aim. He may wish to equalise things, preferring a situation in which all players are of equal status.

No other measure of power which is based on status considerations is known, but Thibaut and Kelley have considered games in which a player's payoff was measured with respect to his past payoffs. In computing these payoffs no consideration was given to the payoffs of other players and though these authors applied the idea of Fate Control they did not attempt a strict measure of this.[7]

Our measure always lies between zero and unity, all negative values being considered as zero. It will be noticed that these values are often very small and will be especially so when payoffs are very small compared to stocks. In such cases the amount of Conflict is also very small and the issue is thus of comparatively minor importance. We should not be too surprised therefore if players did not stick to the maximisation principle here because the outcomes make little difference to them.

The measure of power will be put to the test in the next chapter when it is used in a model for predicting coalitions.

The measure of Conflict can be compared with another measure of Conflict developed by Axelrod.[8] This is outlined in Appendix IV. One advantage of our measure is that for all possible games its maximum value is one and its minimum, zero. Axelrod's measure always has a minimum of zero but its maximum value varies depending on both the type of game and number of players and it is difficult to put an absolute upper limit upon it. Further it gives rise to some odd results. Consider a game such as that in fig. xliv.

Fig. xliv.

	B	
A	2, 5	0, 2
	4, 3	4, 1

Plotting the payoffs as in fig. xlv. Axelrod would measure the shaded area and normalise it by dividing it by

$$\begin{pmatrix} \text{A's best payoff } \textit{minus} \\ \text{A's guaranteed payoff} \end{pmatrix} \text{ x } \begin{pmatrix} \text{B's best payoff } \textit{minus} \\ \text{B's guaranteed payoff} \end{pmatrix}$$

The first bracket is zero so we end up with an infinite value of Conflict.

Our measure would give a zero value since one player can obtain his best payoff irrespective of what the other does.

Fig. xlv.

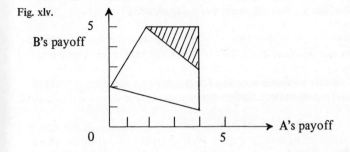

B's payoff

A's payoff

Axelrod tested his measure by examining the correlation between the percentage of "defective" choices in certain experiments involving Prisoner's Dilemma games, and the Conflict value for these games. We would expect a high positive correlation since the temptation to defect and the Conflict measure are both expected to increase as the value of t in the matrix (fig. xlvi.) increases.

This aside, we expect that the more important a game appears to be in terms of winning and losing the more intent will the players be on upholding their demands and not making concessions. Further such situations would be accompanied by higher values of Conflict so that we would expect there to be positive correlation between the amount of aggressive play and the Conflict value. In these games it is the "defective" choice which represents aggressive play.

Fig. xlvi.

B

	r, r	s, t
A	t, s	p, p

The experiments, which were conducted by Rapoport and others, included both two-person and three-person games. A large number of trials, using matrices with various parameter values, were played using students as decision makers.

The difficulty in using these results to test our measure arises from the fact that ours is not constant over time but depends on stocks. However, if we are only interested in the rank ordering of games, as

Axelrod was, it may be that after a point, as stocks increase, the ordering based on the Conflict value remains constant.

In Appendix III we show that the amount of Conflict in the two-person Prisoner's Dilemma game using our measure is

$$\left[\frac{bt-as}{(a+b+s+t)(a+b)} - \frac{p(b-a)}{(a+b)(a+b+2p)} \right] \times \left[\frac{at-bs}{(a+b)(a+b+s+t)} - \frac{p(a-b)}{(a+b)(a+b+2p)} \right]$$

and this usually increases as p and t increase and s decreases.

Axelrod's measure of Conflict for the same game is

$$\frac{(t-r)\ (t-s)}{(t-p)^2}$$

This is affected in the same way as our measure for changes in s, t and p, but it is also affected by changes in r. It is independent of the stocks a and b so it does not take account of possible changes in Conflict and therefore the play of the individuals as a result of many wins or many losses etc. The experimental results used however consisted of a figure for the percentage of defective choices for the whole game. The percentage was seen to vary for different values of r. Without making any calculations we can expect that our measure will not be a good predictor. However, as we have no knowledge of the changes in stocks over time, it is still possible that if we could take these into account the average amount of Conflict over all trials would be well correlated with the percentage of defective choices for the whole game.

One possible way out of the problem regarding stocks is to consider the players equal. It is possible that players would tend to remain approximately equal as time went on because no one would be likely to continually co-operate while the other defected. Assuming stocks of both players are of value a, our Conflict measure becomes

$$(\frac{t-s}{4a})^2$$

which is now also independent of p. 'a' could be some sort of average winnings. The rank order of games, based on the Conflict measure, is invariant as 'a' changes but we do not know whether the same 'a' would be appropriate for all games, and most likely it would not be since winnings would vary as parameters changed. Assuming that a is constant from game to game, table VII gives the parameter values, the percentage of defective responses and Conflict values with ranks.

TABLE VII. *Rank Orderings of Two-Person Prisoners Dilemma Games Based on Percentage of Defective Responses and the Conflict Measure.* [9]

Parameters				% Defective		Conflict	
r	s	t	P	Value	Rank	Value	Rank
1	−10	10	−9	23	1	20	2
9	−10	10	−1	27	2	20	2
1	−2	2	−1	34	3	4	1
5	−10	10	−1	36	4	20	2
1	−10	10	−5	41	5	20	2
1	−10	10	−1	54	6	20	2
1	−50	50	−1	73	7	100	7

The coefficient of rank correlation for our measure is 0.61 compared with 0.84 for that of Axelrod.[11] This relatively poor performance is perhaps excusable in view of what has been said.

The three-person Prisoner's Dilemma has the general matrices

Fig. xlvii.

R, R, R	s, T, s
T, s, s	t, t, S

s, s, T	S, t, t
t, S, t	P, P, P

The measure of Conflict developed by Axelrod is

$$\frac{(T-s)^3 - (t-s)(R-s)(T-S)}{(T-P)^3}$$

Again assuming players are all equal in resources and the same stock 'a' is relevant for all games, each player has a best status change of

$$\frac{a+T}{3a+T+2s} - \frac{1}{3} = \frac{2}{3} \frac{(T-s)}{(3a+T+2s)}$$

and a guaranteed status change of zero. The Conflict value is

163

TABLE VIII. Rank Orderings of Three-Person Prisoner's Dilemma Games Based on Three Measures of Conflict and Percentages of Defective Choices.

Game	Parameters						% Defectives		Rapoport		Axelrod		Wilkinson	
	R	S	T	s	t	P	Value	Rank	Value	Rank	Value	Rank	Value	Rank
9	1	−2	2	−2	2	−1	75	1	16	1	0.59	1	$\dfrac{8}{3(3a-2)}$	1
13	1	−2	6	−2	6	−1	84	2	32	4–6	0.93	3	$\dfrac{16}{3(3a+2)}$	4
12	1	−2	4	−2	4	−1	85	3	24	2–3	0.86	2	$\dfrac{4}{3a}$	2
10	1	−4	2	−4	2	−1	86	4	24	2–3	1.33	5	$\dfrac{4}{(3a-6)}$	3
16	1	−4	4	−4	4	−1	88	5	32	4–6	1.53	6	$\dfrac{16}{3(3a-4)}$	5
14	1	−6	6	−6	6	−3	89	6	48	7–8	0.99	4	$\dfrac{8}{3a-6}$	7–8
15	1	−6	2	−6	2	−1	90	7–8	32	4–6	2.07	7	$\dfrac{16}{3(3a-10)}$	6
11	1	−6	6	−6	6	−1	90	7–8	48	7–8	2.10	8	$\dfrac{8}{(3a-6)}$	7–8

164

$$\left(\frac{2}{3} \; \frac{(T-s)}{(3a + T + 2s)} \right)^3$$

The experimental results used by Axelrod were those obtained by Rapoport and others in their second series of games, already referred to in chapter 3, page 79. These authors themselves developed an index:

$$i = 2(T - S) + 2(t - s)$$

Table VIII lists the games with their parameters and rank orderings according to our measure and those of Rapoport and Axelrod, as well as that resulting from the experiment. The rank ordering of the games by our measure is invariant so long as a is greater than 10.

The coefficients of Rank Correlation are

Rapoport's measure	0.720
Axelrod's measure	0.890
Our measure	0.875

Our own measure gives a better performance here than in the two-person case. This may be due to the fact that since the parameters were not varied to the same extent as in the two-person games, the 'a' value or average stocks or winnings would be more likely to have approximately the same value for each game.

To really test our measure we need statistics which include player's stocks as time goes on. Assuming that these increase, we find that Conflict falls as time goes on (assuming fixed payoffs) and we might expect the percentage of defective responses to fall since the importance of exerting Fate Control, i.e. playing the defective strategy, diminishes. On the other hand, if stocks do not increase appreciably the Conflict value would remain high and the percentage of defective responses would remain high. This might account for the tendency for some games to 'lock in' on CC responses while others lock in on DD responses. It would be interesting to perform similar experiments with these ideas in mind.

The Conflict measure is applicable to any interaction in which the payoffs can be measured, and it is easily extended to n-person interactions. It is of course only a descriptive measure, but many have some limited use in predictir.g behaviour.

Notes

1. We shall refer to the amount of conflict by writing Conflict with capital letter.
2. Elizabeth Converse, "The War of All Against All", *Journal of Conflict*

Resolution, XII, 4 (1968), 471–532.

3. Paul J. Hoffman, Leon Festinger and Douglas H. Lawrence, "Tendencies toward Group Comparability in Competitive Bargaining", *Human Relations,* 7, (1954), 141–159.

4. J. S. Minas, A. Scodel, D. Marlowe and H. Rawson, "Some Descriptive Aspects of Two-Person Non-Zero-Sum Games, II", *Journal of Conflict Resolution,* IV, 4 (1960), 193–197.

5. John W. Thibaut and Harold H. Kelley, *The Social Psychology of Groups* (New York: John Wiley & Sons Inc., 1959).

6. For any reader not familiar with the use of the symbol $\prod$, $\prod_I X I$ means the *product* of the variable X for each individual I.

7. John W. Thibaut and Harold H. Kelley, *The Social Psychology of Groups* (New York: John Wiley & Sons Inc., 1959).

8. Robert Axelrod, "Conflict of Interest: An Axiomatic Approach", *Journal of Conflict Resolution* XI, 1 (1967), 87–89.

9. The results are based on an experiment by Rapoport and Chammah; see Anatol Rapoport and Albot M. Chammah, *Prisoner's Dilemma* (Ann Arbor, Michigan: University of Michigan Press, 1965).

10. With denominator $16a^2$.

11. For an explanation of these calculations see Appendix V.

CHAPTER 6

APPLICATION OF THE MEASURE TO TRIADIC INTERACTIONS

6.1 INTRODUCTION

In earlier chapters we established that power is an important variable in determining which coalition will form. Other variables are of course also important but power seems to be a very basic one. Whether players form a coalition or not depends on the correspondence of their interests, and if power is the criterion we must consider how much power two players can exert, or how much they can each increase their power, by forming a coalition. We are going to build a model to predict coalition formation on the basis of power or Fate Control. Having decided which coalition will form in particular circumstances we can examine the relationship between the amount of Conflict and coalition formation.

Each player in the three-person game is faced initially with the question, "Shall I seek a coalition and if so with whom?" When two players have decided to form a coalition they may have to make further decisions with regard to the division of the payoff. It is the first decision which we are interested in since this determines the stability of the triad, but the subsequent possible division of payoffs will also have an important influence on this decision.

There are several different kinds of triad, based on patterns of influence between coalition and isolate. It may sometimes be the case that a coalition, once formed, gets a certain payoff irrespective of what the isolate does, whilst in other cases the isolate and coalition (acting as one party) may indulge in some bargaining game for example. Each case must be examined for stability. The matrix representation is sometimes used but often, as in traditional Game Theory, it is dropped.

Not only will our model predict whether a triad is stable or not, it will also predict which particular coalition will form and we are able to put it to the test where experimental results are available.

Having decided whether a coalition will form we have to decide whether it is likely to be permanent or whether it is likely to break up before the issue is settled. This is accomplished partly in this chapter and partly in chapter 7 where we consider the isolate as a possible disrupting force.

The model in this chapter is of course very simplified. It assumes that the exercise of Fate Control is the only consideration of the players and it overlooks any possible obstacles to certain coalitions which might be found in the real world, in so far as these are not taken care of in the reward-cost structure.

6.2   FATE CONTROL AS THE BASIS OF A MODEL

As in chapter 4 the approach will be to outline a particular game and build an analytic model to predict the outcome in terms of coalition formation. For any triadic interaction involving players A, B and C there are four possible outcomes. These are any of the coalitions $\overline{AB}$, $\overline{AC}$ or $\overline{BC}$, or no coalition.[1] Each player must decide his order of preference for these four. We shall assume that in order to do this, each player considers the power relationship between himself and each other player resulting from each possible outcome. Let us look therefore at the dyadic power relationship in a little more detail.

Suppose A exerts Fate Control over B to a value 0.100. We could then say that −0.100 represents the extent to which B is controlled, i.e. we use the negative value of Fate Control to represent domination, For each player we can obtain a positive (or zero) value representing the amount of Fate Control he exerts over another as a result of his decision and a negative (or zero) value representing the amount of Fate Control exerted over him by his opponent. The former acts as an incentive for the decision, the latter as a disincentive. The sum of the two represents his *Net Fate Control* or NFC. Thus in the present example, if B's Fate Control over A had been 0.067 his NFC over A would be 0.067 − 0.100 or −0.033. A's NFC over B would be +0.033. The sum of all NFCs is zero.

It should be noted that if a player exerts a positive NFC, it does not follow that he ends up better off than the player with a negative NFC. The former may actually experience a decline in status whilst the latter makes a gain. It all depends on the structure of the game.

When there are three players A will exert NFC over B and NFC over C. A's total Net Fate Control is taken as the sum of these. We assume that the NFC exerted over a coalition partner counts for just as much as the NFC over the isolate since the player is only interested in his own status and this may be influenced by both of the other players.

When the division of payoff within the coalition has to be determined by bargaining, we assume that the first decision is which coalition to form and in order to make this decision players consider both their best possible payoff and guaranteed payoff attainable from membership in each coalition.

The model is based on the hypothesis that players consider the amount of Net Fate Control they are exerting as a result of each possible outcome and make decisions in an attempt to maximise this amount. The games we shall consider are mainly zero-sum in terms of statuses (i.e. all players are considered comparable) so the maximisation of NFC implies the protection or betterment of one's own position. If two players both wish to form a particular coalition, i.e. the same coalition is their first preference, that coalition should form. If only one player desires that coalition however, it will not form.

The rules of the particular game will determine the payoffs involved and how they are made. Sometimes it will be possible to split a player's (say A's) payoffs into amounts received from the separate interactions with each of the others (B and C) but sometimes it will have to be considered as a whole and if this is the case, in computing their NFCs, the players B and C are assumed to act as if the whole of A's payoff was determined by themselves alone.

6.3 CALCULATING NET FATE CONTROL

Firstly, let us consider a very general game. For each outcome in terms of coalition formation we compute each player's best possible and guaranteed status change and build up a *Matrix of Status Changes* as follows.

Outcome		Status Change of		
		A	B	C
$\overline{AB}$	(	a_1	b_1	c_1
	(	a_2	b_2	c_2
$\overline{AC}$	(	a_3	b_3	c_3
	(	a_4	b_4	c_4
$\overline{BC}$	(	a_5	b_5	c_5
	(	a_6	b_6	c_6
No coalition	(	a_7	b_7	c_7
	(	a_8	b_8	c_8

169

The a_i, b_i and c_i are the status changes. In this case the decision to form a coalition does not imply the immediate determination of any player's payoff so that for each outcome all players have a best possible status change ($i = 1, 3, 5$ or 7) and a guaranteed status change ($i = 2, 4, 6, 8$).

For each player in turn we must now decide just which payoffs of the other players he can influence. The first special case we will consider is that in which all players' payoffs are exactly determined no matter what outcome results. For each outcome there is just one payoff for each player i.e. the best and guaranteed payoffs coincide. The matrix becomes

Outcomes	Status Change of		
	A	B	C
$\overline{AB}$	a_2	b_2	c_2
$\overline{AC}$	a_4	b_4	c_4
$\overline{BC}$	a_6	b_6	c_6
No Coalition	a_8	b_8	c_8

Consider player A. He can affect B's payoff if any of the outcomes $\overline{AB}$, $\overline{AC}$ or no coalition results. The decision to form $\overline{BC}$ is however nothing to do with A and as payoffs are exactly determined once a coalition forms, A cannot affect B's payoff in this outcome.

How much Fate Control does A exert over B if $\overline{AB}$ is the outcome? By not forming $\overline{AC}$ he exerts an amount $b_4 - b_2$. By not forming "no coalition" he exerts an amount $b_8 - b_2$. The amount he is actually exerting is therefore the maximum of $(b_4 - b_2)$ and $(b_8 - b_2)$. If both happen to be negative, his Fate Control is zero.

B can influence A's payoffs in any of the outcomes $\overline{AB}$, $\overline{BC}$ or no coalition, and so his Fate Control over A if $\overline{AB}$ results is the maximum of $(a_6 - a_2)$ and $(a_8 - a_2)$.

A can influence C's payoffs in any of the outcomes $\overline{AB}$, $\overline{AC}$ or no coalition, and so his Fate Control over C is the maximum of $(c_4 - c_2)$ and $(c_8 - c_2)$ if AB results. In turn C's Fate Control over A is the maximum of $(a_4 - a_2)$, $(a_6 - a_2)$ and $(a_8 - a_2)$, since C can affect any of the payoffs a_4, a_6 and a_8.

In similar fashion all players' Fate Controls can be calculated for all outcomes. For instance A's Fate Control over B if $\overline{AC}$ forms is the maximum of $(b_2 - b_4)$ and $(b_8 - b_4)$. A whole matrix of NFCs can be built up.

Next we consider a game in which some payoffs are determined when a coalition forms and some are not. The Vinacke and Arkoff type games were of this kind.[2] If a coalition formed, the isolate's payoff was certain to be zero but the coalition members still had to bargain over the division of their points. Following these games we will assume that the payoffs in the no coalition outcome are all exactly determined. The Matrix of Status Changes is therefore

Outcome	Status Change of		
	A	B	C
$\overline{AB}$	$(\ a_1$ $(\ a_2$	b_1 b_2	c_2
$\overline{AC}$	$(\ a_3$ $(\ a_4$	b_4	$(\ c_3$ $(\ c_4$
$\overline{BC}$	a_6	$(\ b_5$ $(\ b_6$	c_5 c_6
No Coalition	a_8	b_8	c_8

Again A can affect B's payoffs in any of the outcomes $\overline{AB}$, $\overline{AC}$ or no Coalition. If $\overline{AB}$ results, assuming that no division of the prize has taken place, A's Fate Control over B is the maximum of $(b_1 - b_2)$, $(b_4 - b_2)$ and $(b_8 - b_2)$. B's status change, if $\overline{AB}$ results, is at least b_2 so these values represent the greatest possible amounts of Fate Control A can exert over B.

A's Fate Control over the isolate, C, is obtained as follows. By not forming $\overline{AC}$ he cuts C's payoff from a possible maximum of c_3 down to c_2. Thus the most Fate Control he can exert by not forming $\overline{AC}$ is $c_3 - c_2$. By not forming "no coalition" he exerts an amount $c_8 - c_2$ so the amount he actually exerts if $\overline{AB}$ results is the maximum of $(c_3 - c_2)$ and $(c_8 - c_2)$. C's Fate Control over A is a possible $a_3 - a_2$ exerted by not forming $\overline{AC}$, a possible $a_6 - a_2$ exerted by not forming $\overline{BC}$ and a possible $a_8 - a_2$ exerted by not forming "no coalition". These are the absolute maximum amounts which C can exert. He cannot stop A getting a possible a_2 and though A will very likely get something greater than a_2 when the A–B interaction is completed, we assume at this stage that he will get a_2. So when the payoffs are not exactly determined, we assume those payoffs which make Fate Control a maximum.

The next game is that in which no payoffs are exactly determined by the decision to form a coalition and all players interact separately,

171

so that we can split up the a_i's, b_i's and c_i's into parts separately determined by the interaction with each other player. The matrix is identical in structure to that on page 155 but the payoffs must be altered depending on which dyadic interaction we are considering. Thus if we consider the A-B interaction, a_1 represents the best status change which B could unilaterally give to A and a_2 is the status change which A could guarantee himself against B. We note now that a player can influence another's outcomes in all situations so A's Fate Control over B if AB forms is the maximum of $(b_1 - b_2)$, $(b_3 - b_2)$, $(b_5 - b_2)$ and $(b_7 - b_2)$.

Finally we shall consider the game in which no payoffs are exactly determined but the isolate interacts with the coalition as a whole so the a_i's etc. cannot be split up into a part affected by one player and a part affected by another. The matrix is again that on page 155, the status changes being the same for all dyadic interactions.

One further point must be noted with respect to the concept of NFC in the game with all payoffs completely determined. It turns out that for any player, that outcome which maximises NFC is also that outcome which maximises his status change. In other words one could simply look at the matrix of status changes and from this determine which coalition would form. It is unnecessary to calculate the values of NFC.

The proof of this is now given.[3]

Consider the following matrix and for simplicity assume that a player always does at least as well for himself as in a coalition, so that the No Coalition outcome can be ignored.

Outcome	Status Change of		
	A	B	C
$\overline{AB}$	x_1	y_1	z_1
$\overline{AC}$	x_2	y_2	z_2
$\overline{BC}$	x_3	y_3	z_3

If $\overline{AB}$ forms, A's NFC over B is

$$[y_2 - y_1] - [x_3 - x_1] = \alpha$$

(where the terms in square brackets are taken as zero if they turn out to be negative).
and A's NFC over C is

$$[z_2 - z_1] - [\{x_2, x_3\} - x_1] = \beta$$

where $\{p, q\}$ is the maximum of p and q.
If $\overline{AC}$ forms, A's NFC over B is

172

$$[y_1 - y_2] - [\left\{x_1, x_3\right\} - x_2] = \gamma$$

and A's NFC over C is

$$[z_1 - z_2] - [x_3 - x_2] = \delta$$

A will prefer $\overline{AB}$ to $\overline{AC}$ if $\alpha + \beta > \gamma + \delta$
We will assume that $y_2 > y_1$ and $z_2 > z_1$ so that the terms $[y_1 - y_2]$
and $[z_1 - z_2]$ are zero. Consider the following four cases.

i) $x_3 > x_1$ and x_2

$\qquad \overline{AB}$ is preferred to $\overline{AC}$ if

$\qquad (y_2 - y_1) + (z_2 - z_1) - 2(x_3 - x_1) + 2(x_3 - x_2) > 0$

$\qquad$ which, since $x_i + y_i + z_i = 0$ for all i, reduces to $x_1 > x_2$.

ii) $x_2 > x_3 > x_1$

$\qquad \overline{AB}$ is preferred to $\overline{AC}$ if

$\qquad (y_2 - y_1) + (z_2 - z_1) - (x_3 - x_1) - (x_2 - x_1) > 0$

$\qquad$ i.e. if $3x_1 > x_3 + 2x_2$ which is impossible as x_1 is the smallest x.

iii) $x_1 > x_3 > x_2$

$\qquad \overline{AB}$ is preferred to $\overline{AC}$ if

$\qquad (y_2 - y_1) + (z_2 - z_1) + (x_1 - x_2) + (x_3 - x_2) > 0$

$\qquad$ i.e. if $x_3 + 2x_1 > 3x_2$ which is true since x_2 is smallest x.

iv) x_2 and $x_1 > x_3$

$\qquad \overline{AB}$ is preferred to $\overline{AC}$ if

$\qquad (y_2 - y_1) + (z_2 - z_1) - (x_2 - x_1) > 0$

$\qquad$ i.e. if $x_1 > x_2$

So $x_1 > x_2$ is a necessary and sufficient condition for $\overline{AB}$ to be
preferred to $\overline{AC}$ by player A. The proof is easily extended to take the
No Coalition outcome into account if necessary.

It is therefore unnecessary to invoke the concept of NFC to predict
coalitions in a game where all payoffs are determined as soon as a
coalition forms. Nevertheless in the following section we do consider
such a game, partly for completeness and partly in order to make
comparisons with other games.

It remains to show in this section that in games which involve
indeterminate payoffs, maximising NFC is not necessarily equivalent to
maximising status change. Consider a game in which all payoffs are

173

determined except those of A and B if the coalition $\overline{AB}$ results.

Outcome	Status Change of		
	A	B	C
$\overline{AB}$	(x_1	(y_1	z_1
	(x_4	(y_4	
$\overline{AC}$	x_2	y_2	z_2
$\overline{BC}$	x_3	y_3	z_3

Where x_1 and y_1 are the best possible payoffs and x_4 and y_4 are the guaranteed payoffs when the coalition $\overline{AB}$ forms.

If $\overline{AB}$ forms A's NFC over B is

$$[\{y_1, y_2\} - y_4] - [\{x_1, x_3\} - x_4] = \alpha$$

using the same notations as earlier. Over C, A's NFC is

$$[z_2 - z_1] - [\{x_2, x_3\} - x_4] = \beta$$

If $\overline{AC}$ forms, A's NFC over B is

$$[y_1 - y_2] - [\{x_1, x_3\} - x_2] = \gamma$$

and over C

$$[z_1 - z_2] - [x_3 - x_2] = \delta$$

A prefers $\overline{AB}$ to $\overline{AC}$ if $\alpha + \beta > \gamma + \delta$

It is sufficient to show that upon a consideration of NFC, if $x_1 > x_2$ $\overline{AB}$ is not necessarily preferred to $\overline{AC}$. It seems reasonable to suppose that a player would get more from being included in a coalition than being the isolate, so assume $y_1 > y_2$ and $z_2 > z_1$.

Suppose $x_1 > x_2 > x_3$. Then A prefers $\overline{AB}$ to $\overline{AC}$ if

$$(y_1 - y_4) - (x_1 - x_4) + (z_2 - z_1) - (x_2 - x_4) > (y_1 - y_2) - (x_1 - x_2)$$

If we assume firstly that $x_4 > x_2$ the fourth term on the left is zero and the equation reduces to

$$(y_2 - y_4) + (z_2 - z_1) - (x_2 - x_4) > 0$$

i.e. $x_1 + x_4 > 2x_2$, since $x_1 + y_4 + z_1 = 0$.[4]

This is true, so $\overline{AB}$ is always preferred here. But now suppose that $x_2 > x_4$. The equation becomes

$$(y_2 - y_4) + (z_2 - z_1) - 2(x_2 - x_4) > 0$$

or $x_1 + 2x_4 > 3x_2$

174

This does not necessarily hold, and so we have shown that a case is possible where $\overline{AC}$ is preferred even though the greatest status change possible occurs when the outcome is $\overline{AB}$. The NFC concept is therefore not redundant here. The analysis is easily extended to games with more than one indeterminate outcome.

In the following sections we shall consider examples of the four types of games. Whilst other types can be synthesised by combining elements of these, it is hoped that the following will be sufficient to illustrate the method of analysis and to gain some ideas about stability.

6.4 THE TRIPOLAR WORLD GAME

We consider here a world of three powers where any two can combine to eliminate the third. The three powers A, B and C have resources a, b and c respectively where $a \geqslant b \geqslant c$. The payoff structure is

Outcome	Payoff to		
	A	B	C
$\overline{AB}$	0	0	$-c$
$\overline{AC}$	0	$-b$	0
$\overline{BC}$	$-a$	0	0
No Coalition	0	0	0

The Matrix of Status Changes is

Outcome	Status Change of		
	A	B	C
$\overline{AB}$	$\dfrac{ac}{(a+b)K}$	$\dfrac{bc}{(a+b)K}$	$\dfrac{-c}{K}$
$\overline{AC}$	$\dfrac{ab}{(a+c)K}$	$\dfrac{-b}{K}$	$\dfrac{bc}{(a+c)K}$
$\overline{BC}$	$\dfrac{-a}{K}$	$\dfrac{ab}{(b+c)K}$	$\dfrac{ac}{(b+c)K}$
No Coalition	0	0	0

where $K = a + b + c$ i.e. the total resources in the system. Note that all payoffs are exactly determined. As stated in 6.3 coalitions can be predicted from this matrix without going a further step and calculating NFCs.

175

A will prefer $\overline{AB}$ to $\overline{AC}$ if

$$\frac{ac}{(a+b)\,K} > \frac{ab}{(a+c)\,K}$$

i.e. if $-a > (b+c)$ which is untrue, so $\overline{AC}$ is preferred.

Similarly it can be shown that B prefers $\overline{BC}$ to $\overline{AB}$ if $(a+c) > -b$ which is true, and C prefers $\overline{BC}$ to $\overline{AC}$ if $(a+b) > -c$ which is also true. So $\overline{BC}$ is the predicted coalition.

The game is very simple and does not allow for side-payments or appeasement payments. Would the triad still be unstable if these were allowed? Suppose we include an additional rule which says that appeasement payments can be made to prevent attack and these are effective.

Player A is generally the most vulnerable. Is there some amount x of his resources which he can pay to B or C to prevent their forming a coalition against him? As C gets the smaller status change if $\overline{BC}$ results, A would have to make a smaller payment to him than to B (assuming $b > c$). If he pays C an amount x the row of the Matrix of Status Changes corresponding to No Coalition becomes:

Outcome	A	B	C
No Coalition	$\dfrac{-x}{K}$	0	$\dfrac{x}{K}$

C prefers No Coalition to $\overline{BC}$ if $\dfrac{x}{K} > \dfrac{ac}{(b+c)\,K}$

i.e. if $x > \dfrac{ac}{b+c}$

We conclude that A could prevent the $\overline{BC}$ coalition by offering some payment x, greater than $\dfrac{ac}{b+c}$, to C. Note that had A made the payment to B it would have had to exceed $\dfrac{ab}{b+c}$ which is greater. This illustrates once more how the triad tends to favour the weak over the strong.

Under the present rules the triad in this game is not necessarily unstable. But suppose the rules were such that even after appeasement payments were made, attacks were still possible. If the game was divided into a number of trials or decision points at each of which a coalition could form or an appeasement payment could be made it might proceed as follows.

So long as A remained the strongest in terms of resources he would make payments to the weaker of B and C. Should either of these become the strongest member then they, rather than A, would begin to make payments. The tendency would be towards equalisation and when in this case any of the three coalitions (now all likely) threatened to form, the isolate would have to make payments to one of them in order to stay in the game. So a situation in which all players were near equal and in which there was a continual re-distribution of a small amount of resources would persist. It is likely therefore that appeasement payments would keep such a triad stable.

The amount of Conflict in this game is given by

$$\Pi_I \text{ (I's best status change } minus \text{ I's guaranteed status change)}$$

$$I = A, B, C$$

In the original game this would be

$$[\frac{ab}{(a+c)K} + \frac{a}{K}] \ [\frac{ab}{(b+c)K} + \frac{b}{K}] \ [\frac{ac}{(b+c)K} + \frac{c}{K}]$$

a player's guarantee being that resulting from exclusion from a coalition. This reduces to

$$\frac{a\,b\,c}{(a+c)\,(b+c)^2}$$

We might also consider the amount of Conflict between any two players. To do this we must only consider the outcomes which are relevant e.g. in the A–B interaction A's best status change is $\frac{ab}{(a+c)K}$ and B's is $\frac{bc}{(a+b)K}$, not $\frac{ab}{(b+c)K}$, since A cannot affect B's status change when $\overline{BC}$ forms.

Conflict between A and B is of value

$$[\frac{ab}{(a+c)K} + \frac{a}{K}] \ [\frac{bc}{(a+c)K} + \frac{b}{K}] = \frac{ab}{(a+b)^2}$$

Similarly between A and C it has a value $\frac{ac}{(a+c)^2}$ and between B and C its value is $\frac{bc}{(b+c)^2}$. The coalition therefore threatens to form between those members in whose interaction there is least conflict.

When A offers a payment to C he increases the Conflict in the total system since C's best outcome improves. Similarly Conflict between A and C goes up but that between B and C remains unchanged. After the payment has been made however, arriving at the next decision point, there is now greater Conflict between B and C since C's stocks have

177

increased. So in a way A prevents the $\overline{BC}$ coalition by increasing the potential conflict between B and C. As the process goes on and equalisation takes place, the total Conflict in the system approaches its minimum value of one-eighth.

6.5   THE TRIPOLAR WORLD GAME WITH SIDE PAYMENTS

We assume now that appeasement payments are not possible but side payments are. This variant of the game is given a separate section because it takes us into the realm of those games with only a partial determination of payoffs.

If $\overline{BC}$ threatens to form A may try to tempt C away by offering some extra payment, y, to C if C will form $\overline{AC}$. This payment is made out of A's stocks. The row of the Matrix of Status Changes corresponding to outcome $\overline{AC}$ becomes

Outcome	A	B	C
$\overline{AC}$	$\dfrac{a-y}{a+c} - \dfrac{a}{K}$	$\dfrac{-b}{K}$	$\dfrac{c+y}{a+c} - \dfrac{c}{K}$

C prefers $\overline{AC}$ to $\overline{BC}$ if

$$\frac{c+y}{a+c} - \frac{c}{K} > \frac{ac}{(b+c)\,K}$$

$$\frac{c+y}{a+c} > \frac{c}{b+c}$$

$$y(b+c) > c(a+c) - c(b+c)$$

i.e. if $\quad y > \dfrac{c(a-b)}{(b+c)}$

The other limitation on y is that it should not exceed a since it is impossible for A to pay C more than he possesses. These limitations are compatible if

$$a > \frac{c(a-b)}{b+c} \quad \text{or } ab > -bc \text{ which is true.}$$

So A could break the $\overline{BC}$ coalition which threatened to form by offering a side-payment to C. The triad is of course still unstable for it is only a different coalition which is now forming. The amount of

178

Conflict is raised by the possibility of a side payment since C's best status change has improved.

But if A can make side payments so can B or any member who is faced with elimination, and an endless chain of bargaining may ensue. In a way this would make for stability since it makes for indecision with regard to coalition formation. But some members of the triad may ultimately refuse to accept side-payments when they see what is happening. How does our model predict which coalition will form, if this in fact does happen? We assume that in theory at least, one coalition member could transfer his entire resources to another by means of side-payments. So in the AB coalition for example A could give B a best status change of $\frac{a+b}{a+b} - \frac{b}{K} = \frac{a+c}{K}$, whilst B could guarantee himself a status change of $\frac{b}{a+b} - \frac{b}{K} = \frac{bc}{(a+b)K}$, corresponding to his making no side-payment to A. The payoffs to coalition members are therefore no longer exactly determined but depend on a bargaining process. While it appears that the decision on the division would be made before the decision on which coalition, nevertheless, as the three dyadic processes are so mixed up this becomes less clear cut, and it seems just as reasonable to regard the decision to form a coalition as coming first.

The Matrix of Status Changes is:

Outcome	Status Change of		
	A	B	C
$\overline{AB}$	$\left\{\begin{array}{l} \dfrac{b+c}{K} \\[2ex] \dfrac{ac}{(a+b)K} \end{array}\right.$	$\begin{array}{l} \dfrac{a+c}{K} \\[2ex] \dfrac{bc}{(a+b)K} \end{array}$	$\dfrac{-c}{K}$
$\overline{AC}$	$\left\{\begin{array}{l} \dfrac{b+c}{K} \\[2ex] \dfrac{ab}{(a+c)K} \end{array}\right.$	$\dfrac{-b}{K}$	$\begin{array}{l} \dfrac{a+b}{K} \\[2ex] \dfrac{bc}{(a+c)K} \end{array}$

179

$\overline{BC}$	$\dfrac{-a}{K}$	$\left\{\begin{array}{l}\dfrac{a+c}{K}\\[2mm]\dfrac{ab}{(b+c)K}\end{array}\right.$	$\begin{array}{l}\dfrac{a+b}{K}\\[2mm]\dfrac{ac}{(b+c)K}\end{array}$
No Coalition	0	0	0

The amount of Conflict in the system is now

$$\left(\frac{b+c}{K} + \frac{a}{K}\right)\ \left(\frac{a+c}{K} + \frac{b}{K}\right)\ \left(\frac{a+b}{K} + \frac{c}{K}\right)\ \text{or one, which is the maximum}$$

value.

Consider now the amounts of Fate Control exerted. If $\overline{AB}$ forms A can alter C's status change from a possible $\dfrac{a+b}{K}$ (from the $\overline{AC}$ outcome) to $\dfrac{-c}{K}$ so his Fate Control is of value one. C can alter A's payoff from a possible $\dfrac{b+c}{K}$ (in the $\overline{AC}$ outcome) to $\dfrac{ac}{(a+b)K}$. So A's NFC over C is

$$1 - \frac{b+c}{K} + \frac{ac}{(a+b)K}\ \text{ or }\ \frac{a}{a+b}$$

Others are calculated similarly and we arrive at the matrix

Outcome	NFC exerted by		
	A	B	C
$\overline{AB}$	$\dfrac{2a-b}{a+b}$	$\dfrac{2b-a}{a+b}$	-1
$\overline{AC}$	$\dfrac{2a-c}{a+c}$	-1	$\dfrac{2c-a}{a+c}$
$\overline{BC}$	-1	$\dfrac{2b-c}{b+c}$	$\dfrac{2c-b}{b+c}$
No Coalition	$\dfrac{2a-(b+c)}{K}$	$\dfrac{2b-(a+c)}{K}$	$\dfrac{2c-(a+b)}{K}$

From this it is easily shown that A's preferences are in order

$$\overline{AC}, \ \overline{AB}, \ \text{None}, \ \overline{BC}$$

B's are $\qquad\qquad \overline{BC}, \ \overline{AB}, \ \text{None}, \ \overline{AC}$

and C's are $\qquad\quad \overline{BC}, \ \overline{AC}, \ \text{None}, \ \overline{AB}.$

Again the weak coalition is the predicted outcome. Side payments then do not produce stability in this game.

6.6   THE VINACKE AND ARKOFF GAMES

We refer broadly here to those games used in experiments by these researchers and others mentioned in chapter 3. The games are examples of those in which the decision to form a coalition means the immediate determination of some player's payoff whilst those of the others are only determined within limits and further decisions are necessary. The payoffs in the No Coalition outcome are also completely determined.

Firstly we shall consider the Vinacke and Arkoff games in algebraic form. The rules are varied slightly for different resource structures i.e. weights. Again assume $a \geqslant b \geqslant c$. The payoff at stake is an amount x which we shall assume is comparable to a, b and c in magnitude. The rules of the games are

1. Applicable to all Types (i.e. weight structures)
   $\overline{AB}$ receives x and C gets 0 if $\overline{AB}$ forms
   $\overline{AC}$ receives x and B gets 0 if $\overline{AC}$ forms

2. Applicable to Types I, II, III and V.
   $\overline{BC}$ receives x and A gets 0 if $\overline{BC}$ forms
   Applicable to Types IV and VI
   $\overline{BC}$ receives 0 and A gets x if $\overline{BC}$ forms
   Applicable to Types VII and VIII
   $\overline{BC}$ receives $\frac{x}{2}$ and A receives $\frac{x}{2}$ if $\overline{BC}$ forms

3. Applicable to Types II, IV, V, VI, VII and VIII
   A receives x and B and C get 0 if no coalition forms
   Applicable to Type I
   Each player receives $\frac{x}{3}$ if no coalition forms
   Applicable to Type III
   A and B each receive $\frac{x}{2}$ and C receives 0 if no coalition forms.

If AB forms the coalition receives an amount x and its members must subsequently decide on the division of this. Each can guarantee a status change of zero corresponding to no decision, when it is assumed that the new resources have not entered the system for comparison. C, the isolate, suffers a fall in status whatever the division. A and B can each obtain a best status change corresponding to their receiving the whole of x.

The complete Matrix of Status Changes is

Types	Outcome	Status Change of		
		A	B	C
All	$\overline{AB}$	$\begin{cases} \dfrac{x(b+c)}{K(K+x)} \\ 0 \end{cases}$	$\begin{cases} \dfrac{x(a+c)}{K(K+x)} \\ 0 \end{cases}$	$\dfrac{-cx}{K(K+x)}$
All	$\overline{AC}$	$\begin{cases} \dfrac{x(b+c)}{K(K+x)} \\ 0 \end{cases}$	$\dfrac{-bx}{K(K+x)}$	$\begin{cases} \dfrac{x(a+b)}{K(K+x)} \\ 0 \end{cases}$
I, II, III, V	$\overline{BC}$	$\dfrac{-ax}{K(K+x)}$	$\begin{cases} \dfrac{x(a+c)}{K(K+x)} \\ 0 \end{cases}$	$\begin{cases} \dfrac{x(a+b)}{K(K+x)} \\ 0 \end{cases}$
IV, VI	$\overline{BC}$	$\dfrac{x(b+c)}{K(K+x)}$	$\dfrac{-bx}{K(K+x)}$	$\dfrac{-cx}{K(K+x)}$
VII, VIII	$\overline{BC}$	0	$\begin{cases} \dfrac{x(a-b)}{K(K+x)} \\ 0* \end{cases}$	$\begin{cases} \dfrac{x(a-c)}{K(K+x)} \\ 0* \end{cases}$
I	No Coalition	0	0	0
III	No Coalition	$\dfrac{cx}{2K(K+x)}$	$\dfrac{cx}{2K(K+x)}$	$\dfrac{-cx}{K(K+x)}$
Others	No Coalition	$\dfrac{x(b+c)}{K(K+x)}$	$\dfrac{-bx}{K(K+x)}$	$\dfrac{-cx}{K(K+x)}$

*The guarantee of 0 here corresponds to division of x in proportion to weights. If there was no division, B and C would lose out to A.

182

From this the matrix of NFC is easily calculated. For $\overline{AB}$ for instance it is obtained as follows.

C's best status change is $\dfrac{x(a+b)}{K(K+x)}$ obtained for $\overline{AC}$ or $\overline{BC}$. His payoff is fixed at $\dfrac{-cx}{K(K+x)}$ if the coalition forms against him. A's Fate Control over C if $\overline{AB}$ forms is therefore $\dfrac{x(a+b)}{K(K+x)} - \left(\dfrac{-cx}{K(K+x)}\right)$

$$= \frac{x}{K+x}$$

C's Fate Control over A is $\dfrac{x(b+c)}{K(K+x)}$ since C could give A a possible status change of $\dfrac{x(b+c)}{K(K+x)}$ by forming $\overline{AC}$ and allowing A to get the whole of x. But if $\overline{AB}$ formed C could not prevent A getting a status change of at least 0. A's NFC over C is therefore

$$\frac{x}{K+x} - \frac{x(b+c)}{K(K+x)} = \frac{xa}{K(K+x)}$$

Within the coalition itself, assuming the decision on divisions is made later, at the time of forming the coalition A exerts an amount of Fate Control of $\dfrac{x(a+c)}{K(K+x)} - 0$ over B and B exerts an amount $\dfrac{x(b+c)}{K(K+x)} - 0$ over A. The Complete Matrix of NFCs is

Type	Outcome	NFC exerted by		
		A	B	C
All	$\overline{AB}$	$\dfrac{x(2a-b)}{K(K+x)}$	$\dfrac{x(2b-a)}{K(K+x)}$	$\dfrac{-x(a+b)}{K(K+x)}$
All	$\overline{AC}$	$\dfrac{x(2a-c)}{K(K+x)}$	$\dfrac{-x(a+c)}{K(K+x)}$	$\dfrac{x(2c-a)}{K(K+x)}$
I, II, III, V	$\overline{BC}$	$\dfrac{-x(b+c)}{K(K+x)}$	$\dfrac{x(2b-c)}{K(K+x)}$	$\dfrac{x(2c-b)}{K(K+x)}$

		A	B	C
IV, VI	$\overline{BC}$	$\dfrac{2x}{K+x}$	$\dfrac{-x}{K+x}$	$\dfrac{-x}{K+x}$
VII, VIII	$\overline{BC}$	$\dfrac{x(2a-b-c)}{K(K+x)}$	$\dfrac{x(2b-c-a)}{K(K+x)}$	$\dfrac{x(2c-a-b)}{K(K+x)}$
I	No Coalition	0	0	0
III	No Coalition	$\dfrac{x(2a+c)}{2K(K+x)}$	$\dfrac{x(2a+c)}{2K(K+x)}$	$\dfrac{-x(2a+c)}{K(K+x)}$
Others	No Coalition	$\dfrac{2x}{K+x}$	$\dfrac{-x}{K+x}$	$\dfrac{-x}{K+x}$

Now let us look at each Type individually.

Type I. $a = b = c$ and the power of any member in any coalition is $\dfrac{x}{3(3a+x)}$. Any coalition is therefore likely and is preferred to no coalition by its members.

Type II. $a > b$, $b = c$ and $(b + c) > a$. A will desire firstly no coalition and secondly the coalition $\overline{AC}$ or $\overline{AB}$ in each of which his NFC is $\dfrac{x(2a-b)}{K(K+x)}$. B and C will however both prefer $\overline{BC}$ where they exert greater NFC than in coalition with A. The prediction is therefore that $\overline{BC}$ will form.

Type III. $a = b$, $b > c$. $\overline{AC}$ and $\overline{BC}$ will always be preferred to $\overline{AB}$ by A and B respectively but will these coalitions be preferred to No Coalition? They will be preferred if

$$\dfrac{x(2a-c)}{K(K+x)} > \dfrac{x(2a+c)}{2K(K+x)}$$

i.e. if $\quad 4ax - 2cx > 2ax + cx$

or $\quad c < \dfrac{2}{3}a$

So if C is quite near to A and B in resources they will prefer No Coalition to coalition with C.

Type IV. $a > b$, $b = c$ and $(b + c) < a$. All players exert the same amount of NFC in the $\overline{BC}$ and No Coalition outcomes. The $\overline{BC}$

184

coalition is useless so the decision is effectively A's. He will prefer No Coalition to coalition with B or C if

$$\frac{2x}{K+x} > \frac{x(2a-b)}{K(K+x)}$$

i.e. if $\quad 2b > -3c$

This is always true so the prediction is No Coalition.

Type V where $a > b > c$ and $(b+c) > a$ is similar to Type II. A desires the coalition $\overline{AB}$ but B and C both choose $\overline{BC}$ as their first preference so the prediction is $\overline{BC}$.

Type VI where $a > b > c$ and $a > (b+c)$ is similar to Type IV with A preferring No Coalition and $\overline{BC}$ being useless.

Type VII $a > b > c$ and $a = (b+c)$. C will prefer $\overline{AC}$ to $\overline{BC}$ if $2c - a > - (a+b-2c)$ or if $0 > - b$ which is true. A will prefer $\overline{AC}$ to $\overline{AB}$ but he will prefer No Coalition to $\overline{AC}$ if

$$\frac{2x}{(K+x)} > \frac{x(2a-c)}{K(K+x)}$$

i.e. if $\quad 3b > - 3c.$

This is true but if A does not form a coalition $\overline{BC}$ will form because B and C prefer this to No Coalition. A prefers $\overline{AC}$ to $\overline{BC}$ so we conclude that A will form a coalition and it will be $\overline{AC}$.

Type VIII where $a > b$, $b = c$ and $(b+c) = a$, is similar to Type VII, the only difference being that A is indifferent between coalitions with B or C so the prediction is $\overline{AC}$ or $\overline{BC}$.

The triad in games such as these appears to be unstable in all cases save Types IV and VI and sometimes Type III. It will be noticed that our predictions are identical to those of Caplow for his continuous case with the exceptions of Type V where he predicts $\overline{BC}$ or $\overline{AC}$, and Type VII where he predicts $\overline{AC}$ or $\overline{BC}$. One of our principle objections to Caplow's model was that he did not quantify power. This made it impossible to decide between $\overline{BC}$ and $\overline{AC}$ in Type V. By considering control over another's payoff we have achieved a quantification and resolved this difficulty.

Vinacke and Arkoff's first experiment gave the players weights which ranged from 1 to 4 and the payoff, x, was 100 points. There was evidence that the players related these weights to their chances of winning. One of our assumptions was that x was of some size comparable to a, b and c but this assumption is not integral to our conclusions.

Vinacke and Caplow equated power with resources; the player with weight a was always taken to be the most powerful. But it was noticed that as far as getting into a coalition was concerned and therefore winning, this player was not the most powerful at all. How do we interpret this in terms of our model? If we look at the No Coalition outcome we see that the player with greatest resources is always the one who exerts greatest Fate Control. So he is the most powerful if no coalition forms. But as coalitions tend to form against him, when they are effective the coalition members exert greater NFC than he does. Resources are correlated with the exertion of NFC in so far as, when a coalition forms, the member with greater resources exerts more NFC.

If we insert the weights used by Vinacke into our model we find the predictions for Types I to VI very well corroborated by his experimental results (See Appendix I). This lends some support to the predictive capacity of our model. In Type V we note that we predicted $\overline{BC}$ which is the coalition which occurred most frequently. The coalition $\overline{AC}$, which occurred next most frequently, would be our second prediction since it is the second preference of both A and C.

Considering the amount of Conflict in these games we immediately note that in Types IV and VI A can guarantee his best status change so there is no Conflict. In Types I, II, III and V A's best status change is $\dfrac{x(b+c)}{K(K+x)}$ and his guarantee is $\dfrac{-ax}{K(K+x)}$ — when a coalition forms against him. B's best status change is $\dfrac{x(a+c)}{K(K+x)}$ with a guarantee of $\dfrac{-bx}{K(K+x)}$ and so on. The Conflict measure for the whole system is

$$\left[\frac{x(b+c)}{K(K+x)} - \left(\frac{-ax}{K(K+x)}\right)\right]\left[\frac{x(a+c)}{K(K+x)} - \left(\frac{-bx}{K(K+x)}\right)\right]\left[\frac{x(b+a)}{K(K+x)} - \left(\frac{-cx}{K(K+x)}\right)\right]$$

$$\text{or} \qquad \left(\frac{x}{K+x}\right)^3$$

Unlike the Tripolar World Game the amount of Conflict is independent of the orderings of a, b and c. Further, for any one particular Type the amount of Conflict depends only on K e.g. the Type V structures 4, 3, 2 and 4, 3½, 1½ are equivalent.

The Conflict between any pair in the present games is $\dfrac{x}{K+x}$. On this consideration we might expect any coalition to form but this neglects one thing. The decision to form a coalition, though it means the end of the triadic interaction, does not mean the resolution of

186

the issue, for the coalition has still to decide on the division of x. This is of course what we mean when we say that all players' payoffs are not completely determined. In other words there is some Residual Conflict after the decision to form a coalition.

Suppose $\overline{AB}$ forms. C's payoff is now determined at $\frac{-x(a+b)}{K(K+x)}$ and A and B can each guarantee a zero status change. The best status change of each player is as before. The amount of Residual Conflict is

[A's best status change *minus* A's new guarantee]

$\times$ [B's best status change *minus* B's new guarantee]

$\times$ [C's best status change *minus* C's actual status change]

$$= \left[\frac{x(b+c)}{K(K+x)} \right] \left[\frac{x(a+c)}{K(K+x)} \right] \left[\frac{x}{K+x} \right]$$

$$= \left(\frac{x}{K+x}\right)^3 \left[\frac{(b+c)(a+c)}{K^2} \right]$$

or $C_t \left[\dfrac{(b+c)(a+c)}{K^2} \right]$

where C_t is the original Conflict value. If $\overline{AC}$ forms, the Residual Conflict is $C_t \dfrac{(b+c)(a+b)}{K^2}$ and if $\overline{BC}$ forms it is $C_t \dfrac{(a+c)(a+b)}{K^2}$.

Except in Type I where all coalitions are equivalent, the predicted coalitions are always those which reduce Conflict least. This is perhaps not surprising, since our predictions were based on the maximisation of NFC and the greater the NFC at a point where some payoffs are not determined the greater the amount of Conflict.

In Types VII and VIII the difference from the above is that A can guarantee himself a zero status change from the start. Thus

$$C_t = \left(\frac{x}{K+x}\right)^3 \left(\frac{b+c}{K}\right)$$

$$= \left(\frac{x}{K+x}\right)^3 \frac{1}{2}$$

(since $a = b+c = \dfrac{K}{2}$)

So Conflict in a game with orderings of resources as in Types VII and VIII is half what it is with orderings of Types I, II, III and IV. Again consideration of Residual Conflict shows that the predicted coalition is that which reduces Conflict by the smallest amount.

The conclusions of this section apply of course only to the particular games considered and their particular rules. But again we have shown that the tendency is for coalitions to form and hence for the triad to be unstable. We have also further demonstrated the capacity of the model to prescribe certain play and on the basis of these prescriptions to make predictions about which coalitions will form.

6.7 A GENERALISED GAME WITH PAYOFFS PARTIALLY DETERMINED

So far the payoffs made to coalitions have either been constant (as in the Vinacke and Arkoff games) or have varied in such a way that they have been greatest, when translated into status changes, for the weakest coalition (as in the Tripolar World Game). The tendency in both types was for weak coalitions to form. To some extent this tendency must be a result of the payoff structure and to some extent a result of a desire to catch up with players of higher status.

In this Generalised Game we will assume that the payoffs to each coalition are different and initially we will further assume that all players get a zero payoff if no coalition forms. Again the payoffs to coalition members will not be immediately determined by the decision to form a coalition. The Vinacke and Arkoff games and the Tripolar World games are particular cases of this Generalised Game.

The rules of the game are simply:

If $\overline{AB}$ forms the coalition receives a payoff x and C gets nothing.
If $\overline{AC}$ forms the coalition receives a payoff y and B gets nothing.
If $\overline{BC}$ forms the coalition receives a payoff z and A gets nothing.
If No Coalition forms, all players get nothing.

As we have already effectively covered an example in which $z > y > x$ in section 6.4 we will assume that $x \geqslant y \geqslant z$. This seems reasonable as we might expect that a coalition with greater resources can achieve greater rewards.

The Matrix of Status Changes is

Outcome	Status Change of		
	A	B	C
$\overline{AB}$	$\begin{cases} \dfrac{x(b+c)}{K(K+x)} \\[2mm] 0 \end{cases}$	$\begin{cases} \dfrac{x(a+c)}{K(K+x)} \\[2mm] 0 \end{cases}$	$\dfrac{-cx}{K(K+x)}$
$\overline{AC}$	$\begin{cases} \dfrac{y(b+c)}{K(K+y)} \\[2mm] 0 \end{cases}$	$\dfrac{-by}{K(K+x)}$	$\begin{cases} \dfrac{y(a+b)}{K(K+y)} \\[2mm] 0 \end{cases}$
$\overline{BC}$	$\dfrac{-az}{K(K+z)}$	$\begin{cases} \dfrac{z(a+c)}{K(K+z)} \\[2mm] 0 \end{cases}$	$\dfrac{z(a+b)}{K(K+z)}$, 0
No Coalition	0	0	0

The matrix of NFCs, calculated in the usual way is

Outcome	NFC of		
	A	B	C
$\overline{AB}$	$\dfrac{y(a-c)}{K(K+y)} + \dfrac{x(a+c-b)}{K(K+x)}$	$\dfrac{z(b-c)}{K(K+z)} + \dfrac{x(b+c-a)}{K(K+x)}$	negative
$\overline{AC}$	$\dfrac{x(a-b)}{K(K+x)} + \dfrac{y(a+b-c)}{K(K+y)}$	negative	$\dfrac{z(c-a)}{K(K+z)} + \dfrac{y(b+c-a)}{K(K+y)}$
$\overline{BC}$	negative	$\dfrac{x(b-a)}{K(K+x)} + \dfrac{z(a+b-c)}{K(K+z)}$	$\dfrac{y(c-a)}{K(K+y)} + \dfrac{z(a+c-b)}{K(K+z)}$
No Coalition	$\dfrac{x(a-b)}{K(K+x)} + \dfrac{y(a-c)}{K(K+y)}$	$\dfrac{x(b-a)}{K(K+x)} + \dfrac{z(b-c)}{K(K+z)}$	$\dfrac{y(c-a)}{K(K+y)} + \dfrac{z(c-b)}{K(K+z)}$

It is at once apparent that players prefer coalitions in which they take part to No Coalition.

189

A prefers $\overline{AC}$ to $\overline{AB}$ if

$$\frac{x(a-b)}{K(K+x)} + \frac{y(a+b-c)}{K(K+y)} > \frac{y(a-c)}{K(K+y)} + \frac{x(a+c-b)}{K(K+x)}$$

i.e. if $\quad \dfrac{yb}{K+y)} > \dfrac{xc}{K+x}$ .... (1)

B prefers $\overline{BC}$ to $\overline{AB}$ if

$$\frac{za}{(K+z)} > \frac{yb}{K+x} \quad\text{... (2)}$$

and C prefers $\overline{BC}$ to $\overline{AC}$ if

$$\frac{za}{K+z} > \frac{yb}{K+y} \quad\text{... (3)}$$

As a special case, before going further let us consider a game in which payoffs are directly proportional to resources i.e.

$$x = p(a+b) \qquad y = p(a+c) \qquad z = p(b+c)$$

where p is a constant.
Then A prefers $\overline{AC}$ to $\overline{AB}$ if

$$\frac{bp(a+c)}{K + p(a+c)} > \frac{cp(a+b)}{K + p(a+b)}$$

or $\quad p(a+c)(a+b)(b-c) > aK(c-b)$.
Since the right hand side is negative this is true, and A's first choice is $\overline{AC}$. Similarly it can be shown that B and C have $\overline{BC}$ as their first preference. So the weak coalition is still likely to form and it seems the tendency to form a coalition against the players with highest status is very strong.

Referring to the inequalities in (1), (2) and (3) above let

$$\frac{yb}{K+y} = \alpha, \qquad \frac{xc}{K+x} = \beta \qquad \text{and} \qquad \frac{za}{K+z} = \gamma .$$

Then if $\alpha > \beta$ A prefers $\overline{AC}$ to $\overline{AB}$
  if $\gamma > \beta$ B prefers $\overline{BC}$ to $\overline{AB}$

190

if $\gamma > \alpha$ C prefers $\overline{BC}$ to $\overline{AC}$.

There are six possible forms for these inequalities.

(i) $\alpha > \beta > \gamma$
A and C both desire $\overline{AC}$, B desires $\overline{AB}$, so $\overline{AC}$ forms.

(ii) $\gamma > \beta > \alpha$
B and C both desire $\overline{BC}$, A desires $\overline{AB}$, so $\overline{BC}$ forms.

(iii) $\alpha > \gamma > \beta$
A and C both desire $\overline{AC}$, B desires $\overline{BC}$, so $\overline{AC}$ forms.

(iv) $\beta > \gamma > \alpha$
A and B both desire $\overline{AB}$, C desires $\overline{BC}$, so $\overline{AB}$ forms.

(v) $\beta > \alpha > \gamma$
A and B both desire $\overline{AB}$, C desires $\overline{AC}$, so $\overline{AB}$ forms.

(vi) $\gamma > \alpha > \beta$
B and C both desire $\overline{BC}$, A desires $\overline{AC}$, so $\overline{BC}$ forms.

In all cases some coalition will form. There is no possible instance where all three members desire different coalitions so that there is no reciprocal choice. The triad is therefore always unstable in such games.

When $x = y = z$, as in the Vinacke and Arkoff game, the form which holds is (vi) so that the tendency is for the weak coalition $\overline{BC}$. But it is easily seen that by allowing a, b, c, x, y and z to vary, strong coalitions as well as a weak one may at times form. If the payoff from a coalition with a strong partner is sufficiently great the tendency to form a coalition to oppose that partner is overcome.

In ruling that the payoffs in the No Coalition outcome were zero it may be fairly said that we created a situation in which coalitions were favoured and bound to form. This was not necessarily so however until we established that situations in which there was no reciprocal choice of coalition partner could not exist. Now this has been established we must look further at the No Coalition outcome.

In the Vinacke and Arkoff Game the player strongest in resources could secure the prize in the No Coalition outcome. Suppose, in the Generalised Game, that if No Coalition forms A's prize is w, B's u and C's is v. The final row in the Matrix of Status Changes becomes

Outcome	Status Change of		
	A	B	C
No Coalition	$\dfrac{wK-ak}{K(K+k)}$	$\dfrac{uK-bk}{K(K+k)}$	$\dfrac{vK-ck}{K(K+k)}$

where k = u + v + w.

It seems reasonable to assume that w, u and v are all less than z so that no player receives his best status change from the No Coalition outcome. NFCs for the No Coalition outcome are

For A $\dfrac{x(a-b)}{K(K+x)} + \dfrac{y(a-c)}{K(K+y)} + \dfrac{(2w-u-v)\,K + (b+c-2a)\,k}{K(K+k)}$

For B $\dfrac{z(b-c)}{K(K+z)} + \dfrac{x(b-a)}{K(K+x)} + \dfrac{(2u-w-v)\,K + (a+c-2b)\,k}{K(K+k)}$

For C $\dfrac{z(c-b)}{K(K+z)} + \dfrac{y(c-a)}{K(K+x)} + \dfrac{(2v-w-u)\,K + (b+a-2c)\,k}{K(K+k)}$

Assuming he prefers $\overline{BC}$ to $\overline{AB}$, B would prefer No Coalition to $\overline{BC}$ if

$$\frac{za}{K+z} \; < \; \frac{3u\,(a+c) - 3b\,(w+v)}{K+k}$$

and C would prefer No Coalition to $\overline{BC}$ if

$$\frac{za}{K+z} \; < \; \frac{3v\,(a+b) - 3c\,(w+u)}{K+k}$$

Broadly, these inequalities are the more likely to hold the smaller the player's own resources, the larger his payoff from No Coalition with respect to those payoffs of other players, and the smaller the total payoff to the coalition. One or two cases will be considered briefly

1. Where payoffs are proportional to resources i.e. x = p (a+b), y = p (a+c), z = p (b+c), w = pa, u = pb, v = pc.
   C prefers No Coalition to $\overline{BC}$ if

$$\frac{3pc(a+b) - 3pc(a+b)}{(K+k)} \; > \; \frac{za}{K+z}$$

i.e. if $0 > \dfrac{za}{K+z}$

This is never true and a similar analysis and conclusion holds for B, and so $\overline{BC}$ still forms.

2. Consider the Type V structure with a=4, b=3 and c=2 and suppose that x=y=z=2. The $\overline{BC}$ coalition was originally predicted. How large a payoff in the No Coalition outcome is necessary to break $\overline{BC}$? B prefers No Coalition to $\overline{BC}$ if

$$\frac{3u(6) - 3(4)(k-u)}{9+k} > \frac{8}{11}$$

i.e. if $(18u - 12(k-u))11 > 72 + 8k$

or $330u - 140k > 72$

The payoff structure $k = 2$ and $u = 1.1$ would satisfy this. C prefers No Coalition if

$$297v - 74k > 72$$

which could be satisfied by the payoff structure $k = 2$, $v = 0.8$. So a payoff structure for the No Coalition situation of $(0.1, 1.1, 0.8)$ would guarantee the stability of the triad in this game. Of course other payoff structures may offer a similar guarantee and sometimes no such structure will exist.

Suppose u had been 1.3 so the most v could be was 0.7. C would still prefer $\overline{BC}$. The question arises, if B does not offer to form $\overline{BC}$ does C prefer $\overline{AC}$ to No Coalition? He does so if

$$\frac{yb}{K+y} > \frac{3v(a+b) - 3c(w+u)}{K+k}$$

i.e. if $\dfrac{6}{11} > \dfrac{21(0.7) - 6(1.3)}{11}$

or $6 > 6.9$

which is untrue and so No Coalition is the outcome. Had C preferred $\overline{AC}$ B would presumably have had to form $\overline{BC}$, since he would get a better payoff here than in the $\overline{AC}$ outcome.

In short, it may sometimes be sufficient for only one member of the prospective coalition to prefer No Coalition to prevent the coalition forming, but if the partner then prefers a coalition with the isolate the original coalition should form. This example has demonstrated that payoff structures can sometimes be found which are consistent with maximisation of Fate Control and at the same time prevent coalitions forming.

6.8   THE MODEL APPLIED TO MATRIX GAMES

The game chosen here is one in which all players' payoffs remain undetermined by the decision to form a coalition but each player interacts separately with each other. While the coalition members may co-ordinate their actions, the isolate's payoff can be split up into a part affected by one member and a part affected by the other. Similarly the payoffs of the coalition members are partly determined by their interaction with each other and partly by their separate inter-action with the isolate.

The conventional matrix representation for three-person games has been described earlier. This is not very suitable here since it does not allow a player to make one choice in his interaction with one of the other players and another choice in this interaction with the third. Therefore we take each pair and describe their interaction with a separate matrix game. Of course their decisions in one game may influence their decisions in another and sometimes certain decisions will be incompatible. But these problems are overlooked in the game under consideration.

We represent the three dyadic interactions by identical Prisoner's Dilemma type matrices. The interaction between A and B is shown in fig. xlviii.

Fig. xlviii.

		B	
		β_1	β_2
A	α_1	2, 2	0, 3
	α_2	3, 0	1, 1

We will consider a numerical example where the players have stocks 4, 3 and 2 respectively.

Acting alone player A can give B a certain best status change and there is a certain status change which B can guarantee himself. By playing co-operatively while B defects, A can give B a payoff of 3. In addition B can get at least 1 from the A—C game and so the most player A can expect to give B is 4. A could also try to reduce the payoffs to himself and C in order to improve B's status. A may there-fore defect in the A—C game but he could not stop C co-operating and giving A a payoff of 3. Then assuming the outcome (1, 1) in the B—C game A can give B a best status change corresponding to the payoffs, 4 to B and 4 to the others (in total). Any player can give any other a best status change corresponding to similar payoffs, since the games are identical.

Acting together A and C could both behave co-operatively toward B and defect against each other, thereby giving B a best status change corresponding to the payoffs, 6 to B and 1 each to A and C.

Whether A and C act together or not B can always guarantee him-self a status change corresponding to the payoffs, 2 to B, 3 each to A and C. The Matrix of Status Changes is:

Outcome	Status Change of		
	A	B	C
$\overline{AB}$	$\begin{cases} -0.026 \\ -0.092 \end{cases}$	$\begin{matrix} 0.080 \\ -0.040 \end{matrix}$	$\begin{matrix} 0.249 \\ 0.013 \end{matrix}$
$\overline{AC}$	$\begin{cases} -0.026 \\ -0.092 \end{cases}$	$\begin{matrix} 0.200 \\ -0.040 \end{matrix}$	$\begin{matrix} 0.131 \\ 0.013 \end{matrix}$
$\overline{BC}$	$\begin{cases} 0.144 \\ -0.092 \end{cases}$	$\begin{matrix} 0.080 \\ -0.040 \end{matrix}$	$\begin{matrix} 0.131 \\ 0.013 \end{matrix}$
No Coalition	$\begin{cases} -0.026 \\ -0.092 \end{cases}$	$\begin{matrix} 0.080 \\ -0.040 \end{matrix}$	$\begin{matrix} 0.131 \\ 0.013 \end{matrix}$

The status changes of the isolate refer to his interaction with coalition members acting together. The status changes of coalition members and all players in the No Coalition outcome refer to their interaction with one other player.

Coming to Fate Control we find all players exert no NFC in all outcomes. Thus there is no point in forming coalitions. This is explained by pointing out that although a coalition can affect the isolate's payoff in a certain way, the coalition members could do this without forming a coalition i.e. there is no special advantage in forming a coalition here as there usually was in the previous games considered.

The game is therefore somewhat trivial but it does illustrate the method, a method which could be used for any matrix games. The three matrices need not be identical either in form or in magnitude of pay-offs.

6.9 OTHER GAMES WITH PAYOFFS UNCERTAIN

The games to be dealt with in this section again refer to situations where the decision to form a coalition does not imply the immediate determination of anyone's payoff, but a coalition once formed inter-acts as one player with respect to the isolate. The isolate has a hand in determining the payoffs to the coalition as a whole but the division of this payoff within the coalition depends only upon the coalition members. Thus all players can influence each other's payoffs in all four outcomes.

A possible game of this type is that where a player (or coalition) in his interaction with another may either lose all his resources or win all of those of his opponent. This differs from the Vinacke and Arkoff game where the coalition (or strongest player in Types IV and VI) is certain to win. The payoffs in the No Coalition outcome pose a problem, for what would they be if, say, both B and C defeated A or if A defeated C but C defeated B? We will assume just two possible payoffs for each player in the No Coalition outcome. Either he beats both of his opponents or he loses. We also assume that if a coalition forms, its members no longer interact in a war game but rather over the division of the isolate's resources if they win.

The Matrix of Status Changes, using the usual notations, is

Outcome	Status Change of		
	A	B	C
$\overline{AB}$	$\dfrac{c}{K}$	$\dfrac{c}{K}$	$\dfrac{a+b}{K}$
	$\dfrac{-a}{K}$	$\dfrac{-b}{K}$	$\dfrac{-c}{K}$
$\overline{AC}$	$\dfrac{b}{K}$	$\dfrac{a+c}{K}$	$\dfrac{b}{K}$
	$\dfrac{-a}{K}$	$\dfrac{-b}{K}$	$\dfrac{-c}{K}$
$\overline{BC}$	$\dfrac{b+c}{K}$	$\dfrac{a}{K}$	$\dfrac{a}{K}$
	$\dfrac{-a}{K}$	$\dfrac{-b}{K}$	$\dfrac{-c}{K}$
No Coalition	$\dfrac{b+c}{K}$	$\dfrac{a+c}{K}$	$\dfrac{a+b}{K}$
	$\dfrac{-a}{K}$	$\dfrac{-b}{K}$	$\dfrac{-c}{K}$

Again if we compute NFCs we find that each player exerts the same amount no matter what outcome results, so there is no point in forming a coalition. This is because a player's best possible status change

196

accrues when he is the isolate or in the No Coalition outcome, while his guarantee is the same for all outcomes.

We have however ignored the chances of winning. In real life the probability of winning would probably vary for different coalitions. This probability is not necessarily related to resources possessed, however, for status may be calculated in resources quite different from those used in fighting.

If the above were a bargaining game between coalition and isolate there would be a large number of possible payoffs to the coalition and isolate i.e. a large number of points of possible settlement. As it is in fact a win or lose game, given the probabilities of winning and losing it is not difficult to compute expected values of payoffs. The coalition's expected payoff forms the basis of the bargaining game between its members.

Suppose we have the following probabilities.

P_1 = the probability that $\overline{AB}$ beats C

P_2 = the probability that $\overline{AC}$ beats B

P_3 = the probability that $\overline{BC}$ beats A

P_4 = the probability that A beats B and C

P_5 = the probability that B beats A and C

P_6 = the probability that C beats A and B

The expected value of the payoff from a particular outcome is calculated as

(payoff) $\times$ (probability of that payoff being made)

summed over all possible payoffs for that outcome. The payoff which we shall consider is the status change, since this is what we have assumed the players consider.

For outcome $\overline{AB}$, C's expected status change is

$$\left(\frac{a+b}{K}\right) \left(1 - P_1\right) - \frac{c}{K} P_1 = \frac{(a+b) - KP_1}{K}$$

The coalition's expected status change is $\dfrac{KP_1 - (a+b)}{K}$. Remembering that status change is the ratio $\dfrac{\text{Change in resources of player}}{\text{Total resources in system}}$ the change in resources here is $KP_1 - (a+b)$. In the ensuing bargaining game between the coalition members each could obtain a best status change by getting the whole of $KP_1 - (a+b)$ (assuming this term is positive)

197

and could guarantee a status change of zero. If the term was negative the best status change would be 0 and the guarantee $KP_1 - (a+b)$ implying that all costs are imposed on that player.

The complete Matrix of Status Changes is

Outcome		Status Change of	
	A	**B**	**C**
$\overline{AB}$	$\begin{cases} \dfrac{KP_1 - (a+b)}{K} \\[2mm] 0 \end{cases}$	$\dfrac{KP_1 - (a+b)}{K}$ 0	$\dfrac{(a+b) - KP_1}{K}$
$\overline{AC}$	$\begin{cases} \dfrac{KP_2 - (a+c)}{K} \\[2mm] 0 \end{cases}$	$\dfrac{(a+c) - KP_2}{K}$	$\dfrac{KP_2 - (a+c)}{K}$ 0
$\overline{BC}$	$\dfrac{(b+c) - KP_3}{K}$	$\begin{cases} \dfrac{KP_3 - (b+c)}{K} \\[2mm] 0 \end{cases}$	$\dfrac{KP_3 - (b+c)}{K}$ 0
No Coalition	$(\frac{b+c}{K})P_4 - \frac{a}{K}(P_5+P_6)$	$(\frac{a+c}{K})P_5 - \frac{b}{K}(P_4+P_6)$	$(\frac{b+a}{K})P_6 - \frac{c}{K}(P_4+P_5)$

This structure looks the same as that of the Generalised game in section 6.7 but in computing NFCs it is treated differently. It must be remembered that now a player can affect another's payoff in *all* outcomes. To calculate NFCs it is necessary to know which payoff represents a player's best possible payoff, but as there are so many parameters involved this is very difficult to ascertain. For further analysis we will make further assumptions.

Assume that probabilities are proportional to the ratio $\dfrac{\text{resources}}{\text{total resources}}$

i.e. $P_1 = \alpha(\frac{a+b}{K})$ $P_2 = \alpha(\frac{a+c}{K})$ $P_3 = \alpha(\frac{b+c}{K})$

where α is constant and $\alpha \leqslant \dfrac{K}{a+b}$. Further assume $P_4 = \dfrac{a}{K}$, $P_5 = \dfrac{b}{K}$ and $P_6 = \dfrac{c}{K}$.

The Matrix of Status Changes is now

Outcome	Status Change of		
	A	B	C
$\overline{AB}$	$\begin{cases}\dfrac{(a+b)(\alpha-1)}{K}\\ 0\end{cases}$	$\begin{cases}\dfrac{(a+b)(\alpha-1)}{K}\\ 0\end{cases}$	$\dfrac{(1-\alpha)(a+b)}{K}$
$\overline{AC}$	$\begin{cases}\dfrac{(a+c)(\alpha-1)}{K}\\ 0\end{cases}$	$\dfrac{(1-\alpha)(a+c)}{K}$	$\begin{cases}\dfrac{(a+c)(\alpha-1)}{K}\\ 0\end{cases}$
$\overline{BC}$	$\dfrac{(1-\alpha)(b+c)}{K}$	$\begin{cases}\dfrac{(b+c)(\alpha-1)}{K}\\ 0\end{cases}$	$\begin{cases}\dfrac{(b+c)(\alpha-1)}{K}\\ 0\end{cases}$
No Coalition	0	0	0

If $\alpha > 1$ obviously A's best status change comes from outcome $\overline{AB}$, B's comes from $\overline{AB}$ and C's from $\overline{AC}$.

The Matrix of NFCs is

Outcome	NFC of		
	A	B	C
$\overline{AB}$	$\dfrac{(K-b)(\alpha-1)}{K}$	$\dfrac{(K-b)(\alpha-1)}{K}$	$\dfrac{2(b-K)(\alpha-1)}{K}$
$\overline{AC}$	$\dfrac{(K+c-2b)(\alpha-1)}{K}$	$\dfrac{(b+c-2K)(\alpha-1)}{K}$	$\dfrac{(K+b-2c)(\alpha-1)}{K}$
$\overline{BC}$	$\dfrac{(-3b-c)(\alpha-1)}{K}$	$\dfrac{2c(\alpha-1)}{K}$	$\dfrac{(3b-c)(\alpha-1)}{K}$
No Coalition	$\dfrac{(c-b)(\alpha-1)}{K}$	$\dfrac{(c-b)(\alpha-1)}{K}$	$\dfrac{2(b-c)(\alpha-1)}{K}$

$\overline{AB}$ is the outcome which maximises NFC for both A and B so this is the predicted coalition. We note that was on the assumption that $\alpha > 1$. If α were unity all NFCs would be zero and no coalition would be likely. If α were less than unity the best payoffs of each player would accrue when in the position of isolate, and so no coalition would be likely here either because no one would make any initiating offer. We conclude that the probability of the coalition winning must be something larger than the ratio $\dfrac{\text{Coalition's resources}}{\text{Total resources}}$ in order to make it worthwhile for both members and then strong coalitions are likely.

In the Tripolar World Game where weak coalitions were predicted, we recall that all coalitions were certain to win. In the Generalised Game it was shown that strong coalitions would form if payoffs to coalitions varied and those made to strong coalitions were sufficiently high compared to those made to weaker ones. As a variant of the Tripolar World Game consider the following which is more easily compared with the present probabilistic game since payoffs are not completely determined.

If coalitions form they win an amount equal to the isolate's resources over the division of which they must bargain.

The Matrix of Status Changes is

Outcome	Status Change of		
	A	B	C
$\overline{AB}$	$\begin{cases} \dfrac{c}{K} \\ 0 \end{cases}$	$\begin{matrix} \dfrac{c}{K} \\ 0 \end{matrix}$	$\dfrac{-c}{K}$
$\overline{AC}$	$\begin{cases} \dfrac{b}{K} \\ 0 \end{cases}$	$\dfrac{-b}{K}$	$\begin{cases} \dfrac{b}{K} \\ 0 \end{cases}$
$\overline{BC}$	$\dfrac{-a}{K}$	$\begin{cases} \dfrac{a}{K} \\ 0 \end{cases}$	$\dfrac{a}{K}$
No Coalition	0	0	0

The Matrix of NFCs is

Outcome	NFC of		
	A	B	C
$\overline{AB}$	$\dfrac{2c-b}{K}$	$\dfrac{b}{K}$	$\dfrac{-2c}{K}$
$\overline{AC}$	$\dfrac{b}{K}$	$\dfrac{-2b}{K}$	$\dfrac{b}{K}$
$\overline{BC}$	$\dfrac{-2a}{K}$	$\dfrac{a}{K}$	$\dfrac{a}{K}$
No Coalition	0	0	0

Obviously BC is still the predicted coalition. Now we return to the probabilistic model but we will assume that nothing happens if No Coalition is the outcome, i.e. no player is strong enough to go to war himself. The Matrices and Status Changes and NFCs are still those on page 185, and as we showed, if $\alpha > 1$ strong coalitions will form, but otherwise no coalition is likely.

If all probabilities are equal, the Matrix of Status Changes becomes

Outcome	Status Change of		
	A	B	C
$\overline{AB}$	$\left\{\begin{array}{l}\dfrac{KP-(a+b)}{K}\\[2mm]0\end{array}\right.$	$\left.\begin{array}{l}\dfrac{KP-(a+b)}{K}\\[2mm]0\end{array}\right\}$	$\dfrac{(a+b)-KP}{K}$
$\overline{AC}$	$\left.\begin{array}{l}\dfrac{KP-(a+c)}{K}\\[2mm]0\end{array}\right\}$	$\dfrac{(a+c)-KP}{K}$	$\left\{\begin{array}{l}\dfrac{KP-(a+c)}{K}\\[2mm]0\end{array}\right.$
$\overline{BC}$	$\dfrac{(b+c)-KP}{K}$	$\left\{\begin{array}{l}\dfrac{KP-(b+c)}{K}\\[2mm]0\end{array}\right.$	$\dfrac{KP-(b+c)}{K}$
No Coalition	0	0	0

201

A's best status change comes from $\overline{AC}$ or $\overline{BC}$. It comes from the former if

$$KP - (a+c) \; > \; (b+c) - KP$$

i.e. if $\quad P \; > \; \dfrac{K+c}{2K}$

Similarly B prefers $\overline{BC}$ to $\overline{AC}$ if $P \; > \; \dfrac{K+c}{2K}$ and C prefers $\overline{BC}$ to $\overline{AB}$ if

$P \; > \; \dfrac{K+b}{2K}$. The subsequent analysis of this game, covered in Appendix VI, yields the following conclusions

1. When $P \; < \; \dfrac{K+c}{2K}$

    If $P \; < \; \dfrac{b+c}{K}$ no coalition will form

    If $P \; > \; \dfrac{b+c}{K}$ $\overline{BC}$ will form

2. When $\dfrac{K+b}{2K} \; > \; P \; > \; \dfrac{K+c}{2K}$

    If $P \; < \; \dfrac{a+c}{K}$ $\overline{BC}$ will form

    If $P \; > \; \dfrac{a+c}{K}$ $\overline{AC}$ will form

3. When $P \; > \; \dfrac{K+b}{2K}$ $\overline{BC}$ will form

We can represent the prediction on a scale for P as in fig. xlix.

Fig. xlix.

P value	0	$\dfrac{b+c}{K}$	$\dfrac{K+c}{2K}$	$\dfrac{a+c}{K}$	$\dfrac{K+b}{2K}$	1
Coalition predicted	None	$\overline{BC}$	$\overline{BC}$	$\overline{AC}$	$\overline{BC}$	

$\dfrac{a+c}{K}$ may well fall to the right of $\dfrac{K+b}{2K}$ on this scale in which case $\overline{AC}$ would not be feasible.

Even if they believe all coalitions have an equal chance of winning, players may perceive P differently. It depends very much on how the weak player perceives it. If he sees it as being very low no coalition is likely whether the others perceive it as being high or low. This is illustrated in the Appendix where we represent the players' lower as well as first preference for various values of P.

It may seem odd that a player should sometimes desire a coalition which could bring about his own destruction. It should be noted here that outcomes are not exactly determined and we are dealing with expected values. Such coalitions are never desired in the non-probabilistic game.

Regarding Conflict in the probabilistic game, it is calculated in the usual way, but because the player's best outcomes vary as P changes, no general formula can be cited. Referring to the player's best outcomes we can easily calculate the Conflict values, as we do in Appendix VI and we can represent them on a rough sketch graph as in fig. L.

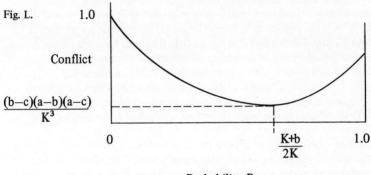

Fig. L.

Conflict is seen to fall as P increases reaching a minimum value of $\dfrac{(b-c)\,(a-b)\,(a-c)}{K^3}$ when $P = \dfrac{K+b}{2K}$. After this it rises as P increases further. This is not surprising since when P is large the coalition has a high chance of winning and a high best expected status change, and when P is small the isolate has a high chance of winning and a high best expected status change. When $P = 0$, Conflict has its maximum value of unity, but such a situation must be purely theoretical. When $P = 1$ its value is $\dfrac{(K-c)^2\,(K-b)}{K^3}$. Further we note that the point of minimal Conflict always occurs at a value of P greater than one half, and it is the point after which the $\overline{BC}$ coalition is certain to form on a consideration of first preferences.

Again it is true that that coalition will form which leaves the greatest amount of Residual Conflict.

In the game with probabilities proportional to shares of resources, for $\alpha > 1$ the Conflict value is

$$\left[\frac{(\alpha-1)\,(K+b)}{K}\right] \times \left[\frac{(\alpha-1)\,(K+a)}{K}\right] \times \left[\frac{(\alpha-1)\,(K+a)}{K}\right]$$

for $\alpha < 1$ it is

$$\left[\frac{(1-\alpha)\,(K+b)}{K}\right] \times \left[\frac{(1-\alpha)\,(K+a)}{K}\right] \times \left[\frac{(1-\alpha)\,(K+a)}{K}\right]$$

and for $\alpha = 1$ it is zero. Conflict then rises from minimum value of 0 as α gets greater or less than one.

6.10 SUMMARY

In this chapter we have built a model based on the idea of maximization of power and have used it to predict whether coalitions will form, and if so, which coalition. The games considered by no means cover all possibilities but it is hoped that they will be sufficiently representative firstly to demonstrate the use of the model and secondly to gather some ideas about the stability of the triad.

We have concentrated chiefly on those games in which a coalition acting as a single decision maker could get some payoff which neither of its members could obtain alone and which had to be divided in a subsequent bargaining game. These games fall strictly into two divisions –– those in which the decision to form a coalition is sufficient to secure the payoff and those in which the coalition, once formed, must enter some interaction with the isolate, possibly bargaining or fighting for the payoff. We have concentrated on these cases because it is felt they are nearer to those found in real life.

Two drives seem to be at work in determining coalition formation. One of these springs from the basic assumption of the model that players are concerned with status. This accounts for the fact that coalitions tend to form against the player strongest in resources, when all coalitions get equal payoffs. The other drive springs from a consideration of the absolute payoffs or resources at stake. This payoff is often likely to be correlated with coalition resources and may sometimes be sufficiently large for a strong coalition, to combat the tendency for the strong player to become the isolate. When weak coalitions receive greater payoffs than strong ones the latter tendency is reinforced.

We saw that in the Generalised Game some coalition will always form unless there are certain payoff structures which can be found for

204

the No Coalition outcome, to prevent this. Such a payoff structure may not always be possible.

In the probabilistic game equal probabilities of winning for all coalitions sometimes give rise to no coalitions, if the probabilities are small enough, and otherwise give rise to the coalition $\overline{BC}$. Unequal probabilities which favour strong coalitions give rise to their formation if these probabilities are sufficiently high, i.e. greater than the ratio $\dfrac{\text{Coalition's Resources}}{\text{Total Resources}}$, otherwise no coalition forms. We may safely add that unequal probabilities favouring weak coalitions would give rise to weak coalitions so long as these probabilities were high enough, and that otherwise no coalition would form.

The triad playing the probabilistic game would seem to be more stable as the possibility of "No Coalition" arises even without a special payoff structure for that outcome. The reason for this is that the isolate can sometimes end up better off than the coalition, and so he desires a coalition between the other two. Each member of the triad may desire to be the isolate and provided that their payoffs in the No Coalition outcome exceed their payoffs in the two other outcomes, i.e. there is no reciprocal coalition choice based on second preferences, no coalition will form.

Such a state of affairs could have existed in the Generalised Game by structuring the payoffs to favour the isolate. Where the isolate's payoff is exactly determined this would seem rather unrealistic but where we are dealing with expected values and with probabilities estimated by the players, it seems more in keeping with the real world.

No particular relationship between the amount of Conflict and coalition formation was found to exist save that when the decision to form a coalition does not imply the immediate settlement of the issue, that coalition tends to form which reduces Conflict by the smallest amount.

Notes

1. For our purposes a triple alliance is equivalent to no coalition.
2. See Section 3.7.
3. For this proof I am indebted to Mr. N.S. Forward.
4. This is not always so — sometimes $x_1 + y_4 + z_1 > 0$ e.g. see the games in section 6.6. Our main conclusion is unaffected by this however.

CHAPTER 7

FURTHER APPLICATIONS OF THE MODEL

7.1 INTRODUCTION

The model was originally built to predict coalition formation where any of the four outcomes $\overline{AB}$, $\overline{AC}$, $\overline{BC}$ or No Coalition was possible and where it was assumed that players were concerned with status and took decisions aimed at maximising their power or net Fate Control over others.

In Chapter 2 we saw that many triadic situations exist where either coalition formation is not the relevant criterion for decisions or where only certain coalitions are feasible. As we are interested in the stability of the triad, and given that a triad is unstable if a coalition forms, we might also enquire how such a coalition may be broken or prevented by the would-be isolate. In chapter 6 appeasement payments were considered as one possibility. Now we turn to the situations of chapter 2 and apply our model to these in the hope that they will throw some light on how the stability of the triad may be prevented, restored or preserved. At the same time we may gain insights into the processes of mediation, divide and rule etc.

Basically there are four situations which we will consider.

1. Just two coalitions are possible, these being say between A and B or A and C. But $\overline{BC}$ is not feasible. A may be the balancer or the third party in competition for allegiance.

2. Just one coalition is possible say $\overline{BC}$, A being the divider.
   Alternatively, there may be a conflict between A and C, B being a

206

possible ally of C.

3. No coalition is possible or desired. C and B are in some conflict and A wishes either to mediate or to intensify the conflict. In a way resolution of the conflict does mean a sort of coalition between C and B.

4. No coalition is possible but the interaction is changed by a third party e.g. delegation.

Section 5.5 on Systems of Reference is relevant to much of what we say in some of the following sections and it will be a good idea for the reader to refer back to this.

7.2 MEDIATION

Mediation is of course relevant to those situations where there is a conflict between two players say B and C. A, desiring a resolution of this conflict, is the mediator. In a way this resolution may be thought of as the formation of a coalition, and we have said that this triad is unstable. This is a case therefore where instability is perhaps desirable.

We shall consider two types of conflict between B and C, that over the division of some new resources, and that over the re-distribution of some resources already possessed by the players. Firstly some new resources of amount x are at stake. Consider two possible outcomes:

(1) Continuation of the conflict

(2) Resolution of the conflict with B getting an amount z and C an amount w. (where $w + z = x$).

The Matrix of Status Changes is

Outcome	Status Change of	
	B	C
(1)	$\begin{cases} \dfrac{cx}{(b+c)(b+c+x)} \\ 0 \end{cases}$	$\dfrac{bx}{(b+c)(b+c+x)}$ 0
(2)	$\dfrac{cz - bw}{(b+c)(b+c+x)}$	$\dfrac{bw - cz}{(b+c)(b+c+x)}$

The best outcomes correspond to their receiving the whole of x and the guarantees correspond to no division.

If (1) results B's NFC over C is $\dfrac{(b-c)\,x}{(b+c)\,(b+c+x)}$

If (2) results B's NFC over C is $\dfrac{(b-c)\,x}{(b+c)\,(b+c+x)}$

So in both cases C's NFC over B is $\dfrac{(c-b)\,x}{(b+c)\,(b+c+x)}$

Neither player has any preference between (1) and (2) and since we are in the conflict situation i.e. (1), there is no reason to move out of it.

Suppose there is some player A who can influence the payoffs in (2) by performing some mediative function — perhaps suggesting values of z and w. As A cannot influence the value of x he exerts no NFC over B or C if (2) is the outcome.

Assuming $cz > bw$, if (1) is the outcome A exerts NFC over B of value $\dfrac{cz-bw}{(b+c)\,(b+c+x)}$. His NFC over C is negative and therefore zero.

B's total NFC from (1) is now $\dfrac{(b-c)+bw-cz}{(b+c)\,(b+c+x)}$ and C's is $\dfrac{(c-b)\,x}{(b+c)\,(b+c+x)}$.

B will thus prefer (2) to (1) since his NFC is now greater in (2). But C will still be indifferent and have no reason to relax his demand and move away from (1), thereby accepting a fall in status.

If $bw > cz$ it is easily shown that C will prefer (2), but B will now be indifferent and have no reason to depart from (1). In short, both B and C must prefer the outcome (2) in order to resolve the conflict.

Now suppose there exists a player A who is comparable in resources with B and C. The Matrix of Status Changes becomes

Outcome	Status Change of		
	A	B	C
(1)	$\dfrac{-ax}{K(K+x)}$	$\begin{cases}\dfrac{x(a+c)}{K(K+x)}\\[2mm] 0\end{cases}$	$\begin{array}{c}\dfrac{x(a+b)}{K(K+x)}\\[2mm] 0\end{array}$
(2)	$\dfrac{-ax}{K(K+x)}$	$\dfrac{z(a+c)-bw}{K(K+x)}$	$\dfrac{w(a+b)-cz}{K(K+x)}$

A must accept a fall of status under both outcomes because x resources have been added to the system and whether they are divided or not between B and C makes no difference to A.

Suppose A exerts no influence over the payoffs in (1) and (2).

If (1) results B's NFC over C is $\dfrac{x(b-c)}{K(K+x)}$

If (2) results B's NFC over C is $\dfrac{x(b-c)}{K(K+x)} + \dfrac{z(a+2c) - w(a+2b)}{K(K+x)}$

Obviously, since C's NFC is the negative of that of B one player will prefer (1) and the other will prefer (2) depending on the sign of $\dfrac{z(a+2c) - w(a+2b)}{K(K+x)}$.

Now suppose that A can influence the payoffs in (2), i.e. he exercises some mediative function. Assuming both B's and C's status changes in (2) are positive, if (1) results A's NFC over B is $\dfrac{z(a+c) - bw}{K(K+x)}$ and over C it is $\dfrac{w(a+b) - cz}{K(K+x)}$.

B's total NFC in (1) is thus $\dfrac{x(b-c) - z(a+c) + bw}{K(K+x)}$.

C's total NFC in (1) is $\dfrac{x(c-b) - w(a+b) + cz}{K(K+x)}$.

NFCs in (2) are as before so B prefers (2) to (1) if

$$x(b-c) + z(a+2c) - w(a+2b) > x(b-c) - z(a+c) + bw$$

i.e. if $\dfrac{w}{z} < \dfrac{2a + 3c}{a + 2b}$

C prefers (2) to (1) if

$$x(c-b) + w(a+2b) - z(a+2c) > x(c-b) + cz - w(a+b)$$

i.e. if $\dfrac{w}{z} > \dfrac{a + 3c}{2a + 3b}$.

For both B and C to prefer (2), the inequality

$$\frac{2a + 3c}{a + 3b} > \frac{w}{z} > \frac{a + 3c}{2a + 3b}$$

must hold. Any division of x which satisfies this inequality should be preferred by B and C to continuation of the conflict. Before such a solution can exist A must be comparable in resources and must influence the payoffs in (2). It is not sufficient for A to be merely comparable, so no implicit mediation can arise from the consideration of A as a reference individual.

The reason for the success of the mediator is that the loss of status appears to fall on him. Though either B or C lose status to the other both can gain at A's expense so there is less 'loss of face'. Both prefer to settle the conflict because they are exerting more NFC here than they would be under its continuation. A of course is not maximising his Fate Control if (2) is the outcome but since he suffers the same loss of status in (1) and (2) his use of Fate Control does not affect his own position, and so there is not the same incentive for him to use it.

As a gets larger, the range of values for $\frac{w}{z}$ increases, approaching the the limits $2 > \frac{w}{z} > \frac{1}{2}$. Now the larger this range, the easier should the task of the mediator be.

Fig. Li.

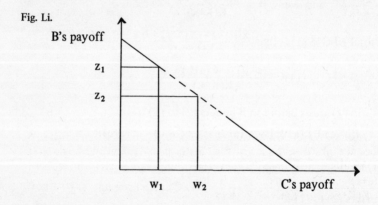

The sloping line in fig. Li. represents various feasible solution points (w, z) and the dotted segment represents those for which the inequality holds. This of course is the ordinary diagram applicable to a bargaining model. C looks at B's initial demand, z_1, and finds he would get an amount w_1 which does not fall in the range so he prefers the conflict to continue. Had B's demand been z_2 however, the corresponding w_2 is within the range and the solution is acceptable. The wider the range the more likely is a solution or the sooner will it be reached as concessions are made.

Thus the higher is a, the wider the range and the easier the mediation. This may suggest something about the quality of 'distance' in the mediator. However a should not be too large, otherwise he becomes irrelevant as a reference individual and mediation will not succeed. Further as a increases, so does K, and the amount of Conflict falls. So it is perhaps not surprising that the mediation process is easier. Finally we note that a does not necessarily have to be greater than b or c. It could be less, though being very much less would land us in a similar position to being very much greater i.e. incomparability.

The above referred to a bargaining process between B and C. Had this been a fight their guarantees under the continued conflict may have been less and in the extreme case they might lose the whole of x. It is easily shown that in the absence of a mediator A, B and C still prefer the conflict situation. If there exists some comparable individual A, the Matrix of Status Changes becomes

Outcome   Status Change of

	A	B	C
(1)	$\dfrac{-ax}{K(K+x)}$	$\begin{cases} \dfrac{x(a+c)}{K(K+x)} \\[2mm] \dfrac{-bx}{K(K+x)} \end{cases}$	$\begin{array}{c} \dfrac{x(a+b)}{K(K+x)} \\[2mm] \dfrac{-cx}{K(K+x)} \end{array}$
(2)	$\dfrac{-ax}{K(K+x)}$	$\dfrac{z(a+c)-bw}{K(K+x)}$	$\dfrac{w(a+b)-cz}{K(K+x)}$

Again it is easy to show that either B or C prefers (1) so long as A does not influence the payoffs in (2). Suppose A does this however. If (1) results there is no NFC between B and C, but A exerts an amount $\dfrac{z(a+c)-bw}{K(K+x)} - (\dfrac{-bx}{K(K+x)}) = \dfrac{z}{K+x}$ over B and an amount $\dfrac{w}{K+x}$ over C. As B's NFC over C in (z) is

$$\frac{x(b-c) + z\,(a+2c) - w\,(a+2b)}{K(K+x)} \quad \text{B prefers (2) if}$$

$$x(b-c) + z(a+2c) - w(a+2b) \; > \; -zK$$

Substituting x = w + z the expression becomes

$$\frac{w}{z} < 2$$

Similar analysis yields that C prefers (2) if $\dfrac{w}{z} > \dfrac{1}{2}$.

211

So for a settlement the inequality

$$2 > \frac{w}{2} > \frac{1}{2}$$

must hold. The range does not now depend on the values of a, b, and c but we note that it is the maximum it could be when a was allowed to vary in the bargaining game. This implies that, for a given a, mediation should generally be easier here. This is because the players' guarantees have fallen. Mediation is more difficult, the higher the guarantees.

Suppose now that we have a conflict involving a redistribution of resources between B and C. Such a conflict is more likely to involve fighting. Suppose C can gain at most an amount x and B can gain at most an amount y. x and y are therefore the greatest losses of B and C respectively and we assume these are their guaranteed payoffs. A is again the mediator and the suggested solution gives B an amount z and C an amount w where $z + w = 0$ and $y \geqslant z > -x$ and $x \geqslant w > -y$. The Matrix of Status Changes is

Outcome	Status Change of		
	A	B	C
(1)	0	$\begin{cases} \dfrac{y}{b+c} \\[2mm] \dfrac{-x}{b+c} \end{cases}$	$\begin{cases} \dfrac{x}{b+c} \\[2mm] \dfrac{-y}{b+c} \end{cases}$
(2)	0	$\dfrac{z}{b+c}$	$\dfrac{w}{b+c}$

This is all right if A is incomparable in resources, but even if he is comparable he suffers no status change, since we are dealing with a redistribution between B and C. If A is comparable the only difference is an addition of an a term in the denominators, and as this makes no difference to the analysis we shall stick to the simpler case.

Under outcome (1) there is no NFC between B and C but A exerts an amount $\frac{w+y}{b+c}$ over C and $\frac{z+x}{b+c}$ over B.

Under outcome (2) B's NFC over C is $\frac{x-y}{b+c} + \frac{z-w}{b+c}$ so B prefers (2) to (1) if

$$x-y + z-w > -z - x$$

Substituting $z = -w$ we arrive at

$$w < \frac{2x-y}{3}$$

Similarly C prefers (2) to (1) if

$$w > \frac{x-2y}{3}$$

so for both to prefer (2) to (1) w must satisfy the inequality

$$\frac{x-2y}{3} < w < \frac{2x-y}{3}$$

The range for w is $\frac{1}{3}(2x-y - (x-2y)) = \frac{x+y}{3}$. It is therefore greater the greater are x and y, and is maximum when $x = b$ and $y = c$. The ratio $\frac{\text{Range for w}}{\text{Total resources at stake}}$ remains constant at $\frac{1}{3}$ so possibly the chances of mediation succeeding do not vary.

If the conflict involves fighting the fighting may go on after the mediation attempt until w falls between the above limits. If w is still within these limits when the mediation bid is made, it should succeed. But if w is outside, one of the parties will prefer to continue fighting. The solution $w = 0$ exists if $\frac{1}{2} < \frac{x}{y} < 2$ i.e. the payoffs do not differ in ratio greater than $2 : 1$. Here mediation can succeed without any re-distribution, but if such a solution does not exist there must first be some re-distribution through fighting or appeasement. The importance of the timing of the mediation bid becomes apparent.

While the conflict involving re-distribution is more likely to be resolved by fighting (or competition) it is possible that a bargaining process might take place. In this the players can guarantee a status change of zero. The situation is similar if fighting is taking place but has reached a stalemate where each side can prevent the other advancing but still believes that it can itself win. For these cases the Matrix of Status Changes is

Outcome   Status Change of

Outcome	B	C
(1)	$\left\{\begin{array}{l}\dfrac{y}{b+c}\\[2mm] 0\end{array}\right.$	$\begin{array}{l}\dfrac{x}{b+c}\\[2mm] 0\end{array}$
(2)	$\dfrac{z}{b+c}$	$\dfrac{w}{b+c}$

213

Under outcome (1) B now exerts NFC of amount $\frac{x+y}{b+c}$ over C and A exerts an amount $\frac{z}{b+c}$ over B and $\frac{w}{b+c}$ over C.

Under (2) B's NFC over C is as before, so B prefers (2) if

$$x - y + z - w > x - y - z$$

i.e. if $\quad z > 0$

C prefers (2) if $w > 0$ but w and z cannot both exceed 0, so no solution exists.

Mediation then has a chance of succeeding in a bargaining game involving new resources but not in a bargaining game involving a re-distribution of resources. The latter is however less likely in practice and is more likely to be replaced by fighting, where mediation can succeed, unless the situation is one of stalemate with players able to guarantee their present status indices. Should this guarantee fall, mediation again becomes a possibility.

The games considered so far have assumed the resources at stake were always divisible so that a compromise settlement was possible. This is not always true in the real world. In conflicts involving new resources the only solution points are then $z = 0$, $w = x$ and $z = x$, $w = 0$ which do not lie in the required range, and mediation will not succeed. In conflicts involving re-distribution there is also the solution point $z = 0$, $w = 0$, and we showed that this lies in the required range if $\frac{1}{2} < \frac{x}{y} < 2$; so mediation may succeed here even if resources are indivisible.

7.3 DIVIDE AND RULE

Unlike the mediator, the divider desires the dyad to continue in a state of conflict i.e. he prefers outcome (1). If the divider takes active steps to influence the payoffs in (2) he tries to promote values of z and w which lie outside the range for settlement. However, in the foregoing situations, as the conflict state would be preferred anyway if he did nothing, such action would be futile and this case becomes rather trivial.

Of more interest is the case where the divider gets some payoff in resources similar to those of B and C and this payoff is greater if B and C remain in conflict. Suppose B and C are engaged in some bargaining game of resources x. If they stay in conflict A gets a payoff y, if there is a settlement A gets a payoff v, where $y > v$.

The Matrix of Status Changes is

Outcome   Status Change of

A   B   C

(1) $\dfrac{(b+c)y-ax}{K(K+x+y)}$ $\begin{cases} \dfrac{(a+c)x-by}{K(K+x+y)} & \dfrac{(a+b)x-cy}{K(K+x+y)} \\[2ex] \dfrac{-by}{K(K+y)} & \dfrac{-cy}{K(K+y)} \end{cases}$

(2) $\dfrac{(b+c)v-ax}{K(K+x+v)}$ $\dfrac{(a+c)z-b(w+v)}{K(K+x+v)}$ $\dfrac{(a+b)w-c(z+v)}{K(K+x+v)}$

Firstly suppose that A takes no steps to influence the payoffs to B and C. If outcome (1) results, B's NFC over C is

$$\frac{(b-c)x+(b-c)y}{K(K+x+y)} + \frac{(c-b)y}{K(K+y)} \ .$$

If (2) is the outcome B's NFC over C is

$$\frac{(b-c)\,(x+y)}{K(K+x+y)} + \frac{z(2c+a) - w\,(a+2b) + v\,(c-b)}{K(K+x+v)}$$

B and C each exert NFC over A, if (2) is the outcome. Its value is

$$\frac{(b+c)\,y - ax}{K(K+x+y)} - \frac{(b+c)\,v - ax}{K(K+x+v)}$$

B's total NFC in (2) is thus

$$\frac{(b-c-a)\,x + 2by}{K(K+x+y)} + \frac{2z(a+c) - 2b(v+w)}{K(K+x+v)}$$

and he prefers (2) to (1) if

$$\frac{(b-c-a)\,x + 2by - (b-c)\,(x+y)}{K(K+x+y)} + \frac{2z(a+c) - 2b(v+w)}{K(K+x+v)} + \frac{(b-c)y}{K(K+y)} > 0$$

i.e. if $z > \dfrac{K+x+v}{2(a+c)} \left[\dfrac{(c-b)y}{K+y} + \dfrac{ax - (b+c)y}{K+x+y} \right] + \dfrac{b(v+w)}{a+c}$

Similarly C prefers (2) to (1) if

$$z < \frac{K+x+v}{2c} \left[\frac{(b+c)\,y - ax}{(K+x+y)} + \frac{(c-b)y}{K+y} \right] + \frac{w(a+b) - cv}{c}$$

Substituting w = x−z and combining these inequalities we find that B and C both prefer settlement if z satisfies

$$\frac{K+x+v}{2K} \left[\frac{(b+c)y-ax}{K+x+y} + \frac{(c-b)y}{K+y} \right] + \frac{x(a+b)-cv}{K} > z >$$

$$\frac{K+x+v}{2K} \left[\frac{(c-b)y}{K+y} + \frac{ax-(b+c)y}{K+x+y} \right] + \frac{b(v+x)}{K}$$

The length of the range for z is

$$\frac{K+x+v}{2K} \left[\frac{2(b+c)\,y - 2ax}{K+x+y} \right] + \frac{ax - (b+c)\,v}{K}$$

A similar range can of course be computed for w.

The range for z exceeds zero i.e. exists if

$$(K+x+v) \; [\,(b+c)\,y - ax\,] > (K+x+y) \; [\,(b+c)\,v - ax\,]$$

i.e. if ax(y−v) > (K+x) (b+c) (v−y)

As y > v this is true, so some range always exists. Further, it is wider, the larger the value of a.[1]

A can therefore cause the settlement of the conflict even though he takes no active steps to influence the payoffs. He acts as an implicit mediator. Because B and C consider A's resources and his payoffs they will accept a settlement in this range. This could not occur when A did not get a material payoff, as mentioned in the previous section. Implicit mediation is more likely to be effective, the greater the resources of A.

As he may cause a settlement by remaining aloof, if A is to promote the conflict between B and C he must take some steps to influence the payoffs. Firstly we assume that he cannot affect the amount x but can influence the division i.e. the outcome (2).

B's and C's NFCs are as before but if outcome (1) results, A exerts an amount $\frac{(a+c)\,z-b\,(w+v)}{K(K+x+v)} + \frac{by}{K(K+y)}$ over B and an amount $\frac{(a+b)\,w-c\,(z+v)}{K(K+x+v)} + \frac{cy}{K(K+y)}$ over C.

B's total NFC from outcome (2) is now

$$\frac{(b-c)\,(x+y)}{K(K+x+y)} + \frac{b(w+v) - z\,(a+c)}{K(K+x+v)} + \frac{(c-2b)y}{K(K+y)}$$

and he prefers (2) to (1) if

$$z > \frac{K+x+v}{3K} \left[\frac{ax-(b+c)y}{K+x+y} + \frac{(c-2b)y}{K+y} \right] + \frac{b(v+x)}{K}$$

Similarly it can be shown that C prefers (2) to (1) if

$$z < \frac{K+x+v}{3K} \left[\frac{(b+c)y-ax}{K+x+y} + \frac{(2c-b)y}{K+y} \right] + \frac{x(a+b)-cv}{K}$$

The new range for z is of length

$$\left[\frac{K+x+v}{3K} \right] \left[\frac{2(b+c)y-2ax}{K+x+y} + \frac{(b+c)y}{K+y} \right] + \frac{xa-(b+c)v}{K}$$

Compare this with the range when A exerted no influence i.e.

$$\left[\frac{K+x+v}{2K} \right] \left[\frac{2(b+c)y-2ax}{K+x+y} \right] + \frac{xa-(b+c)v}{K}$$

The latter is larger if

$$\frac{1}{3} \left[\frac{2(b+c)y-2ax}{K+x+y} + \frac{(b+c)y}{K+y} \right] < \frac{(b+c)y-ax}{K+x+y}$$

i.e. if $\dfrac{(b+c)y}{K+y} < \dfrac{(b+c)y-ax}{K+x+y}$

which is obviously not true. By exerting an influence on the outcome (2), A causes the range for settlement to increase rather than diminish, so this is not a good tactic for the divider.

Suppose now that A can influence the outcome in (1) i.e. he can affect the value of x. x and y may be thought of as expected values like those in the game in section 6.9.

If (1) results, A's NFC over B is

$$\frac{(a+c)x-by}{K(K+x+y)} + \frac{by}{K(K+y)}$$

and over C

$$\frac{(a+b)x-cy}{K(K+x+y)} + \frac{cy}{K(K+y)}$$

B's NFC over C is as before.

B's total NFC if (1) results is therefore

$$\frac{(b-a-c)x + (2b-c)y}{K(K+x+y)} + \frac{(c-2b)y}{K(K+y)}$$

If (2) results, A's NFC over B is

$$\frac{(a+c)x - by}{K(K+x+y)} + \frac{b(w+v) - (a+c)z}{K(K+x+v)}$$

B's total NFC in (2) is therefore

$$\frac{(b-2-2a)x + 3by}{K(K+x+y)} + \frac{z(3K) - 3b\,(x+v)}{K(K+x+v)}$$

and it is easily shown that B prefers (2) to (1) if

$$z > \frac{K+x+v}{3K} \left[\frac{(a+c)x + (b+c)y}{K+x+y} + \frac{(c-2b)y}{K+y} \right] + \frac{b(x+v)}{K}$$

Similarly it can be shown that C prefers (2) to (1) if

$$z < \frac{K+x+v}{3K} \left[\frac{(b+c)y - (a+b)x}{K+x+y} + \frac{(2c-b)y}{K+y} \right] + \frac{(a+b)x-cv}{K}$$

The new range for z for a solution is of length

$$\left(\frac{K+x+v}{3K}\right) \left[\frac{(b+c)y}{K+y} - \frac{(2a+b+c)x}{K+x+y} \right] + \frac{xa - v(b+c)}{K}$$

This is obviously smaller than the range when A only influenced the payoffs in (2). So A stands a better chance of succeeding at divide-and-rule if he can influence the total amount at stake rather than just its division. This might be expected intuitively.

But does A's attempt at influencing x decrease the range for z comparing it with its value if he does nothing? It does so if

$$\left(\frac{K+x+v}{3K}\right) \left[\frac{(b+c)y}{K+y} - \frac{(2a+b+c)x}{K+x+y} \right] - \frac{xa-v(b+c)}{K} <$$

$$\frac{K+x+v}{3K} \left[\frac{(b+c)y-ax}{K+x+y} \right] - \frac{xa-v(bK)}{K}$$

i.e. if $(a-b-c)\,xK + axy < 2\,(b+c)\,(K+y)\,y$

This is more likely to hold the smaller is a compared to b and c and the larger is y and the smaller is x.

We conclude that A's divide-and-rule bid is more likely to be successful i.e. reduce the range for z and w, if A is of low resources compared to B and C. This is all the more noteworthy since the ranges for z and w are smaller to begin with, the lower is a.

Returning to mediation for a slight digression, suppose that the mediatior had received a material payoff y or v similar to that of B and C. The difference from divide-and-rule is that $v > y$ — the mediator gets his greatest payoff from a settlement. Analysis shows that w and z must satisfy the same inequalities as in the case of divide-and-rule, but as we showed on page 202 the range for z (and w) is only greater than zero if $y > v$. So no solution can exist and mediation will not succeed. If the range gets larger if A influences the payoffs in (2), mediation

218

may succeed here, and is the range could be increased if A influences the payoffs in (1) there is some possibility of succeeding here; but it is always the case that if it has a chance of success here it would have a better chance if A only influenced the outcome (2).

So when the third party himself gets a material payoff similar to that of the disputants, he can best achieve his end, whether it be mediation or division, by influencing the payoffs of the dyad in that outcome where his own payoff is greatest.

Now we shall consider divide-and-rule applied to conflicts involving a re-distribution of resources. Again assume that B gets some best payoff y and C gets x. A gets an amount u if the conflict exists and v if it is settled. $u > v$.

The Matrix of Status Changes is

Outcome	Status Change of		
	A	B	C
(1)	$\dfrac{u(b+c)}{K(K+u)}$	$\left\{\begin{array}{c}\dfrac{Ky - bu}{K(K+u)} \\[2ex] \dfrac{-Kx - bu}{K(K+u)}\end{array}\right.$	$\begin{array}{c}\dfrac{Kx - cu}{K(K+u)} \\[2ex] \dfrac{-Ky - cu}{K(K+u)}\end{array}$
(2)	$\dfrac{v(b+c)}{K(K+v)}$	$\dfrac{Kz - bv}{K(K+v)}$	$\dfrac{Kw - cv}{K(K+v)}$

where $z + w = 0$ $-x < z < y$ and $-y < w < x$.

Firstly let us look at the case where A exerts no influence on the payoffs. If outcome (1) results no one exerts NFC. If (2) results B's NFC over C is

$$\frac{K(x-y) - u(c-b)}{K(K+u)} + \frac{K(z-w) - v(b-c)}{K(K+v)}$$

and B and C each exert an amount

$$\frac{u(b+c)}{K+u} - \frac{v(b+c)}{K+v} \quad \text{over A.}$$

B prefers (2) to (1) if

$$\frac{K(x-y) - u(c-b) + u(b+c)}{K(K+u)} + \frac{K(z-w) - v(b-c) - v(b+c)}{K(K+v)} > 0$$

i.e. if $\quad w < \dfrac{K+v}{2K} \left[\dfrac{K(x-y) + 2ub}{K+u} \right] - \dfrac{vb}{K}$

C prefers (2) if

$$w > \frac{K+v}{2K} \left[\frac{K(x-y) - 2uc}{K+u} \right] - \frac{vc}{K}$$

For a solution w must satisfy the inequality

$$\frac{vc}{K} + \frac{K+v}{2K} \left[\frac{K(x-y)-2uc}{K+u} \right] < w < \frac{K+v}{2K} \left[\frac{K(x-y)+2ub}{K+u} \right] - \frac{vb}{K}$$

The range for w is therefore

$$\frac{K+v}{K} \left[\frac{(b+c)u}{K+u} \right] - \frac{v(b+c)}{K}$$

This is independent of x and y but the larger is x compared to y, the nearer to C's end of the scale of payoffs will the range be, i.e. the more must C receive in a settlement. Again there may be a sort of implicit mediation, resulting from A's being considered as a comparable individual.

Now suppose that A influences the payoffs in (2). NFCs are as above with the addition that if (1) results, A exerts an amount $\dfrac{Kz - bv}{(K+v)K} + \dfrac{Kx + bu}{(K+u)K}$ over B and an amount $\dfrac{Kw - cv}{K(K+v)} + \dfrac{Ky - cu}{K(K+u)}$ over C. It is easily shown that B prefers (2) if

$$w < \left[\frac{2Kx - Ky - 3ub}{K+u} \right] \frac{K+v}{3K} - \frac{vb}{K}$$

and C prefers (2) if

$$w > \left[\frac{Kx - 2Ky - 3uc}{K+u} \right] \frac{K+v}{3K} + \frac{cv}{K}$$

The length of the new range for w is

$$\left[\frac{K(x+y) + 3ub + 3uc}{K+u} \right] \frac{K+v}{3K} - \frac{v(b+c)}{K}$$

which, as in the previous type of conflict, is greater than it would be if A did nothing.

Suppose then that A influences the payoffs in (1).

If (1) is the outcome A's NFC over B is

$$\frac{Ky - bu}{K(K+u)} + \frac{Kx + bu}{K(K+u)}$$

If (2) results A exerts an amount

$$\frac{Ky - bu}{K(K+u)} - \frac{Kz - bv}{K(K+v)} \quad \text{over B.}$$

B's NFC over C and A is as before and in the usual way it can easily be shown that B prefers (2) to (1) if

$$w < \left[\frac{3ub + 2Kx - Ky}{K+u}\right] \frac{K+v}{3K} - \frac{vb}{K}$$

Computing A's NFC over C in a similar fashion we arrive at C preferring (2) to (1) if

$$w > \frac{cv}{K} - \frac{K+v}{3K} \left[\frac{3uc + 2Ky - Kx}{K+u}\right]$$

The new range for w is hence of length

$$\frac{K+v}{3K} \left[\frac{K(x+y) + 3u(b+c)}{K+u}\right] - \frac{v(b+c)}{K}$$

This range is the same as that when A influenced the outcome (2) and again represents an increase on what it would have been had A not interfered. An active policy of divide-and-rule tends to be self defeating in such a conflict.

Referring briefly again to the case of mediation where the mediator gets a material payoff, in the case of conflict over a re-distribution the range for w is again non-existent if $v > u$ and A does nothing, i.e. there is no implicit mediation. But depending on the magnitude of the parameters, as the range increases in length when A influences the payoffs in (1) or (2), mediation may stand a chance of success if A does this.

Finally we will consider the conflict involving a re-distribution where either a bargaining process is taking place or fighting has pro-duced a stalemate i.e. each player can guarantee the situation with no re-distribution. Since A continues to get his payoff u, the guarantees of B and C are $\frac{-bu}{K(K+u)}$ and $\frac{-cu}{K(K+u)}$ respectively.

Assuming firstly that A exerts no influence, B's NFC over C is $\frac{K(x-y)}{K(K+u)}$ in (1) and as in the previous case in (2).

B prefers (2) to (1) if

$$w < \frac{K+v}{2K} \left[\frac{2ub}{K+u}\right] - \frac{vb}{K}$$

and C prefers (2) if

$$w > \frac{K+v}{2K} \left[\frac{-2uc}{K+u} \right] + \frac{vc}{K}$$

The length of the range is thus

$$\frac{K+v}{K} \left[\frac{u}{K+u} \right] (b+c) - \frac{v(b+c)}{K}$$

which is the same as in the case with the lower guarantees though this time the position of the range on the w, z scale is invariant to x and y.

If A exerts an influence on outcome (2), if (1) is the outcome h exerts NFC of value $\frac{Kz - bv}{K(K+v)} + \frac{bu}{K(K+u)}$ over B and $\frac{Kw - cv}{K(K+v)} +$

$\frac{cu}{K(K+u)}$ over C. Other NFCs are as above and B will prefer (2) if

$$w < \frac{ub}{K+u} \left[\frac{K+v}{K} \right] - \frac{vb}{K}$$

The new range is of length $\frac{u}{K+u} \left[\frac{K+v}{K} \right] (b+c) - \frac{v(b+c)}{K}$ which is exactly the same as the case above where A exerted no influence.

If A influences the payoffs in (1) it can be shown that the same inequalities hold and the length of the range is unchanged. As the range is not increased the policy of actions aimed at division may be worthwhile, for though it is desirable to decrease the range for settlement, part of the policy is to promote claims by the disputants which are incompatible and to discourage concessions, thereby keeping w out of the range.

Mediation in this case, where the mediator's payoff u exceeds his payoff v, will not succeed since the range for settlement never exists.

7.4   THE ALLY AND THE BALANCER
B and C are still assumed to be the parties in conflict and A is a player who may join just one side, or possibly either, in order to improve that side's chances of winning or that side's payoff. In the games in chapter 6 we effectively covered the case of the ally who gets a payoff and joins another to improve that payoff, at the same time improving the payoff of the other. The partner's payoff is not the thing which matters to the ally in this case.

Consider now a conflict of re-distribution between B and C where B's best payoff is x and C's is y. To be more general suppose that their guarantees are s and t respectively. (Note that not both s and t can exceed zero.)

Whether A is comparable in resources or not does not matter since only the denominators in the following matrix would be changed. Using the usual notations the Matrix of Status Changes is

Outcome		Status Change of
	B	C
(1) Conflict	$\dfrac{x}{b+c}$ $\dfrac{s}{b+c}$	$\dfrac{y}{b+c}$ $\dfrac{t}{b+c}$
(2) Resolution	$\dfrac{z}{b+c}$	$\dfrac{w}{b+c}$

If A is the ally of B he will try to make the w (or z) range favour B, i.e. he will try to make C settle for a lower w. Assuming A affects the payoffs in (1), if (1) results A's NFC over B is $\dfrac{x-s}{b+c}$ and over C, $\dfrac{y-t}{b+c}$. B's NFC over C is $\dfrac{y-x+s-t}{b+c}$. If (2) results, A exerts an amount $\dfrac{y-w}{b+c}$ over C and $\dfrac{x-z}{b+c}$ over B. B's NFC over C is $\dfrac{y-x+z-w}{b+c}$. C prefers (2) to (1) if

$$\frac{(x-y+w-z)+(w-y)}{b+c} \;>\; \frac{(x-y+t-s)+(t-y)}{b+c}$$

i.e. if $\quad w \;>\; \dfrac{2t-s}{3}$

A must attempt to reduce this limit so that C will settle for as small a w as possible. It is the guarantees which he must influence, attempting to make t as small as possible and s as large as possible.

It can be shown that B prefers (2) if $w < \dfrac{t-2s}{3}$. The length of the range for w is therefore $\dfrac{1}{3}$ (−t−s). This range will be increased by making t and s as small as possible so in reducing t and increasing s the ally may reduce or increase the length of range besides moving it in the direction of lower values of w.

If t and s are both zero and C can maintain things that way the alliance is useless. If the alliance means that t and s are affected in the required direction, it should form. Therefore if we begin with some B-C conflict over redistribution, and A the ally of B able to influence the payoffs, a coalition is likely if A can affect the guarantees, thereby enforcing a settlement in favour of B. Of course a settlement may sometimes result without the coalition, and if a coalition forms it does not imply an immediate settlement. The conclusion is that the coalition will form only if A can influence either s or t or both, and in this case the triad may be considered unstable.

It was assumed in the above that A was always present and therefore always a party to be considered even though he would not necessarily form a coalition. If A was not present no settlement would be possible. It may happen in such a situation that B, say, calls in some party A who is able to affect the payoffs but not the guarantees. This may be considered a coalition between A and B, though it is a coalition to get any settlement, not necessarily one in favour of B. But this case is not of real interest to us because we never really have a triad, but rather firstly a dyad and then a dyad with one side re-inforced.

We now turn to a conflict involving new resources, x. As we showed in the section on mediation there is no possibility of settlement unless A is comparable. If A is comparable and influences the payoffs we showed that C prefers a settlement if $w > (\frac{3c+a}{3K})$ x. To make this as small as possible B should call in a party A with small resources a. B prefers (2) if $w < (\frac{2a+3c}{3K})x$, so if C were calling in a third party A, he should have high resources. Again these cases are not really of interest since a triad as such never really exists, so we gain nothing on stability.

Suppose however that A was always present and relevant for comparison. Further suppose it was possible that he might side with B. We note that he could only alter the lower limit of w by altering x. But this would also mean a reduction in what B could get so the alliance would be ineffective. Underlying this is the point made above — that if A cannot change the guarantees, the alliance is pointless. This is so here where both players can always guarantee the zero status change.

The Balancer may be thought of as an ally who may join either side. Perhaps we may think of him doing this in order to maintain the status quo or point of zero status change. He therefore requires the range of settlement to include the point w = 0, if it is a conflict over redistribution.

Suppose the lower limit of w, i.e. $\frac{2t-s}{3}$, were greater than 0. The balancer must reduce t and raise s, i.e. improve B's chances or make C's possible loss greater. He therefore effectively forms an alliance with B, assuming he can influence the guarantees. Similarly if the upper limit of w is too small, A must join C. Further, assuming the range does include the status quo point the balancer may attempt to reduce this range so that no solution is too far from this point. He may do so by making both t and s small, in this case favouring neither side.

In the conflict involving new resources, if A is comparable he will himself always suffer a decline in status. He may however wish to preserve a balance in the B-C system. Thus he seeks a solution.

$w = \dfrac{c}{b+c}$ x. For a solution, w must lie between the limits:

$$\frac{x(3c+a)}{3K} < w < \frac{(2a+3c)x}{3K}$$

i.e.
$$\frac{3c+a}{3K} < \frac{c}{b+c} < \frac{2a+3c}{3K}$$

i.e. c must satisfy the inequalities

$$\frac{b}{2} < c < 2b$$

7.5 COMPETITION

Competition is a process by which the amount of Conflict may be changed. It is relevant to coalition formation as far as competition for an ally is concerned. This has been dealt with in Chapter 6 where side payments were made in order to tempt another party into a coalition. In this section we apply the model to other cases of competition. The question of the stability of the triad does not arise but we still have an interesting triadic situation and a further illustration of the application of the model.

What distinguishes competition from bargaining or fighting is that the prize is in the hands of a third party who decides on its ultimate division. The resource at stake may be fairly divisible e.g. it may be money, people or a market. On the other hand it may be completely indivisible as in the case of competition for an ally. Where division is possible and especially where the third party consists of many individuals e.g. a market, so that there is no single decision maker, the competitive process is rather similar to the bargaining process. In bargaining, one player making a concession is rather like the other player winning part of the prize through, say, advertising. The third party makes the choice but that choice is influenced by the competitors' actions.

Suppose we consider competition for a fixed market. The number of customers is the resource upon which status is calculated. Firstly consider the case of a market already divided up between firms B and C so that B has b customers and C has c customers. Competition is assumed to go on indefinitely through time making for a redistribution of resources. Time is divided into a number of periods in each of which each firm must decide on its tactics such as advertising and sales promotion. The matrix of Status Changes is

Status Change of

B   C

$$\text{Outset of period} \quad \left\{ \begin{array}{cc} \dfrac{c}{b+c} & \dfrac{b}{b+c} \\[2ex] \dfrac{-b}{b+c} & \dfrac{-c}{b+c} \end{array} \right.$$

$$\text{End of period} \quad \dfrac{z}{b+c} \qquad\qquad \dfrac{w}{b+c}$$

where $z + w = 0$, z and w being the changes in the number of customers for B and C during the period. A choice has to be made here, and so whilst B and C have some influence over the payoffs z and w they cannot remain indefinitely in the state of conflict as they could in previous games. For this reason we only consider the NFC exerted at the end of the period.

B's NFC over C is $\dfrac{b-w-c+z}{b+c}$

The market exerts an amount $\dfrac{c-z}{b+c}$ over B and $\dfrac{b-w}{b+c}$ over C.

Suppose at the end of the first period $z = t$ and $w = -t$, i.e. B has gained customers from C. B's NFC is $\dfrac{b-2c+3t}{b+c}$ and C's is $\dfrac{c-2b-3t}{b+c}$. B's is larger, and as long as he gains customers from C it will increase. The incentive is therefore for C to increase his advertising expenditure etc. in order to improve his share. The incentive still exists even if $t = 0$ or is negative (up to a point) since B's NFC is greater so long as $b > c$.

The amount of Conflict in the system remains constant at 1.0.

Competition may sometimes take place for new resources or a new market of value x. Further, in the competitive process itself the competitors may use up resources similar to those at stake. We may for example consider duopoly in which the market is measured in terms of money, as are selling costs.

Again the firms have existing markets of values b and c and a new market x arises. Suppose they spend amounts s and t respectively in an attempt to gain that market. They have two choices — either compete or opt out and let the opponent get all the market. The Matrix of Status Changes is

Status Change of

	B	**C**
(1) Outset	$\dfrac{c(x-s) + bt}{(b+c)\,(b+c+x-s-t)}$	$\dfrac{b(x-t) + cs}{(b+c)\,(b+c+x-s-t)}$
	$\dfrac{-cs-bx+bt}{(b+c)\,(b+c+x-s-t)}$	$\dfrac{-bt-cx+cs}{(b+c)\,(b+c+x-s-t)}$
(2) Choice made	$\dfrac{(b+c)\,z+bt-bc-sc}{(b+c)\,(b+c+x-s-t)}$	$\dfrac{(b+c)\,w+cs-cx-bt}{(b+c)\,(b+c+x-s-t)}$

— using the usual notations.

When the choice is made B's NFC over C is

$$\frac{2z\,(b+c) -\ (b+c)\,x}{(b+c)\,(b+c+x-s-t)}$$

The market's NFC over B is $\dfrac{(b+c)\,x - (b+c)\,z}{(b+c)\,(b+c+x-s-t)}$ so B's total is

$$\frac{3z-2x}{(b+c+x-s-t)}\ .$$

If x were indivisible and went entirely to B, this would be of value $\dfrac{x}{(b+c+x-s-t)}$ — all being exerted over C. This would be the smaller the less C had spent on advertising, but the less C spends on advertising the more likely is x to go to B.

The amount of Conflict in this situation is

$$\left[\frac{c(x-s) + bt + cs + bx - bt}{(b+c)\,(b+c+x-s-t)}\right]\quad\left[\frac{b(x-t) + cs + bt + cx - cs}{(b+c)\,(b+c+x-s-t)}\right]$$

$$=\ \left[\frac{(b+c)x}{(b+c)\,(b+c+x-s-t)}\right]\quad\left[\frac{(b+c)x}{(b+c)\,(b+c+x-s-t)}\right]$$

$$=\ \left[\frac{x}{b+c+x-s-t}\right]^2$$

It is therefore greater the greater the values of x, s, and t. So the fiercer the competition, i.e. the greater the amount spent on advertising etc. and the greater the value of the market at stake, the greater the amount of Conflict, as might be expected.

7.6 DELEGATION

Under delegation one party vests its authority in another to whom its opponent reacts differently. This may improve the bargaining position of the first. Delegation has nothing to do with coalition formation and so again will add nothing to our discussion on stability, but it is interesting in its own right.

Suppose B and C are in conflict over new resources x and the Matrix of Status Changes is that on page 193 under Mediation. We showed there that B and C are indifferent between outcomes (1) and (2) so the conflict would persist. Suppose B delegates his authority to A so that C has to interact with, or believes he is interacting with, A. Suppose further that A is incomparable in resources so that all A's status changes are zero.

C's best possible status change comes from his receiving the whole of x. C still measures himself against B, so that if A gets the whole of x, C believes his own status change is zero. If C gets an amount w out of the final solution he believes B gets 0, so he thinks B's status change is $\dfrac{-bw}{(b+c)\,(b+c+w)}$.

The Matrix of Status Changes, believed by C, is

Outcome		Status Change of	
	A	B	C
(1)	0	$\left\{\begin{array}{l} 0 \\[2ex] \dfrac{-bx}{(b+c)\,(b+c+x)} \end{array}\right.$	$\dfrac{bx}{(b+c)\,(b+c+x)}$ 0
(2)	0	$\dfrac{-bw}{(b+c)\,(b+c+w)}$	$\dfrac{bw}{(b+c)\,(b+c+w)}$

If outcome (1) results A's NFC over C is $\dfrac{bx}{(b+c)\,(b+c+x)}$ and C's NFC over B is $\dfrac{bx}{(b+c)\,(b+c+x)}$ so C's total NFC is zero. If outcome (2) results A's NFC over C is $\dfrac{bx}{(b+c)\,(b+c+x)} - \dfrac{bw}{(b+c)\,(b+c+w)}$. C's NFC

over B is $\dfrac{bw}{(b+c)\,(b+c+w)}$ so C's total is $\dfrac{2bw}{(b+c)\,(b+c+w)} - \dfrac{bx}{(b+c)\,(b+c+x)}$.

C prefers (2) to (1) if

$$\frac{2bw}{(b+c)\,(b+c+w)} - \frac{bx}{(b+c)\,(b+c+x)} > 0$$

i.e. if $w > \dfrac{(b+c)x}{2(b+c) + x}$

So there is some w for which C prefers (2). But is this favourable to B?

B gets an amount $x - w$ so assuming $w = \dfrac{(b+c)x}{2(b+c)+x}$

B gets $\dfrac{(b+c)x + x^2}{2(b+c)+x}$. B's real status change in outcome (2) is

therefore $\dfrac{cx - (b+c)\,w}{(b+c)\,(b+c+x)}$ which, substituting for w, comes out as

$\dfrac{x(c^2 - b^2 + cx)}{(b+c)\,(b+c+x)\,(2(b+c) + x)}$.

This is more likely to be positive the greater the value of x and the smaller is b compared to c. For a given x, a stronger party is less likely to succeed in getting a favourable solution out of his opponent by delegation of his position to some 'non-comparable' outsider.

7.7 CONCLUSIONS ON STABILITY

Many of the games in chapter 6 ended with the formation of a coalition, the members of which had then to decide on the division of the payoff. This issue is not defined as settled however until this division has taken place. If the coalition forms and remains in being until the issue is settled the triad is definitely unstable. However, we must ask, can the coalition survive or will the third party succeed in breaking it before the issue is finally settled? If the third party can prevent a settlement over a long period of time it seems reasonable to suppose that the coalition may disintegrate. If this happens the triad may be considered more stable or more viable in that it persists longer as a system with three separate decision makers.

In this chapter we have attempted to answer the question: "Given that a dyad exists with some conflict between its members, what are the chances of a solution being found, given that a third party intervenes in some way?" Referring to the games of chapter 6 we may think of B and C forming a coalition against A but in more general terms B and C may be any two parties who have come into conflict and A, some third party who attempts to mediate, divide etc. The conclusions reached on mediation, division etc. apply to the general case, whilst those on stability refer to B and C as a coalition i.e. B and C are still a coalition whether the outcome is (1) or (2). In the general case however, especially where A is the divider, the outcome (2) may sometimes be thought of as the formation of a coalition between B and C, since they resolve their conflict and at the same time influence A's payoff in a direction which is beneficial to themselves.

It should not be forgotten of course that all our conclusions are based on the assumptions that players consider status and attempt to maximise their Fate Control over others. The analysis in this chapter set out to see if there was some range of settlements, i.e. solutions, which B and C would prefer to the continued conflict. We examined two basically different types of conflicts — one involving new resources, the other involving a re-distribution of resources. In each case we considered the third party either himself getting a material payoff in similar resources, or getting a payoff in some other resources. The mediator's payoff for instance, may be purely psychological. We also consider the third party affecting the payoff in different ways.

Both types of conflict may be represented diagramatically. We have already done this for the type involving new resources on page 196. The general case for the other type is shown in fig. Lii.

Fig. Lii.

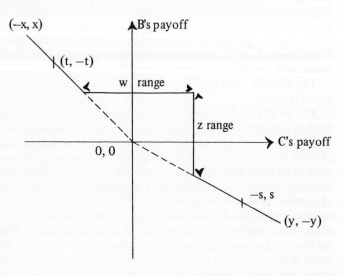

C can guarantee a payoff −s and B can guarantee a payoff −t. All

230

points along the line from $(-x, x)$ to $(y, -y)$ represent possible solutions, x being B's best payoff and y being C's best payoff. The only feasible solutions are those between points $(t, -t)$ and $(-s, s)$. The broken line represents possible solutions in the required range i.e. where B and C prefer settlement to continued conflict.

When the players have made concessions or when fighting has gone on to such an extent that an outcome in the required range results, the conflict will cease. Obviously the wider the range the sooner this will be. The mediator tries to increase the range and stands a better chance of succeeding by say persuading the disputants to make appeasement payments or concessions, the wider is this range. The divider on the other hand tries to persuade the parties to make large demands, attempting to reduce the range. His success is more likely, the smaller is the range. The ally considered in section 7.4 desires a settlement but wishes it to be in favour of his partner. If he is the ally of B he tries in effect to push the dotted line upwards, along the continuous line towards the point $(t, -t)$.

It can be seen from the diagram that if both parties can guarantee the zero status change, point $(0, 0)$, no range for w for settlement will exist so that resolution of the conflict will be difficult.

As far as stability goes section 7.4 is important in describing the triad where all three members can influence the payoffs, but these payoffs, as far as status considerations apply, accrue only to B and C. A joins one side in order to improve that side's payoff. A may get a payoff in some other resource. As we showed, such an alliance will be effective if A can influence the guarantees of one or both disputants. If this is so we may expect the alliance to form and the triad may be considered unstable.

The general conclusions reached on mediation and division are set out in table IX.

The bargaining situations are also equivalent to fighting which has reached a stalemate i.e. the guarantees are zero. Indeed it seems that the guaranteed payoffs are very important in determining the success of these processes and hence stability. Interactions involving fighting seem to be more amenable to mediation, and divide-and-rule policies have less chance of succeeding or are self defeating here. Often a sort of implicit mediation takes place when the third party receives a material payoff and benefits from the conflict. Mediation is more likely to succeed and division less likely to succeed when guarantees are low, so the triads in the games of chapter 6 will tend to be unstable in these cases. In the more general case of a conflicting dyad and a third party trying to divide them, he is unlikely to succeed if their guarantees are small, and the triad in this case may also be

TABLE IX. *Summary on Mediation and Division*

		Conflict over new resources		Conflict involving a re-distribution	
		Bargaining	Fighting	Bargaining	Fighting
A gets no material payoff	Mediation	Possible if A is comparable in resources and influences payoffs in (2). Chances improve as a increases.	Possible if A is comparable and influences outcome (2). Generally easier than in bargaining game and independent of a.	Not likely to succeed. No range for w exists.	Makes no difference whether A is comparable or not. Must influence payoffs in (2). Chances of success independent of amounts at stake.
	Division	Policy tends to be unnecessary since disputants prefer the conflict anyway.		Policy not likely to make any difference.	Tends to be self defeating
A gets a comparable material payoff	Mediation	May succeed if A influences the payoffs in (2).	More likely to succeed than in bargaining case.	Will not succeed.	May succeed if A influences payoffs in (1) and (2).
	Division	More likely to succeed in reducing w range if a is small and A influences outcome (1). May act as an implicit mediator if he takes no action.	Less likely to succeed than in bargaining case.	w range is unaffected. Policy may be effective in keeping demands outside this range.	Self defeating, tending to increase the w range. May act as an implicit mediator if takes no action.

considered unstable. Divide and rule has a better chance of succeeding, however, if the conflict is over new resources rather than a re-distribution.

If the gurantees are high, which is more typical of the bargaining situation, mediation is less likely to succeed, especially if the conflict is one of re-distribution. Division is more likely to succeed here, and so the triads may be more stable.

Notes

1. By calculus $\dfrac{\delta(z\ range)}{\delta a} = \dfrac{K+x+v}{K+x+y} \left(\dfrac{-x}{K}\right) + \dfrac{x}{K}$

This is positive if $x(K+x+y) > (K+x+v)\ x$, which is true.

CHAPTER 8

CONCLUSIONS

The broad aim of this study has been to analyse the triad or three-person group. In order to do this firstly we had to decide what constituted a triadic situation and then to classify the various types. This was accomplished by drawing heavily on examples from the real world and on work undertaken by various authors on such topics as mediation and competition.

We could then ask what were the relevant questions to be answered concerning the various types of triads and it became clear that the main question concerned the tendency for the triad to split up into a coalition of two and an isolate.

Reviewing the accomplished work on the analysis of the triad it emerged in Chapter 3 that the bulk of it relates to this question. Further, given that the split occurs, which of the three possible coalitions will form? It also became clear that power is an important variable in determining coalition formation, but the lack of consensus on what constitutes power and the absence of any satisfactory measure were also apparent. The main body of this thesis sought therefore to establish what we mean by power, to develop a measure of this, and, on the hypothesis that players seek to maximise their power, to examine the stability of the triad in various situations.

Apart from its general aim this work has also produced a certain amount of "spin off" or by-products. These are the measures of Conflict and of power. It is hoped that these might be further examined and made use of elsewhere.

234

Chapter 2 drew together much research from very diverse fields and showed that many apparently different triadic situations are in fact very much alike. Thus something we learn about mediation may throw light on the process of competition and so on. The cases considered were those of a third party instigating a dyadic process or intervening in a dyadic process which already existed. The conduct of such a process depends of course on the rules of the game. Broadly we can recognise three main processes, each with its peculiar system of rules. These are bargaining, fighting and competition. This is not to say that all bargaining games for instance have the same body of rules. All we are saying is that the rules conform to a certain pattern.

Of the three processes a third party is only essential to one, namely competition. This is of course following our particular definition of competition. Though not essential to the other processes there are many ways in which third parties can and do come in on them. Broadly, the purpose of the third party is to put an end to, prolong, or improve one side's position in, the dyadic process.

The research and theory covered in Chapter 3 reveals that much of what has been done follows a logical pattern and the works of some experimenters have been interrelated. But there are some significant contributions from outside this general stream. It is noticeable that some of the experiments considered in Chapter 3, although they used triads, might equally have used larger groups. In other words they were not really interested in the triadic aspect of their experiments. These were included in the thesis because it was thought that in view of the comparatively small amount of research carried out in this field, even these might throw some light on the triad.

One of our earliest tasks was to define the triad and the coalition. We decided that any three decision makers constituted a triad, but were only of real interest if there was some interaction between them. Where all three interact over the same issue the analysis is straight-forward. Where each dyad within the triad interacts over a different issue there are two possibilities. Firstly the issues may be independent, i.e. decisions taken by a player with respect to one issue don't affect his outcomes or possible decisions relating to the other issue in which he is involved. Secondly the issues may be dependent or interrelated, in which case it may be possible to combine them into one overall issue over which all three players interact.

Two parties were said to constitute a coalition with respect to the issue in question if they acted as one decision maker with respect to the third player. This is not to deny that both continue to make separate decisions, but what it means is that their decisions are co-ordinated and conform to some overall plan which may be thought of as being conceived by a single decision maker. It was pointed out that we can only speak of a coalition with respect to some issue, and then we must consider decisions taken with respect to that issue. It is important that we recognise that we can either consider an issue in isolation as we can do in experimental games, or consider all interfering issues and combine these somehow in order to see the real issue in question. Because all three parties must interact over this issue, the question of coalitions does not arise in those triads where dyads interact over separate independent issues, mentioned earlier.

But where coalitions can and do form, the question of the stability of the triad arises. We have said that a triad is unstable if there are no longer three separate decision makers at the completion of the issue, either because one has been eliminated by the others or because two combine and in effect act as one decision maker. Now some issues require many decisions and the possibility should be recognised of a coalition forming to take some decision and then disintegrating. We have defined stability by looking at the configuration of decision makers at the completion of the issue. In most of the games we considered there was no possibility, once a coalition had formed, of going back to the triadic state (though this was considered in Chapter 7). Had the games been more complicated and involved a large number of decisions, we might have been able to speak of the degree of stability of the triad by considering the number of decisions taken by a coalition and the number taken by members acting as single decision makers. We have gone some way towards this by considering the same game played over a large number of trials. But this is only really like making the same decision or choosing from a similar repertoire of decisions, over and over again, so it is not quite the same thing.

Most theory indicated that the triad was unstable, the 2–1 split always tending to occur. This agrees with the informal observation of many real-life phenomena. It is often noticed that where there are three decision makers two tend to be on one side and one on the other. We must be careful to investigate how this state of affairs has come about. If the issue began with all three interacting and then two joined forces the observation is fair enough. But there are also the large number of situations as considered in Chapter 2 where the issue began with two parties and a third was called in as the ally of one of these. Observation of the later stage would again reveal a 2–1 split but it has arisen in an essentially different way. Since we never had a traidic situation in the sense of three separate interacting decision makers this cannot be counted as evidence for the instability of the triad.

The motive for forming a coalition is that both members are able by it to improve the payoff. This may mean increasing their rewards or decreasing their costs. From their point of view the coalition, and hence the instability of the triad, is a good thing. One gets the impression however, from various writings of sociologists, that instability is a bad thing. This may be because of their preoccupation with the triad at the individual level and thinking of the distinctly unpleasant feeling of being the odd man out in a group of three. This would be a reasonable view. But more generally, is instability a bad or a good thing? We can only answer this with respect to the issue in question. If two states combine to eliminate a third by declaring war on it our opinion as to whether this is good or bad depends on how we view the third state. Most people would agree that the alliance between East and West against Nazi Germany was justified. Would so many agree that the alliance of Arab states against Israel is so justified?

Two parties which form a coalition obviously have the common aim of improving their payoffs. But this is not sufficient to unite them, for the third party also has this aim. What is important is the extent to which these aims can be achieved. What the coalition parties have in common is a means of maximising their payoffs. In other words they experience a correspondence of interests. This may occur in any of the three interaction processes mentioned above. Even in competition we may get collusion between two buyers or two sellers and sometimes the aim of the competition is a coalition with the third party. Indeed it is the lack of collusion in competition which benefits the third party here. In a similar way the tertius gaudens benefits from a conflict between two others.

Sometimes the interests of all three members of the triad may correspond in which case there is no reason to form a coalition. Again there may be no correspondence of outcomes for any pair, so no two desire the same coalition and no coalition forms. In Riker's terms the indecision in the situation makes for stability. It has been said that there can be no pure opposition of interests in the traid. This must refer to zero-sum games where zero-sum is used in the broader sense of winners and losers. In the three-person zero-sum game there must be either two winners or two losers so two players always have something in common.

The need for a consideration of zero-sum and non-zero-sum situations was brought home when we considered the contribution of the Balance of Power theories in Chapter 4. This led us into something of a digression before going on to our main model.

A game was considered in Chapter 4 which by altering the rules created zero-sum or non-zero-sum conditions of play. Players were given resources which followed certain orderings and a measure of coercive power which depended on these resources. It was shown that the resource orderings did produce different outcomes, some triads being more stable, others unstable under various conditions. Factors such as time horizons and the possibility of appeasement payments contributed to this in various ways, again depending on the conditions of play. The triad in general was no more stable under the non-zero-sum conditions, defensive coalitions tending to form in the absence of the offensive types.

These results again lend support to the theory that a triad is basically unstable. Our approach in the remainder of the thesis was to consider triads with various resource structures playing a variety of games and to examine where coalitions would form and whether they could be broken in some way. We further considered whether a third party could promote a coalition (or resolve a conflict) between two others.

The models were based on several hypotheses relating to the players' behaviour and it should be always borne in mind that the conclusions reached were based on these hypotheses. Firstly it was assumed that the exercise of power is a very compelling determinant of behaviour. Power was defined in a special way, referring to a player's control over another's payoff (Fate Control), which does not necessarily imply control over another's behaviour. It was also assumed that players are not only concerned with their own payoff but also with that made to other players who are considered comparable. Further, invoking the notion of diminishing marginal utility, it was assumed that players also consider their own stocks of resources as well as the stocks of others. In other words they are interested in their relative standing or status in the system. An index of this status was developed, and, on the assumption that all three players in the game constitute the system of reference for each player, i.e. each player measures his status with respect to the other two, all games were reduced to zero-sum games.

It was generally assumed that players considered comparable were those fairly near in stocks of resources and we might reasonably expect most interactions to be between such players. The fact that all games become zero-sum games and as we have said, these have no pure opposition of interests if triadic, immediately makes for some common interest between two of the players. Fate Control has been defined in such a way that by its exercise players are attempting to improve their own status. The player with the highest status is seen as a target by the others even before the game begins. If payoffs are equal for all coalitions this common opposition of the weaker players to the strong one will prevail and determine the coalition. This demonstrates the

238

often observed phenomenon of the triad favouring the weak over the strong. It should be noted however that this is not necessarily a peculiarity of the triad. It may also be true of higher groups where status considerations are relevant.

If payoffs to different coalitions vary, a coalition with the strong player may promise one of the others a better status change than a coalition with the third, weaker player. The Generalised Game of Chapter 6 demonstrated this, and also showed that certain payoff structures may be possible in the No-Coalition situation which imply that no coalition will form, because either there will no longer be a reciprocal choice or both members of a would-be coalition prefer this outcome. It is suggested that this may be considered further as a possible solution to three-person games.

Of all the games considered in Chapter 6 the Probabilistic Game is probably the most realistic. It is based on the player's estimates of winning so even if a coalition forms its payoff in total is not known with certainty. Unlike the Generalised Game where payoffs were known with certainty, the possibility of non-reciprocal choices now arises and gives rise to greater stability, even without a special payoff structure for the No-Coalition outcome. Further it was shown in Chapter 7 that the divider is more likely to succeed if he can influence the amount the coalition as a whole may receive and so even if coalitions form in the Probabilistic Game the isolate may succeed in breaking them.

There are many drawbacks with our measures and these have been pointed out. The status measure assumes complete information and rules out the psychological and perceptual elements of power. An element of perception was however brought in in Chapter 7 when it was asked, "Is the third party relevant for comparisons?" It was shown that this may make a lot of difference in mediation and division. Our assumption of rationality — that players attempt to maximise their status and therefore maximise their use of power — may be questioned. The motive may be to equalise status, as the female players tended to do in the Vinacke and Arkoff experiments.

We shall not re-state the many minor conclusions which have come out of each chapter and have been listed there. Overall we may say that the triad is an extremely important group and its analysis throws light not only upon the dyad and higher groups, but also on the very basic interaction processes of bargaining, and competition. Where stability is a relevant question it does appear that there are strong forces at work making for a 2–1 split. For this to occur however players must (1) believe they can get more from the coalition than without it and (2) make reciprocal choices of coalition partner, i.e.

there must be some correspondence of interests. If we accept that players consider status, a basis for this correspondence certainly exists and promotes weak coalitions. Payoff structures may be such however that strong coalitions sometimes form. But whatever coalition forms there are still many possible ways of breaking it, such as appeasement payments, divide-and-rule policies, changes in the estimates of the probabilities of winning, and so on.

APPENDIX I

RESULTS OF THE VINACKE AND ARKOFF EXPERIMENT

Type	Weights			Coalition				Caplow's Predic-tions	Our Predic-tions
	A	B	C	AB	AC	BC	None		
I	1	1	1	33	17	30	10	Any	Any
II	3	2	2	13	12	64	1	BC	BC
III	2	2	1	15	40	24	11	AC or BC	AC or BC
IV	3	1	1	11	10	7	62	None	None
V	4	3	2	9	20	59	2	AC or BC	BC
VI	4	2	1	9	13	8	60	None	None

APPENDIX II

A NOTE ON TIME HORIZONS

A well known principle in Economics, in the theory of the firm, is the discount mechanism. When making an investment it is assumed that the firm looks ahead at future costs and returns which accrue episodically and discounts these to find their present value, e.g. £100 which will be made next year might be equivalent to £90 made this year, and the further ahead in the future the £100 is made, the less it will be worth today. Future returns are discounted at the rate $\frac{1}{1+r}$, where r is the rate of interest, so that if returns of amount S are due each year they have a current value of

$$V = \frac{S}{(1+r)} + \frac{S}{(1+r)^2} + \frac{S}{(1+r)^3} + \dots$$

Such a mechanism can be built into our model in the following way.

At every trial a random device operates to determine whether the next trial will take place. Suppose the probability of the next trial is p, then the probability of the trial after that taking place is p^2 and so on. So if a player obtains a payoff S at each trial, his expected payoff over the future is S $(p + p^2 + p^3 + \dots)$. Now if $p = \frac{1}{1+r}$, we effectively have the same mechanism.

We assumed that players considered that t trials would definitely take place, i.e. t trials each have a probability of one and all trials thereafter, a probability of zero. But we did not assume any discounting of future returns. Even if a player only looks ahead over t trials it is probably more realistic to assume that he will consider the more immediate trials more certain than those further in the future. Let us therefore consider the model with discounting. Consider the Type I resource structure played under condition I, i.e. rule 9.

If any coalition forms, by attacking the third player it receives an expected payoff of

$$a \left(k + \sum_{x=1}^{t} p^x \right)$$

where t is the time horizon of the coalition.
If no attack is made the expected payoff is' is

$$2a \left(1 + \sum_{x=1}^{t} p^x \right)$$

Attack is profitable if

$$a \left(k + \sum_{x=1}^{t} p^x \right) > 2a \left(1 + \sum_{x-1}^{t} p^x \right)$$

$$\text{i.e.} \quad \sum_{x=1}^{t} p^x < k - 2$$

In effect we previously assumed that $p = 1$. The smaller is p, the more likely is the inequality to hold and the more likely is an attack to take place. So the effect of discounting is to increase the probability of attack.

Discounting will not affect our predictions of which coalition will form, but it will in general make aggressive coalitions more likely and stability lower.

We will also consider the case of an indefinite time horizon. The expected value of future returns is now

$$S \left(p + p^2 + p^3 + p^4 + \ldots \right)$$

an infinite series whose sum is $\dfrac{Sp}{1 - p}$.

Referring to same situation as above, attack now pays if

$$p < \frac{k - 2}{k - 1}$$

The larger is k and the smaller is p, the more likely is this to hold.

We can consider the effect of discounting on appeasement. Consider the type II resource structure and condition I (rule 9), players looking ahead indefinitely. AB would form for the purpose of attack if

$$p < \frac{k-2}{k-1}$$

The coalition could demand an amount

$$(k + \frac{p}{1-p})\, a - (a+b)\, (\frac{p}{1-p} + 1) \text{ from C.}$$

The expected value of C's future returns is $\frac{b}{1-p}$ so C can make the payment if $\frac{b}{1-p} > ka - (a+b) - \frac{bp}{1-p}$

i.e. if $p > \dfrac{a(k-1) - 2b}{a(k-1)} = p^*$

But we have already assumed that $p < \frac{k-2}{k-1}$ so if p^* exceeds $\frac{k-2}{k-1}$ C cannot make this payment. This means that a must be less than 2b before C can possibly pay it and hence make the triad stable. This is true for the Type II structure, and so appeasement is still a possibility when discounting is considered.

APPENDIX III

CONFLICT IN SOME MATRIX GAMES

In the following games we shall adopt these conventions. The cells of the matrix will be referred to by numbers as shown in fig. Liii. The resources of players A and B will be a and b respectively and total resources in the system, K, is the sum of a and b.

Fig. Liii.

I	II
III	IV

1. *The Zero-Sum Game*

The general matrix is shown in fig. Liv. and we assume that $r > s > t > p$ and $a > s, b > r$.

Fig. Liv.

B

r, −r	−s, s
−t, t	p, −p

A

The Matrix of Status Changes is

Fig. Lv.

B

A

$\dfrac{r}{K}, \dfrac{-r}{K}$	$\dfrac{-s}{K}, \dfrac{s}{K}$
$\dfrac{-t}{K}, \dfrac{t}{K}$	$\dfrac{p}{K}, \dfrac{-p}{K}$

A's best outcome is in cell I and his guarantee is cell III. B's best outcome is in cell II and his guarantee is cell IV.

$$\text{Conflict} = \left[\frac{r}{K} - \left(\frac{-t}{K}\right)\right]\left[\frac{s}{K} - \left(\frac{-p}{K}\right)\right]$$

$$= \frac{(r + t)(s + p)}{K^2}$$

It is easily seen that Conflict falls as total resources increase and rises as any of the payoffs in the game increase. For a fixed total of resources, Conflict does not change for different distributions amongst the players.

2. *Prisoner's Dilemma Game*

The general matrix is shown in fig. xLvi. The payoff orderings are $t > r > p > s$. Assume $b > a$.

The Matrix of Status Changes is

Fig. Lvi.

B

A

$\dfrac{r(b-a)}{K(K+2r)}, \dfrac{r(a-b)}{K(K+2r)}$	$\dfrac{bs-at}{K(K+s+t)}, \dfrac{at-bs}{K(K+s+t)}$
$\dfrac{bt-as}{K(K+s+t)}, \dfrac{as-bt}{K(K+s+t)}$	$\dfrac{p(b-a)}{K(K+2p)}, \dfrac{p(a-b)}{K(K+2p)}$

We have first to decide in which cells the players best and guaranteed outcomes fall. Consider player A. Obviously cell III is preferred to cell II. It is preferred to I if

$(bt - as)(K + 2r) > r(b - a)(K + s + t)$

i.e. if $(ab + b^2)(t - r) + (a^2 + ab)(r - s) + r(a + b)(t - s) > 0$.

which by our assumed payoff orderings is true. Similarly III is preferred to IV if $(ab + b^2)(t - p) + (ab + a^2)(p - s) + (a + b)p(t - s) > 0$. This is always true if p is positive. If p is negative IV will be preferred if $p < \dfrac{as - bt}{(a-b+t-s)}$. Cell IV will be preferred to II if

$(ab + b^2)(s - p) + (ab + a^2)(p - t) + (a + b)p(s - t) < 0$.

which again is true provided p is not too negative. It is easily shown that I is always preferred to II.

We will assume that p is not too negative so the final cell ordering for A is III, IV, I, II. A's best outcome is cell III and his guarantee is cell IV. It follows that B's best outcome is cell II and his guarantee also cell IV.

The amount of Conflict is

$$\left[\frac{bt - as}{K(K+s+t)} - \frac{p(b-a)}{K(K+2p)}\right] \times \left[\frac{at - bs}{K(K+s+t)} - \frac{p(a-b)}{K(K+2p)}\right]$$

Using calculus it is easy to show that for a fixed K, Conflict decreases as a increases provided that $a > b$. Conflict is the greater the nearer the players are in resources and is maximal when they are equal. This is because we are dealing with a symmetrical payoff structure. Were it asymmetrical the point of greatest Conflict would be at some unequal division of K. It is also apparent that Conflict declines with increasing K.

We can investigate also the change in Conflict as the parameters of the matrix change. Considering $\dfrac{\partial C}{\partial t}$ we obtain a numerator

$K^2(p-s) + K(2at+2as+st+pt - (4ap+ps+s^2)) + (2spt+2ast+4a^2p - (2a^2t + 2a^2s + 2ps^2))$.

The first term is positive, the second is positive if $t + s > 2p$ and the last could be positive or negative. It seems highly likely however that the whole expression will generally be positive and as the denominator is positive we conclude the Conflict increases as t increases.

Considering $\dfrac{\partial C}{\partial p}$ the numerator is $(t+s-2p)(a-b)^2$. This will exceed zero if $(t+s) > 2p$. If this is true, Conflict will increase as p increases. We note that for the game called 'Chicken' $(t+s) > 2p$ always.

3. *The Co-operative Game*

The payoff matrix is the same as that in the previous example but now we impose one of the orderings

$p > s > t > r$ where players have a dominant strategy

or $p > t > s > r$ where players do not have such a strategy.

If we consider the preference orderings of the cells we find this is very likely to change, depending on the parameters and a and b, and so no general formula for Conflict is possible here.

4. *The Mixed Motive Game with No Dominance*

This is similar to the Prisoner's Dilemma Game but neither player has a dominant strategy. The payoff matrix can no longer be symmetrical. We assume it is that in fig. Lvii. with the payoff orderings

$$r_1 > p_1 > t_1 > s_1 \text{ and } t_2 > s_2 > p_2 > r_2.$$

Fig. Lvii.

r_1, r_2	s_1, t_2
t_1, s_2	p_1, p_2

When considering the Matrix of Status Changes it is easily shown that the cell preference orderings follow the absolute payoff orderings. Conflict has the value

$$\left[\frac{br_1 - ar_2}{(K+r_1+r_2)} - \frac{bt_1 - as_2}{(K+t_1+s_2)} \right] \left[\frac{at_2 - bs_1}{K+t_2+s_1} - \frac{ap_2 - bp_1}{K+p_2+p_1} \right] \frac{1}{K^2}$$

APPENDIX IV

AXELROD'S MEASURE OF CONFLICT

What follows is intended as a brief summary of the Conflict measure proposed by Axelrod.

Like our measure, this one is based on payoffs and the structure of these. But it does not take account of stocks.

Axelrod begins by listing properties which he considers desirable in such a measure. These are:

a) Symmetry or invariance with respect to an interchange of the players' labels.

b) Independence with respect to the choice of zero and unit points on the player's utility schedules.

c) Continuity i.e. if two games are almost alike they should have almost the same amount of Conflict.

d) Boundedness − there should be an upper and lower limit to the measure.

e) Normalisation − which sets the zero of the scale at the worst the player can get and the unit at the best he can get.

f) Equivalent Reducibility − if the increase in maximum utility one player can get for any given level of utility of the other player is the same in two modified games, then the reduction of Conflict is the same in the two games.

Axelrod first considers the bargaining game and shows that the only measure which satisfies the above five properties is the area in the unit square which lies beyond the region of feasible outcomes. This is the shaded area in fig. Lviii.

Fig. Lviii.

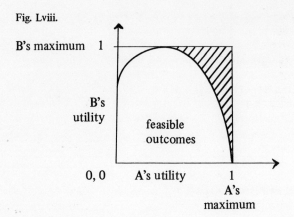

Each player can guarantee the status quo point or no division and his best payoff becomes the unit on the utility schedule. Where the region of feasible outcomes is convex, the maximum value for Conflict is ½. If the region is concave it is unity. Like our measure we can calculate the change in Conflict as players make concessions. Also the measure can be extended to the n-person case by considering the unit hypercube as the region of feasible outcomes.

The measure can also be applied to matrix games. Consider the general Prisoner's Dilemma matrix in fig. xLvi. page 246. The outcomes can be plotted as in fig. Lix.

Fig. Lix.

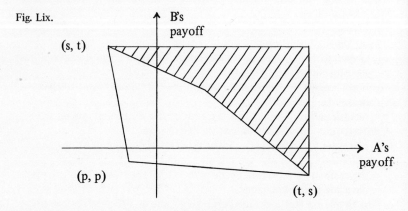

Conflict in this game is measured by calculating the area of the shaded portion and normalising this by dividing it by

250

$$\begin{bmatrix} \text{A's best payoff } \textit{minus} \\ \text{A's guaranteed payoff} \end{bmatrix} \times \begin{bmatrix} \text{B's best payoff } \textit{minus} \\ \text{B's guaranteed payoff} \end{bmatrix}$$

which is $(t - p) \times (t - p)$. The Conflict value comes out as

$$\frac{(t - r)\ (t - s)}{(t - p)^2}$$

APPENDIX V

THE COEFFICIENT OF RANK CORRELATION

If we have a population of n members, and for each one we measure two characteristics x and y, each member can be ranked or ordered depending on his x value or his y value. The difference between the two ranks we denote by d.

Spearman's Coefficient of Rank Correlation, ρ, is given by

$$\rho = 1 - \frac{6 \sum\limits_{i=1}^{n} d_i^2}{(n^2 - 1) n}$$

Seven two-person games were considered in section 5.6 so n = 7. Referring to Table VII, page 163 we note that the ranks were

Rank on % Defection	1	2	3	4	5	6	7
Rank on Conflict measure	2–6	2–6	1	2–6	2–6	2–6	7

As ranks 2, 3, 4, 5 and 6 are all the same in our case, we give each the average rank $\dfrac{2+3+4+5+6}{5} = 4.$

Then $\rho = 1 - \dfrac{6\,(4+9+4+4+0+0+1)}{7(48)}$

$\quad\quad = 1 - \dfrac{11}{28}$

252

$$= 0.61$$

The rank orderings for the three-person games were

Rank on % Defection	1	2	3	4	5	6	7–8	7–8
Rank on Conflict measure	1	4	2	3	5	7–8	6	7–8

Those ranked 7–8 are given the average rank 7½.

$$\text{Then } \rho = 1 - \frac{6(0 + 4 + 1 + 1 + 0 + \frac{9}{4} + \frac{9}{4} + 0)}{8(63)}$$

$$= 1 - \frac{1}{8}$$

$$= 0.875.$$

APPENDIX VI

FURTHER ANALYSIS OF THE PROBABILISTIC GAME

Referring to the Matrix of Status Changes on page 200 we see that A's first choice is $\overline{BC}$, B's is $\overline{AC}$ and C's is $\overline{AB}$, if $p < \dfrac{K+c}{2K}$. With this order no coalition would form. But would all players be better off in the No Coalition outcome than in their next best coalition? The Matrix of NFCs is

Outcome	NFC of		
	A	B	C
$\overline{AB}$	$\dfrac{Kp+a-c-2b}{K}$	$\dfrac{Kp+b-2a-c}{K}$	$\dfrac{(a+b+2c)-2Kp}{K}$
$\overline{AC}$	$\dfrac{Kp+a-b-2c}{K}$	$\dfrac{a+c+2b-2Kp}{K}$	$\dfrac{KP-b+c-2a}{K}$
$\overline{BC}$	$\dfrac{b+c+2a-2Kp}{K}$	$\dfrac{Kp+b-a-2c}{K}$	$\dfrac{Kp-a+c-2b}{K}$
No Coalition	$\dfrac{2a-b-c}{K}$	$\dfrac{2b-a-c}{K}$	$\dfrac{2c-b-a}{K}$

A always prefers $\overline{AC}$ to $\overline{AB}$ and he will prefer No Coalition to $\overline{AC}$ if

254

$$2a - b - c \quad > \quad Kp + a - b - 2c$$

or if $\quad p \quad < \quad \dfrac{a+c}{K}$

We assumed that $p < \dfrac{K+c}{2K}$ and as $\dfrac{a+c}{K} > \dfrac{K+c}{2K}$, $p < \dfrac{a+c}{K}$ and A will prefer No Coalition to $\overline{AC}$.

B obviously will prefer $\overline{BC}$ to $\overline{AB}$ and he will prefer No Coalition to $\overline{BC}$ if $Kp+b-a-2c < 2b-a-c$

or if $\quad p \quad < \quad \dfrac{b+c}{K}$

A similar condition holds for C.

But if $p < \dfrac{K+c}{2K}$ it may or may not also be less than $\dfrac{b+c}{K}$ since $\dfrac{b+c}{K} < \dfrac{K+c}{2K}$ under the assumption that $a > b$.

If $p < \dfrac{b+c}{K}$ No Coalition will be the outcome; but if $p \geqslant \dfrac{b+c}{K}$, though B and C each desire the other to form a coalition with A, as this is not forthcoming both will prefer to form $\overline{BC}$.

Now suppose $\dfrac{K+b}{2K} > p > \dfrac{K+c}{2K}$

C's best status change now comes from $\overline{AB}$, B's from $\overline{BC}$ and A's from $\overline{AC}$. The Matrix of NFCs becomes

Outcome		NFC of	
	A	B	C
$\overline{AB}$	$\dfrac{-Kp+(2a+c-b)}{K}$	$\dfrac{2b-a+c-Kp}{K}$	$\dfrac{2Kp-(a+b+2c)}{K}$
$\overline{AC}$	$\dfrac{2a-Kp}{K}$	$\dfrac{2a+3b-3c-4Kp}{K}$	$\dfrac{5Kp-4a-3b-3c}{K}$
$\overline{BC}$	$\dfrac{a-c}{K}$	$\dfrac{a+3b+2c-3Kp}{K}$	$\dfrac{3Kp-2a-3b-c}{K}$
No Coalition	$\dfrac{3a+c-2Kp}{K}$	$\dfrac{3b+c-2Kp}{K}$	$\dfrac{4Kp-3a-3b-2c}{K}$

Obviously A will prefer $\overline{AC}$ to $\overline{AB}$. $\overline{AC}$ is preferred to No Coalition if

$2a-Kp > a-c$, or $p < \dfrac{a+c}{K}$ which may or may not be true. A will prefer No Coalition to $\overline{BC}$ if

$$3a+c-2Kp > a-c$$

$$\text{or} \quad p < \frac{a+c}{K}$$

and he will prefer None to $\overline{AC}$ if $p < \dfrac{a+c}{K}$

So if $p < \dfrac{a+c}{K}$ A's preference orderings are

$$\text{No Coalition, } \overline{AC}, \overline{BC}, \overline{AB}$$

If $p > \dfrac{a+c}{K}$ A's preference orderings are

$$\overline{BC}, \overline{AC}, \text{No Coalition, } \overline{AB}.$$

For B obviously $\overline{BC}$ is better than $\overline{AB}$ and it is better than No Coalition if

$$a+3b+2c-3Kp > 3b+c-2Kp$$

$$\text{or} \quad p < \frac{a+c}{K}$$

$\overline{BC}$ is preferred to $\overline{AC}$ if

$$a+3b+2c-3Kp > 2a+3b-3c-4Kp$$

$$\text{i.e.} \quad p > \frac{a-5c}{K}$$

which is probably true seeing that $p > \dfrac{K+c}{2K}$.

For C $\overline{AB}$ is his first preference and it can easily be shown that he prefers $\overline{BC}$ to No Coalition if $p < \dfrac{a+c}{K}$; he prefers $\overline{BC}$ to $\overline{AC}$ if $p < \dfrac{a+c}{K}$ and he prefers No Coalition to $\overline{AC}$ if $p < \dfrac{a+c}{K}$.

Amongst first preferences there is no reciprocal choice for coalition partner. If $p < \dfrac{a+c}{K}$, C prefers $\overline{BC}$ to No Coalition, and so he will reciprocate B's choice when he considers his second preference and $\overline{BC}$ will form. But if $p > \dfrac{a+c}{K}$, C will prefer $\overline{AC}$ to No Coalition. As A prefers $\overline{AC}$ to No Coalition, $\overline{AC}$ should form. These conclusions only apply if $\frac{a+c}{K} < \frac{K+c}{2K}$ which may or may not be true.

Suppose finally that $p > \frac{K+b}{2K}$. A's best status change comes from $\overline{AC}$ while B's and C's come from $\overline{BC}$. The matrix of NFCs is

Outcome	NFC of		
	A	B	C
$\overline{AB}$	$\dfrac{Kp+a-3b}{K}$	$\dfrac{Kp-2a}{K}$	$\dfrac{3b+a-2Kp}{K}$
$\overline{AC}$	$\dfrac{Kp+a-c-2b}{K}$	$\dfrac{b-a}{K}$	$\dfrac{b+c-Kp}{K}$
$\overline{BC}$	$\dfrac{2a+2c-2KP}{K}$	$\dfrac{Kp-a-c}{K}$	$\dfrac{Kp-a-c}{K}$
No Coalition	$\dfrac{2(a-b)}{K}$	$\dfrac{b-a}{K}$	$\dfrac{b-a}{K}$

B obviously prefers $\overline{BC}$ to $\overline{AB}$ and C prefers $\overline{BC}$ to $\overline{AC}$ if

$$Kp-a-c > b+c-Kp$$

or $p > \frac{K+c}{2K}$ which is true by assumption. B and C prefer $\overline{BC}$ to No Coalition if

$$Kp-a-c > b-a$$

or $p > \frac{b+c}{K}$.

But $\frac{b+c}{K} < \frac{K+b}{2K}$ so this is true.

The complete list of preference orderings for various values of p is shown in fig. Lx.

Fig. Lx.

	p =	0	$\frac{b+c}{K}$	$\frac{K+c}{2K}$	$\frac{a+c}{K}$	$\frac{K+b}{2K}$
	A	$\overline{BC}$, None	$\overline{BC}$, None	None, $\overline{AC}$, $\overline{BC}$	$\overline{BC}$, $\overline{AC}$, None	$\overline{AC}$, $\overline{AB}$
Preferences	B	$\overline{AC}$, None	$\overline{AC}$, $\overline{BC}$, None	$\overline{BC}$, None	None, $\overline{BC}$	$\overline{BC}$, $\overline{AC}$
	C	$\overline{AB}$, None	$\overline{AB}$, $\overline{BC}$, None	$\overline{AB}$, $\overline{BC}$, None	$\overline{AB}$, $\overline{AC}$, None	$\overline{BC}$, $\overline{AB}$
Prediction		No Coalition	$\overline{BC}$	$\overline{BC}$	$\overline{AC}$	$\overline{BC}$

Conflict in the Probablistic Model

We have to decide on the player's best and guaranteed payoffs. We already know the former for various values of p from the above analysis. When p becomes low some of the payoffs such as Kp − (a+b) will be negative. In these cases such payoffs become the guaranteed payoff and the zero payoff is the best payoff. The negative guarantee is the greatest cost a player would have to bear if the coalition.lost. This cannot however exceed his total resources.

For C when $p > \frac{K+b}{2K}$, the gurantee in $\overline{AC}$ exceeds the payoff in $\overline{AB}$ if

$$Kp - (a+c) > (a+b) - Kp$$

i.e. if $\qquad p > \frac{K+a}{2K}$

so if $p > \frac{K+a}{2K}$, $\overline{AB}$ is his guarantee. When $p < \frac{K+a}{2K}$, $\overline{AC}$ is the guarantee at all times.

For B, when $p > \frac{K+c}{2K}$, the guarantee in $\overline{AB}$ exceeds the payoff in $\overline{AC}$ if $p > \frac{K+a}{2K}$, so $\overline{AC}$ is the guarantee if $p > \frac{K+a}{2K}$. $\overline{AB}$ always gives his guaranteed payoff if $p < \frac{K+c}{2K}$.

For A, when $p > \frac{K+c}{2K}$, the guarantee in $\overline{AB}$ exceeds the payoff in $\overline{BC}$ if $p > \frac{K+b}{2K}$, so $\overline{BC}$ is the guarantee when $p > \frac{K+b}{2K}$. $\overline{AB}$ always gives his guaranteed payoff when $p < \frac{K+c}{2K}$. But the most A can lose is

258

$-a$, so $KP - (a+b)$ must exceed $-a$, i.e. p must exceed $\dfrac{b}{K}$. When p falls below this value A can still only lose $-a$. Similarly when p falls below $\dfrac{a}{K}$, B can only lose $-b$ and C can only lose $-c$.

The measures of Conflict as p varies are

1. $p > \dfrac{K+a}{2K}$

$$C_t \text{ (Conflict)} = \left[\frac{(Kp-a-c)-(b+c-Kp)}{K}\right] \times \left[\frac{(Kp-b-c)-(a+c-Kp)}{K}\right] \times$$
$$\left[\frac{(Kp-b-c)-(a+b-Kp)}{K}\right]$$

$$= \left[\frac{2Kp-K-c}{K}\right]^2 \left[\frac{2Kp-K-b}{K}\right]$$

2. $\dfrac{K+a}{2K} > p > \dfrac{K+b}{2K}$

$$C_t = \left[\frac{(Kp-a-c)-(b+c-Kp)}{K}\right] \times \left[\frac{(Kp-b-c)-(Kp-a-b)}{K}\right] \times$$
$$\left[\frac{(Kp-b-c)-(Kp-a-c)}{K}\right]$$

$$= \left[\frac{2Kp-K-c}{K}\right]\left[\frac{a-c}{K}\right]\left[\frac{a-b}{K}\right]$$

3. $\dfrac{K+b}{2K} > p > \dfrac{K+c}{2K}$

$$C_t = \left[\frac{(Kp-a-c)-(Kp-a-b)}{K}\right] \times \left[\frac{(Kp-b-c)-(Kp-a-b)}{K}\right] \times$$
$$\left[\frac{(a+b-Kp)-(Kp-a-c)}{K}\right]$$

$$= \frac{(b-c)\,(a-c)\,(K+a-2Kp)}{K^3}$$

4. $\dfrac{K+c}{2K} > p > \dfrac{a}{K}$

$$C_t = \left[\frac{(K+c-Kp) - (Kp-a-b)}{K}\right] \times \left[\frac{(a+c-Kp) - (Kp-a-b)}{K}\right]$$

$$\left[\frac{(a+b-Kp) - (Kp-a-c)}{K}\right]$$

$$= \left[\frac{K+b-2Kp}{K}\right] \left[\frac{K+a-2Kp}{K}\right]^2$$

5. $\dfrac{a}{K} > p > \dfrac{b}{K}$

$$C_t = \left[\frac{(a+c-Kp) - (Kp-a-b)}{K}\right] \times \left[\frac{(a+c-Kp) - (-b)}{K\ K}\right] \times$$

$$\left[\frac{(a+b-Kp) - (-c)}{K}\right]$$

$$= \left[\frac{K+b-2Kp}{K}\right] \left[1 - p\right]^2$$

6. $0 < p < \dfrac{b}{K}$

$$C_t = \left[\frac{(b+c-Kp) - (-a)}{K}\right] \times \left[\frac{(a+c-Kp) - (-b)}{K}\right] \times$$

$$\left[\frac{(a+b-Kp) - (-c)}{K}\right]$$

$$= (1 - p)^3$$

A sketch graph can be drawn up as in fig. L. page 203. If we consider a numerical example when a = 4, b = 3, c = 2, we construct the curve in fig. Lxi.

Fig. Lxi.

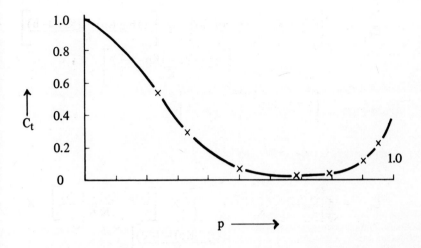

APPENDIX VII

SOME DEFINITIONS

COALITION	A two-person coalition is defined by saying, 'A dyad becomes a coalition with respect to some issue if its members co-ordinate their decisions in their interaction with a third party on this issue in order to improve their outcomes'.
CONFLICT	Two parties are said to be in a state of conflict if they pursue goal states which are incompatible.
FATE CONTROL	Player A has Fate Control over B if he can control B's payoffs in some way by taking certain actions.
INTERACTION	Two parties interact over some issue if the actions of one or both, taken with respect to that issue, influence the outcomes of the other.
INTERACTION PROCESS	The sequence of decisions and actions taken through time and their consequences on the parties involved are called the interaction process.

NET FATE CONTROL (NFC)	If two players A and B each make a decision which results in a certain outcome, A's NFC over B for that outcome is defined as A's Fate Control over B minus B's Fate Control over A.
STABILITY	A triad is said to be stable with respect to some issue if three separate decision makers remain at the completion of the issue.
STATUS	A player's status is defined as the ratio of his own resources to the total resources possessed by all members of a system of reference. Members of this system are considered relevant for comparison purposes in terms of resources.

SELECTED BIBLIOGRAPHY

Adrian, Charles R. "Decision Costs in Coalition Formation". American Political Science Review, LXII, No. 2 (June, 1968), 556–563.

Asch, S. E. "Studies of Independence and Conformity: I. A Minority of One against a Unanimous Majority". Psychological Monographs, 70, No. 9 (1956) Whole No. 416.

Ash, Maurice A. "An Analysis of Power, with Special Reference to International Politics". World Politics, III, 2 (1951), 218–237.

Aubert, Vilhelm. "Competition and Dissensus: Two Types of Conflict and of Conflict Resolution". Journal of Conflict Resolution, VII 1 (March, 1963), 26–42.

—————— "Courts and Conflict Resolution". Journal of Conflict Resolution, XI, 1 (March, 1967), 40–51.

Axelrod, Robert. "Conflict of Interest: an Axiomatic Approach". Journal of Conflict Resolution, XI, 1 (March, 1967), 87–99.

Bales, R. F. Interaction Process Analysis. Cambridge Mass.: Addison-Wesley, 1950.

Barkun, M. "Conflict Resolution through Implicit Mediation". Journal of Conflict Resolution, VIII, 2 (June, 1964), 121–130.

Bernard, Jessie. "Parties and Issue in Conflicts". Journal of Conflict Resolution, I, 2 (June, 1957) 111–121.

—————— "The Theory of Games as a Modern Sociology of Conflict". American Journal of Sociology, 59 (1954) 411–424.

Bishop, R.L. "A Zeuthen Hicks Theory of Bargaining". Quarterly Journal of Economics, 77 (1963), 559–602.

264

Bond, J. R. and W. Edgar Vinacke. "Coalitions in Mixed Sex Triads". Sociometry, 24 (1961), 61–75.

Borgatta, Marie L. and Edgar F. Borgatta. "Coalitions in Three-Person Groups", Journal of Social Psychology, 60 (1963), 319–326.

Boulding, Kenneth E. "Organization and Conflict". Journal of Conflict Resolution, I, 2 (June, 1957), 122–134.

—————— Conflict and Defense. New York: Harper, 1962.

Caplow, Theodore. "A Theory of Coalitions in the Triad". American Sociological Review, 21 (1956), 489–493.

—————— "Further Development of a Theory of Coalitions in the Triad". American Journal of Sociology, 64 (1959), 488–493.

Cartwright, D. and F. Harary. "Structural Balance: A Generalisation of Heider's Theory". In D. Cartwright and A. Zanders (eds.). Groups Dynamics. New York: Harper and Row, 1953.

Chaney, M. V. and W. E. Vinacke. "Achievement and Nurturance in Triads Varying in Power Distributions". Journal of Abnormal Social Psychology, 2 (1960), 175–181.

Chertkoff, Jerome. "The Effect of Probability of Future Success on Coalition Formation". Journal of Experimental and Social Psychology, 2, 3 (July, 1966), 265–277.

—————— "A Revision of Caplow's Coalition Theory". Journal of Experimental and Social Psychology, 3, 2 (1967), 172–177.

Converse, Elizabeth. "The War of All Against All". Journal of Conflict Resolution, XII, 4 (December, 1968), 471–532.

Coser, Lewis A. The Function of Social Conflict. Glencoe, Ill.: The Free Press, 1956.

Cross, John G. "Some Theoretic Characteristics of Economic and Political Coalitions". Journal of Conflict Resolution, XI, 2 (June, 1967), 184–195.

Dahl, Robert A. "The Concept of Power". Behavioural Science, II (1957), 201–215.

De Charms, R. "Affiliation, Motivation and Productivity in Small Groups". Journal of Abnormal Social Psychology, 55 (1957), 222–226.

Deutsch, Morton. "A Theory of Co-operation and Competition". Human Relations, 2 (1949a), 129–152.

—————— and R. M. Krauss. "Studies in Interpersonal Bargaining". Journal of Conflict Resolution, 6 (1962), 52–76.

Douglas, Ann. "What Can Research Tell Us About Mediation?". Labour Law Journal, (August, 1955), 545–552.

Fisher, R., ed. International Conflict and Behavioural Science. New York: Basic Books, 1964.

French, J. R. P., Jr. "A Formal Theory of Social Power". Psychological

Review, 63, 3 (1956), 181–194.

Galtung, Johan. "Institutionalised Conflict Resolution: A Theoretical Paradigm". Journal of Conflict Resolution, IX, 4 (December, 1965), 348–396.

Gamson, William A. "A Theory of Coalition Formation". American Sociological Review, 26, 3 (1961), 373–382.

————— "An Experimental Test of a Theory of Coalition Formation". American Sociological Review, 26, 4 (1961), 565–573.

————— (Ed.) Power and Discontent. Illinois: Dorsey, 1968.

Harary, F. "A Structural Analysis of the Situation in the Middle East in 1956". Journal of Conflict Resolution, V, 2 (June, 1961), 161–178.

Harford, Thomas and John Cheney. "The Effects of Proliferating Punitive Power in a Bargaining Game with Male and Female Triads". Mimeograph (V. A. Outpatients Clinic, Boston, Mass. 1968).

Harsanyi, J. "Game Theory and the Analysis of International Conflict". Australian Journal of Political History, 11, 3 (1965), 292–304.

Heider, F. The Psychology of Interpersonal Relations. New York: Wiley, 1958.

Herniter, J. and J. Wolpert. "Coalition Structures in Three-Person Non-zero-sum Games". Preliminary Draft. Peace Research Meeting. The Hague. (August, 1967).

Hoffman, Paul J., Leon Festinger, and Douglas H. Lawrence. "Tendencies toward Group Comparability in Competitive Bargaining". Human Relations, 7 (1954), 141–159.

Holsti, K. J. "Resolving International Conflicts: A Taxonomy of Behaviour and Some Figures of Procedures". Journal of Conflict Resolutions, X, 3 (September, 1966), 272–296.

Jully, Laurent. "Arbitration and Judicial Settlement — Recent Trends". American Journal of International Law, 48 (1954), 380–407.

Kaplan, Morton A. System and Process in International Politics. New York: John Wiley & Sons Inc., 1957.

Karlsson, G. "Some Aspects of Power in Small Groups", in J. H. Criswell et. al. eds. Mathematical Methods in Small Group Processes. Stanford: Stanford University Press, 1962.

Kelley, H. H. and A. J. Arrowood. "Coalitions in the Triad: Critique and Experiment". Sociometry, 23 (1960), 231–244.

Kerr, C. "Industrial Conflict and Its Mediation". American Journal of Sociology, 60 (1954), 230–245.

Kuhn, H. W. "Game Theory and Models of Negotiation". Journal of Conflict Resolution, VI 1 (March, 1962), 1–4.

Lasswell, H. D. and A. Kaplan. Power and Society. New Haven: Yale University Press, 1950.

Leiserson, Michael. Coalitions in Politics. Unpublished Doctoral

Dissertation, Yale University, 1966.

Lerche, Charles O. Principles of International Politics. New York: Oxford University Press, 1956.

LeVine, Robert A. "Anthropology and the Study of Conflict: Introduction". Journal of Conflict Resolution, V, 1 (March, 1961), 3–15.

Lieberman, Bernhardt. "Experimental Studies of Conflict in Some Two and Three Person Games", in J. H. Crisswell et. al. (eds.) Mathematical Methods in Small Group Processes. Stanford University Press, 1962.

—————— "i–Trust: A Notion of Trust in Three Person Games and International Affairs". Research Memorandum SP–105–R. State University of New York at Stoney Brook, (October, 1963).

Liska, George. Nations in Alliance. Baltimore: Johns Hopkins University Press, 1962.

Luce, Duncan R. and Howard Raiffa. Games and Decisions. New York: Wiley, 1957.

Mack, Raymond W. and Richard C. Snyder. "The Analysis of Social Conflict — Towards an Overview and Synthesis". Journal of Conflict Resolution, I, 2 (June, 1957), 212–248.

McKinsie, J. C. C. Introduction to the Theory of Games. New York: McGraw-Hill Book Co., 1952.

March, J. G. "Theory and Measurement of Influence". American Political Science Review, XXXIX (1955), 431–445.

—————— "Measurement Concepts in the Theory of Influence". Journal of Politics, 19 (1957), 202–226.

Mazur, Allan. "A Nonrational Approach to Theories of Conflict and Coalition". Journal of Conflict Resolution, XII, 2 (June, 1968), 196–205.

Mills, Theodore M. "Power Relations in Three-Person Groups". American Sociological Review, 18 (1953), 351–357.

—————— "The Coalition Pattern in Three-person Groups". American Sociological Review, 19 (1954), 657–667.

Nash, John F. "The Bargaining Process". Econometrica, 18 (1950), 155–162.

Organski, K. and A. F. K. Organski. Population and World Power. New York: Alfred A. Knopf, 1961.

Phillips, James L. and Lawrence Nitz. "Social Contacts in a Three-person 'Political Convention' Situation". Journal of Conflict Resolution, XII, 2 (June, 1968), 206–213.

Rapoport, Anatol. Fights, Games and Debates. Ann Arbor: University of Michigan Press, 1960.

—————— Strategy and Conscience. New York: Harper and Row, 1964.

—————— Two Person Game Theory, Ann Arbor: University of Michigan Press, 1966.

Rapoport, Anatol. Albert M. Chammah, John Dwyer and John Cyr. "Three Person Non-zero-sum Nonnegotiable Games". Behavioural Science, 7 (1962), 38–58.

—————— and Carol Orwant. "Experimental Games: A Review". Behavioural Science, 7 (1962), 1–37.

—————— and Albert M. Chammah. Prisoner's Dilemma. Ann Arbor, Michigan: Michigan University Press, 1965.

Riker, William H. The Theory of Political Coalitions. New Haven: Yale University Press, 1963.

—————— "Bargaining in a Three-Person Game". American Political Science Review, LXI, 3 (1967), 642–656.

—————— and L. S. Shapley. "Weighted Voting: A Mathematical Analysis for Instrumental Judgements". Rand. Meeting of American Society for Political and Legal Philosophy, New York, 1965.

Rush, Myron. Political Succession in the U.S.S.R. New York: Columbia University Press, 1965.

Schelling, Thomas C. The Strategy of Conflict. Cambridge, Mass: Harvard University Press, 1960.

Shapley, L. S. "A Value for N-Person Games". Annals of Mathematics Studies, 28 (1953), 307–317.

Shubik, Martin, ed. Readings in Game Theory and Political Behaviour. Garden City, New York: Doubleday, 1954.

—————— ed. Game Theory and Related Approaches to Social Behaviour. New York: Wiley, 1964.

Simmel, Georg. Conflict and the Web of Group Affiliations. Translated by Kurt H. Wolff and Reinhard Bendix. Glencoe, Ill: The Free Press, 1955.

—————— "The Significance of Numbers for Social Life", in E. P. Hare, E. F. Borgatta and R. F. Bales, eds. Small Groups: Studies in Social Interaction. New York: Knopf, 1955, pp. 9–15.

Simon, H. A. "Notes on the Observation and Measurement of Political Power". Journal of Politics, 15 (1953), 500–516.

Snyder, G. H. "Deterrence and Power". Journal of Conflict Resolution, IV, 2 (June 1960), 163–178.

Solomon, Leonard. "The Psychology of Threat: A Study of Blackmail". Unpublished mimeograph, Tavistock Institute, London.

Stanger, R., ed. Essays in Intervention. Columbus, Ohio: Ohio State University, 1954.

Strodtbeck, Fred L. "The Family as a Three-Person Group". American Sociological Review, 19 (1954), 23–29.

Stryker, Sheldon and George Psathas. "Research in Coalitions in the Triad. Findings, Problems and Strategy". Sociometry, 23, (1960), 217–230.

Thibaut, John W. and Harold H. Kelley. The Social Psychology of Groups. New York: John Wiley and Sons, Inc., 1959.

Torrance, Paul E. "Some Consequences of Power Differences on Decision Making in Permanent and Temporary Three Man Groups", in A. P. Hare, E. F. Borgatta and R. F. Bales, eds. Small Groups: Studies in Social Interactions. New York: Knopf, 1955, pp. 488–489.

Uesugi, T. T. and W. E. Vinacke. "Strategy in a Feminine Game". Sociometry, 26 (1963), 75–88.

Von Neumann, John and Oskar Morgenstern. The Theory of Games and Economic Behaviour. Princeton, N. J.: Princeton University Press, 1947.

Vinacke, Edgar W. "Sex Roles in a Three-Person Game". Sociometry, 22 (1959), 343–360.

—————— "Power, Strategy and Formation of Coalitions in Triads under Four Incentive Conditions". Office of Naval Research Nonr 3748 (02), Technical Report No. 1, 1963.

—————— and Abe Arkoff. "An Experimental Study of Coalitions in the Triad". American Sociological Review, 22 (1957), 406–414.

—————— Doris C. Crowell, Dora Dien and Vera Young. "The Effect of Information about Strategy in a Three-Person Game". Behavioural Science, II (1966), 180–189.

Willis, Richard H. and Norma J. Long. "An Experimental Simulation of an Internation Truel". Behavioural Science, 12 (1967), 24–31.

Wolff, Kurt H., ed. and translator. The Sociology of Georg Simmel. Glencoe: The Free Press, 1950.

Young, Oran. The Intermediaries: Third Party Intervention in International Crises. Princeton N.J.: Princeton University Press, 1967.

Zinnes, Dina A. "An Analytic Study of the Balance of Power Theories". Journal of Peace Research, 3 (1967), 270–287.

INDEX